THE LITERARY
COMPANION
TO LOW LIFE

HP £5

THE LITERARY COMPANION TO LOW LIFE

An anthology of prose and poetry

collected by

Fiona Pitt-Kethley

SINCLAIR-STEVENSON

First published in Great Britain in 1995
by Sinclair-Stevenson
an imprint of Reed Consumer Books Ltd
Michelin House, 81 Fulham Road, London SW3 6RB
and Auckland, Melbourne, Singapore and Toronto

A CIP catalogue record for this book
is available at the British Library
ISBN 1 85619 393 4

Typeset by Falcon, Wallington
Printed and bound in Great Britain by
Clays Ltd, St. Ives plc

CONTENTS

ACKNOWLEDGEMENTS

I would like to express my gratitude to the following publishers, agents and writers for permission to use their work:

The estate of the late Sonia Orwell, Martin Secker and Warburg, and Harcourt, Brace and Jovanovich for extracts from George Orwell's *Down and out in Paris and London*.
To Reed Consumer Books for an extract from Dostoevsky's *House of the Dead*, translated by Constance Garnett and published by William Heinemann Ltd.
To Serpent's Tail and Daniel de Souza for a piece from *Under the Crescent Moon*.
To Peter Owen Ltd., Dacia Maraini and Siân Williams for an extract from *Isolina* by Dacia Maraini.
To Olive Pitt-Kethley, my mother, for her translation of a Martial poem and for some helpful suggestions and much unpaid proof-reading.

I have been unable to trace the rights of the Maxim Gorky piece. If its uncredited translator, or those who own the rights to it, would get in touch I would be grateful.

INTRODUCTION

T HE LITERARY COMPANION TO LOW LIFE is my second essay into the world of anthology-making. In my previous anthology, *The Literary Companion to Sex*, I selected as my criteria: humour, realism and the bizarre. I also felt a kind of duty to include as many types of sex as possible and most of the world's best-known erotic writers, even if I, personally, did not enjoy their work.

In *The Literary Companion to Low Life* I have used a very different approach. While I have again included much that is humorous, realistic or unusual, there was not a fixed canon of low-life writers to draw on. In the period between putting together these anthologies, I reviewed a great many anthologies by other writers. Again and again the ones to which I gave the best reviews were those that contained a certain mixture of ingredients – large chunks of enjoyable narrative writing plus a few unusual items I had never seen before. I believe that the anthology-maker has a certain duty to bring lost or little-known examples of good writing back into general circulation. John Taylor's work, for instance, certainly deserves to be better known. I have thus included his description of the Hamburg executioner.

When I started to think about the phrase 'low life' I realised that its meaning was a lot wider than that ascribed to it in the average dictionary, i.e. 'life among the lowest classes'. Jeffrey Bernard uses the title for his weekly column in the *Spectator*. In origins he is probably of rather better class than many of us, yet his column's title is appropriate because of his forays into pub-life and drunkenness, etc. In slang, describing someone as 'a low-life' has yet another meaning. A low-life is a scum-bag, someone that even the rest of 'the lowest classes' could look down on. When you think of the word 'low' alone, yet more meanings are possible; anything from insect-life to Lilliputians could be included. In the final selection, however, I rejected the Lilliputians in favour of Swift's highly amusing advice to servants.

I structured *The Literary Companion to Low Life* on a similar pattern to Shakespeare's 'seven ages of man', although only two of the ages, or stages, are exactly the same. I have drawn from a narrower range of periods and cultures than I at first intended. While there are a few classical and medieval items included, I soon realised that most of the good, colourful writing on lowness came from later ages. The problem with the Middle Ages was that if nobody took a bath more than once a year, they couldn't complain about (or even notice) the smell of their neighbours. It is precisely the sense of difference that often makes for the best writing about low life. Orwell could observe it sharply in his down-and-out phase simply because he had once been a class up on it all and had hope for the future. Others, such as the Victorian Henry Mayhew, stood outside in their forays into the low-life world. His magnum opus, *London Labour and the London Poor*, is an amazing piece of research. With the help of a couple of mission-workers, he interviewed thousands of people and recorded their conversations word for word. The result has a thoroughly Dickensian flavour. Hardly any of the low-lifes spoke standard English.

Annals of crime such as *The New Newgate Calendar* also provided rich pickings for information on low life. When low-lifes are criminal they often have their own language – one that normal citizens are not supposed to understand. I have included three pieces that give information on this language at various periods – the first, Dekker's 'The Canters Dictionarie', from the seventeenth century. Only a couple of his words have survived, more or less – *dudes* (pretty much the same as duds) for clothes, and *drawers* for hose (now knickers of the old-fashioned sort). There are a few enjoyable but inexplicable phrases in this three-page 'dictionary' – *Margery Prater* (a hen) and *Tib of the Buttry* (a goose). I also liked the phrase for 'to lie down and sleep' – *couch a Hogshead*. Interestingly, Dekker also shows the origin of our modern term of abuse 'pratt'. In seventeenth-century cant it meant 'a buttock'. Curiously, at least as much of Orwell's slang from the 1930s is obsolete; only three of his words have survived. My own grandfather's *The Sign-Language of Tramps*, written at the turn of the century, deals with an entirely obsolete language. Perhaps the fact that he published it in the *Strand* magazine meant that tramps everywhere had to change their code! When I discovered the piece by accident, it revealed the fact that my grandfather had changed our name slightly. While he was never low, in his rise from journalist to rich editor and author, he obviously felt that a hyphen inserted in the middle of the family name, Pitkethley, would add a little class.

It is the British obsession with class that has made us world leaders in writing about lowness. Again and again I found myself throwing out other Europeans in favour of English pieces. This book could easily have been entirely filled up with Dickens, Shakespeare, Mayhew, *The New Newgate Calendar* and a medley of Elizabethan prose items. The only other people that came close to stooping low as agreeably were the Russians – Dostoevsky, Tolstoy and Gorky are all here. But they are definitely less good on the comic side of lowness.

While this anthology has many comic pieces, there are also those that will move the sensitive reader to tears. Some of these are fiction; others, more chillingly, show life at the bottom of the pile in every dreadful human detail. Most horrifying are those that reveal situations in which people are utterly trapped by their circumstances – from Mayhew's prostitute to, worst of all, the slaves mentioned in *The New Newgate Calendar* and Cowper's poems.

There are two kinds of lowness. There's the one that Jeffrey Bernard and I stoop to. Then there is the other kind – the black hole, the terrible twist of fate that engulfs its victim. While slavery was abolished long ago there are still many conditions that come close to it. That sort of 'low life' will continue in the world as long as the spiritual *low-lifes* enforce it.

Reader, you who can afford the price of a book, or can visit a library in a country where these are still free, I shall assume that you only indulge in a little low life from the outside – by observing, as Mayhew and my grandfather did – or at worst indulging in a little Jeffrey Bernard- or Fiona Pitt-Kethley-style research. Remember, reader, next time you fall down drunk (or observe someone else doing it), that the homeless man beside you might be another George Orwell or Villon and that you yourself are only a hair's breadth away from that black hole where a man's luck runs out. Examine the pasts of the men and women on the street today. What they are now often depends upon some turn of ill-luck – first losing their job, then their house when there's a divorce, for instance. In terms of appearance, a few days of poor food and a few nights in the rain are all it takes to convert a well-dressed businessman into the lowest of low-lifes. The only thing that we, the lucky ones, can do is try to ensure that there are steps out of that abyss and ways back to a more comfortable life. One day we may need those steps . . .

MEWLING
AND
PUKING

Looking After a Baby

Two homeless boys, Tommy and Clare, rescue a very young baby left to drown by its mother. They take it to their squat in an old haunted house full of rats. They buy a pennyworth of milk a day to feed it.

BABY STARTED a feeble whimper.

'You must wait now till I've attended to her,' continued Clare. 'If you had got up quietly without waking her, I would have given you your share at once.'

As he spoke, he pulled a blanket off the bed to wrap her in, and made haste to take her up. A series of difficulties followed, which I will leave to the imagination of mothers and aunts, and nurses in general – the worst being that there was no warm water to wash her in, and cold water would be worse than dangerous after what she had gone through with it the night before. Clare comforted himself that washing was a thing non-essential to existence, however desirable for well-being.

Then came a more serious difficulty: the milk must be mixed with water, and water as cold as Clare's legs would kill the drug-dazed shred of humanity! What was to be done? It would be equally dangerous to give her the strong milk of a cow undiluted. There was but one way: he must feed her as do the pigeons. First, however, he must have water! The well was almost inaccessible: to get to it and return would fearfully waste life-precious time! The rain-water in the little pool must serve the necessity! It was preferable to that in the butt!

★　★　★

Clare laid the baby down, and fetched water from the pool. Then he mixed the milk with what seemed the right quantity, again took the baby up, who had been whimpering a little now and then all the time, laid a blanket, several times folded, on his wet knees, and laid her in her blanket upon it. These preparations made, he took a small mouthful of the milk and water, and held it until it grew warm. It was the only way, I condescend to remind any such reader as may think it proper to be disgusted. When then he put his mouth to the baby's, careful not to let too much go at once, they managed so between them that she successfully appropriated the mouthful. It was followed by a second, a third, and more, until, to Clare's delight, the child seemed satisfied, leaving some of the precious fluid for another meal. He put her in the bed again, and covered her up.

Clare eventually contrives a bottle and manages to bath the baby.

Having in his mind revolved the matter many a time that day, he got some sticks together from the garden, and with one of the precious matches lighted a small fire of coals that were not his own, and for which he could merely hope one day to restore amends. But baby! Baby was more than coals! He filled a rusty kettle with water, and while it was growing hot on the fire, such was his fear lest the smoke should betray them, that he ran out every other minute to see how much was coming from the chimney.

While the fire was busy heating the water, he was busier preparing a bottle for baby – making a hole through the cork of a phial, putting the broken stem of a clean tobacco pipe he had found in the street through the hole, tying a small lump of cotton wool over the end of the pipe-stem, and covering that with a piece of his pocket handkerchief, carefully washed with the brown Windsor soap, his mother's last present. For the day held yet another gladness: in looking for a kettle he had found the soap – which probably the rat had carried away and hidden before finding baby. Through the pipe-stem and the wool and the handkerchief he could without difficulty draw water, and hoped therefore baby would succeed in drawing her supper. As soon as the water was warm he mixed some with the milk, but not so much this time, and put the mixture in the bottle. To his delight, the baby sucked it up splendidly. The bottle, thought out between the heavy linen and the hard street, was a success! Labour is not unfriendly to thought, as the annals of weaving and shoe-making witness.

And now at last was Clare equipped for a great attempt: he was going to wash the baby! He was glad that disrespectful Tommy was not in the house. With a basin of warm water and his precious piece of soap he set about it, and taking much pains washed his treasure perfectly clean. It was a state of bliss in which, up to that moment, I presume, she had never been since her birth. In the process he handled her, if not with all the skill of a nurse, yet with the tenderness of a mother. His chief anxiety was not to hurt, more than could not be helped, the poor little rat-eaten toes. He felt he must wash them, but when in the process she whimpered, it went all through the calves of his legs. When the happy but solicitous task was over, during which the infant had shown the submission of great weakness, he wrapped her in another blanket, and laid her down again. Soothed and comfortable, as probably never soothed or comfortable before, she went to sleep.

As soon as she was out of his arms, he took a piece of bread, and with some of the hot water made a little sop for the dog, which the small hero, whose four legs carried such a long barrel of starvation, ate with undisguised pleasure and thankfulness. For his own supper Clare preferred his bread dry, following it with a fine draught of water from the well.

from *A Rough Shaking* by George Macdonald

The Luck of Roaring Camp

THERE WAS COMMOTION in Roaring Camp. It could not have been a fight, for in 1850 that was not novel enough to have called together the entire settlement. The ditches and claims were not only deserted, but 'Tuttle's grocery' had contributed its gamblers, who, it will be remembered, calmly continued their game the day that French Pete and Kanaka Joe shot each other to death over the bar in the front room. The whole camp was collected before a rude cabin on the outer edge of the clearing. Conversation was carried on in a low tone, but the name of a woman was frequently repeated. It was a name familiar enough in the camp – 'Cherokee Sal'.

Perhaps the less said of her the better. She was a coarse, and, it is to be feared, a very sinful woman. But at the time she was the only woman in Roaring Camp, and was just then lying in sore extremity, when she most needed the ministration of her own sex. Dissolute, abandoned, and irreclaimable, she was yet suffering a martyrdom hard enough to bear even when veiled by sympathising womanhood, but now terrible in her loneliness. The primal curse had come to her in that original isolation which must have made the punishment of the first transgression so dreadful. It was, perhaps, part of the expiation of her sin, that, at a moment when she most lacked her sex's intuitive tenderness and care, she met only the half-contemptuous faces of her masculine associates. Yet a few of the spectators were, I think, touched by her sufferings. Sandy Tipton thought it was 'Rough on Sal', and, in the contemplation of her condition, for a moment rose superior to the fact that he had an ace and two bowers in his sleeve.

It will be seen, also, that the situation was novel. Deaths were by no means uncommon in Roaring Camp, but a birth was a new thing. People had been dismissed the camp effectively, finally, and with no possibility of return; but this was the first time that anybody had been introduced *ab initio*. Hence the excitement.

'You go in there, Stumpy,' said a prominent citizen known as 'Kentuck', addressing one of the loungers. 'Go in there, and see what you kin do. You've had experience in them things.'

Perhaps there was a fitness in the selection. Stumpy, in other climes, had been the putative head of two families; in fact, it was owing to some legal informality in these proceedings that Roaring Camp – a city of refuge – was indebted to his company. The crowd approved the choice, and Stumpy was wise enough to bow to the majority. The door closed on the extempore surgeon and midwife, and Roaring Camp sat down outside, smoked its pipe, and awaited the issue.

The assemblage numbered about a hundred men. One or two of these were actual fugitives from justice, some were criminal – and all were reckless. Physically, they exhibited no indication of their past lives and character. The greatest scamp had a Raphael face, with a profusion of blonde hair; Oakhurst, a gambler, had the melancholy air and intellectual abstraction of a Hamlet; the coolest and most courageous man was scarcely over five feet in height, with a soft voice and an embarrassed, timid manner. The term 'roughs' applied to them was a distinction rather than a definition. Perhaps in the minor details of fingers, toes, ears, etc., the camp may have been deficient, but these slight omissions did not detract from their aggregate force. The strongest man had but three fingers on his right hand; the best shot had but one eye.

Such was the physical aspect of the men that were dispersed around the cabin. The camp lay in a triangular valley, between two hills and a river. The only outlet was a steep trail over the summit of a hill that faced the cabin, now illuminated by the rising moon. The suffering woman might have seen it from the rude bunk whereon she lay – seen it winding like a silver thread until it was lost in the stars above.

A fire of withered pine-boughs added sociability to the gathering. By degrees the natural levity of Roaring Camp returned. Bets were freely offered and taken regarding the result. Three to five that 'Sal would get through with it'; even, that the child would survive, side bets as to the sex and complexion of the coming stranger. In the midst of an excited discussion an exclamation came from those nearest the door, and the camp stopped to listen. Above the swaying and moaning of the pines, the swift rush of the river, and the crackling of the fire, rose a sharp, querulous cry – a cry unlike anything heard before in the camp. The pines stopped moaning, the river ceased to rush, and the fire to crackle. It seemed as if Nature had stopped to listen too.

The camp rose to its feet as one man! It was proposed to explode a barrel of gunpowder, but, in consideration of the situation of the mother, better counsels prevailed, and only a few revolvers were discharged; for, whether owing to the rude surgery of the camp, or some other reason, Cherokee Sal was sinking fast. Within an hour she had climbed, as it were, that rugged road that led to the stars, and so passed out of Roaring Camp, its sin and shame, for ever. I do not think that the announcement disturbed them much, except in speculation as to the fate of the child. 'Can he live now?' was asked of Stumpy. The answer was doubtful. The only other being of Cherokee Sal's sex and maternal condition in the settlement was an ass. There was some conjecture as to fitness, but the experiment was tried. It was less problematical than the ancient treatment of Romulus and Remus, and apparently as successful.

When these details were completed, which exhausted another hour, the door was opened, and the anxious crowd of men who had already formed themselves into a queue entered in single file. Beside the low bunk or shell, on which the figure of the mother was starkly outlined below the blankets, stood a pine table. On this a candlebox was placed, and within it, swathed in staring red flannel, lay the last arrival at Roaring Camp. Beside the candlebox was placed a hat. Its use was soon indicated. 'Gentlemen,' said Stumpy, with a singular mixture of authority and *ex officio* complacency – 'Gentlemen will please pass in at the front door, round the table, and out at the back door. Them as wishes to contribute anything toward the orphan will find a hat handy.' The first man entered with his hat on; he uncovered, however, as he looked about him, and so, unconsciously, set an example to the next. In such communities good and bad actions are catching. As the procession filed in, comments were audible – criticisms addressed, perhaps, rather to Stumpy, in the character of showman – 'Is that him?'; 'mighty small specimen'; 'hasn't mor'n got the colour'; 'ain't bigger nor a derringer'. The contributions were as characteristic: a silver tobacco-box; a doubloon; a Navy revolver, silver mounted; a gold specimen; a very beautifully embroidered lady's handkerchief (from Oakhurst the gambler); a diamond breastpin; a diamond ring (suggested by the pin, with the remark from the giver that he 'saw that pin and went two diamonds better'); a slung shot; a Bible (contributor not detected); a golden spur; a silver teaspoon (the initials, I regret to say, were not the giver's); a pair of surgeon's shears; a lancet; a Bank of England note for £5; and about $200 in loose gold and silver coin. During these proceedings Stumpy maintained a silence as impassive as the dead on his left, a gravity as inscrutable as that of the newly born on his right. Only one incident occurred to break the monotony of the curious procession. As Kentuck bent over the candlebox half curiously, the child turned, and, in a spasm of pain, caught at his groping finger, and held it fast for a moment. Kentuck looked foolish and embarrassed. Something like a blush tried to assert itself in his weather-beaten cheek. 'The d—d little cuss!' he said, as he extricated his finger, with, perhaps, more tenderness and care than he might have been deemed capable of showing. He held that finger a little apart from its fellows as he went out, and examined it curiously. The examination provoked the same original remark in regard to the child. In fact, he seemed to enjoy repeating it. 'He rastled with my finger,' he remarked to Tipton, holding up the member, 'the d—d little cuss!'

It was four o'clock before the camp sought repose. A light burnt in the cabin where the watchers sat, for Stumpy did not go to bed that night. Nor did Kentuck. He drank quite freely, and related with great gusto his experience, invariably ending with his characteristic condemnation of the new-comer. It seemed to relieve him of any unjust implication of sentiment, and Kentuck had the weaknesses of the nobler sex. When everybody else had gone to bed, he walked down to the river, and whistled reflectingly. Then he walked up the gulch, past the cabin, still whistling with demonstrative unconcern. At a large red-wood tree he paused and retraced his steps, and again passed the cabin. Half-way down to the river's bank he again paused, and then returned and knocked at the door. It was opened by Stumpy. 'How goes it?' said Kentuck, looking past Stumpy toward the candlebox. 'All serene,' replied Stumpy. 'Anything up?' 'Nothing.' There was a pause – an embarrassing one – Stumpy still holding the door. Then Kentuck had recourse to his finger, which he held up to Stumpy. 'Rastled with it – the d—d little cuss,' he said, and retired.

The next day Cherokee Sal had such rude sepulture as Roaring Camp afforded. After her body had been committed to the hillside, there was a formal meeting of the camp to discuss what should be done with her infant. A resolution to adopt it was unanimous and enthusiastic. But an animated discussion in regard to the manner and feasibility of providing for its wants at once sprung up. It was remarkable that the argument partook of none of those fierce personalities with which discussions were usually conducted at Roaring Camp. Tipton proposed that they should send the child to Red Dog, a distance of forty miles – where female attention could be procured. But the unlucky suggestion met with fierce and unanimous opposition. It was evident that no plan which entailed parting from their new acquisition would for a moment be entertained. 'Besides,' said Tom Ryder, 'them fellows at Red Dog would swap it, and ring in somebody else on us.' A disbelief in the honesty of other camps prevailed at Roaring Camp as in other places.

The introduction of a female nurse in the camp also met with objection. It was argued that no decent woman could be prevailed to accept Roaring Camp as her home, and the speaker urged that 'they didn't want any more of the other kind'. This unkind allusion to the defunct mother, harsh as it may seem, was the first spasm of propriety – the first symptom of the camp's regeneration. Stumpy advanced nothing. Perhaps he felt a certain delicacy in interfering with the selection of a possible successor in office. But when questioned, he averred stoutly that he and 'Jinny' – the mammal before alluded to – could manage to rear the child. There was something original, independent, and heroic about the plan that pleased the camp. Stumpy was retained. Certain articles were sent for to Sacramento. 'Mind,' said the treasurer, as he pressed a bag of gold dust into the expressman's hand, 'the best that can be got – lace, you know, and filigree-work and frills – d—m the cost!'

Strange to say, the child thrived. Perhaps the invigorating climate of the mountain camp was compensation for material deficiencies. Nature took the foundling to her broader breast. In that rare atmosphere of the Sierra foothills – that air pungent with balsamic odour, that ethereal cordial at once bracing and exhilarating – he may have found food and nourishment, or a subtle chemistry that transmuted asses' milk to lime and phosphorus. Stumpy inclined to the belief that it was the latter and good nursing. 'Me and that ass,' he would say, 'has been father and mother to him! Don't you,' he would add, apostrophising the helpless bundle before him, 'never go back on us.'

By the time he was a month old, the necessity of giving him a name became apparent. He had generally been known as 'the Kid', 'Stumpy's boy', 'the Coyote' (an allusion to his vocal powers), and even by Kentuck's endearing diminutive of 'the d—d little cuss'. But these were felt to be vague and unsatisfactory, and were at last dismissed under another influence. gamblers and adventurers are generally superstitious, and Oakhurst one day declared that the baby had brought 'the luck' to Roaring Camp. It was certain that of late they had been successful. 'Luck' was the name agreed upon, with the prefix of Tommy for greater convenience. No allusion was made to the mother, and the father was unknown. 'It's better,' said the philosophical Oakhurst, 'to take a fresh deal all round. Call him Luck, and start him fair.' A day was accordingly set apart for the christening. What was meant by this ceremony the reader may imagine, who has already gathered some idea of the reckless irreverence of Roaring Camp. The master of ceremonies was one 'Boston', a noted wag, and the occasion seemed to promise the greatest facetiousness. This ingenious satirist had spent two days in preparing a burlesque of the church service, with pointed local allusions. The choir was properly trained, and Sandy Tipton was to stand godfather. But after the procession had marched to the grove with music and banners, and the child had been deposited before a mock altar, Stumpy stepped before the expectant crowd. 'It ain't my style to spoil fun, boys,' said the little man, stoutly, eyeing the faces around him, 'but it strikes me that this thing ain't exactly on the square. It's playing it pretty low down on this yer baby to ring in fun on him that he ain't going to understand. And if there's going to be any godfathers round, I'd like to see who's got any better rights than me.' A silence followed Stumpy's speech. To the credit of all humorists be it said, that the first man to acknowledge its justice was the satirist, thus stopped of his fun. 'But,' said Stumpy, quickly, following up his advantage, 'we're here for a christening, and we'll have it. I proclaim you Thomas Luck, according to the laws of the United States and the State of California, so help me God.' It was the first time that the name of the Deity had been uttered otherwise than profanely in the camp.

The form of christening was perhaps even more ludicrous than the satirist had conceived; but, strangely enough, nobody saw it and nobody laughed. 'Tommy' was christened as seriously as he would have been under a Christian roof, and cried and was comforted in as orthodox fashion.

And so the work of regeneration began in Roaring Camp. Almost imperceptibly a change came over the settlement. The cabin assigned to 'Tommy Luck' – or 'The Luck', as he was more frequently called – first showed signs of improvement. It was kept scrupulously clean and white-washed. Then it was boarded, clothed, and papered. The rosewood cradle – packed eighty miles by mule – had, in Stumpy's way of putting it, 'sorter killed the rest of the furniture'. So the rehabilitation of the cabin became a necessity. The men who were in the habit of lounging in at Stumpy's to see 'how The Luck got on' seemed to appreciate the change, and, in self-defence, the rival establishment of 'Tuttle's grocery' bestirred itself, and imported a carpet and mirrors. The reflections of the latter on the appearance of Roaring Camp tended to produce stricter habits of personal cleanliness. Again, Stumpy imposed a kind of quarantine upon those who aspired to the honour and privilege of holding 'The Luck'. It was a cruel mortification to Kentuck – who, in the carelessness of a large nature and the habits of frontier life, had begun to regard all garments as a second cuticle, which, like a snake's, only sloughed off through decay – to be debarred this privilege from certain prudential reasons. Yet such was the subtle influence of innovation that he thereafter appeared regularly every afternoon in a clean shirt, and face still shining from his ablutions. Nor were moral and social sanitary laws neglected. 'Tommy', who was supposed to spend his whole existence in a persistent attempt to repose, must not be disturbed by noise. The shouting and yelling which had gained the camp its infelicitous title were not permitted within hearing distance of Stumpy's. The men conversed in whispers, or smoked with Indian gravity. Profanity was tacitly given up in these sacred precincts, and throughout the camp a popular form of expletive, known as 'D—n the luck!' and 'Curse the luck!', was abandoned, as having a new personal bearing. Vocal music was not interdicted, being supposed to have a soothing, tranquillising quality, and one song, sung by 'Man-o'-War Jack', an English sailor, from Her Majesty's Australian colonies, was quite popular as a lullaby. It was a lugubrious recital of the exploits of 'the Arethusa, Seventy-four', in a muffled minor, ending with a prolonged dying fall at the burden of each verse, 'On b-o-o-o-ard of the Arethusa.' It was a fine sight to see Jack holding The Luck, rocking from side to side as if with the motion of a ship, and crooning forth this naval ditty. Either through the peculiar rocking of Jack or the length of his song – it contained ninety stanzas, and was continued with conscientious deliberation to the bitter end – the lullaby generally had the desired effect. At such times the men would lie at full length under the trees, in the soft summer twilight, smoking their pipes and drinking in the melodious utterances. An indistinct idea that this was pastoral happiness pervaded the camp. 'This 'ere kind o' think,' said the Cockney Simmons, meditatively reclining on his elbow, 'is 'evingly.' It reminded him of Greenwich.

On the long summer days The Luck was usually carried to the gulch, from whence the golden store of Roaring Camp was taken. There, on a blanket spread over pine-boughs, he would lie while the men were working in the ditches below. Latterly, there was a rude attempt to decorate this bower with flowers and sweet-smelling shrubs, and generally someone would bring him a cluster of wild honeysuckles, azaleas, or the painted blossoms of Las Mariposas. The men had suddenly awakened to the fact that there were beauty and significance in these trifles, which they had so long trodden carelessly beneath their feet. A flake of glittering mica, a fragment of variegated quartz, a bright pebble from the bed of the creek, became beautiful to eyes thus cleared and strengthened, and were invariably put aside for 'The Luck'. It was wonderful how many treasures the woods and hillsides yielded that 'would do for Tommy'. Surrounded by playthings such as never child out of fairy-land had before, it is to be hoped that Tommy was content. He appeared to be securely happy, albeit there was an infantine gravity about him, a contemplative light in his round grey eyes, that sometimes worried Stumpy. He was always tractable and quiet, and it is recorded that once, having crept beyond his 'corral' – a hedge of tessellated pine-boughs, which surrounded his bed – he dropped over the bank of his head in the soft earth, and remained with his mottled legs in the air in that position for at least five minutes with unflinching gravity. He was extricated without murmur. I hesitate to record the many other instances of his sagacity, which rest, unfortunately, upon the statements of prejudiced friends. Some of them were not without a tinge of superstition. 'I crep' up the bank just now,' said Kentuck one day, in a breathless state of excitement, 'and dern my skin if he wasn't a talking to a jay-bird as was sittin' on his lap. There they was, just as free and sociable as anything you please, a jawin' at each other just like two cherry-bums.' Howbeit, whether creeping over the pine-boughs or lying lazily on his back blinking at the leaves above him, to him the birds sang, the squirrels chattered, and the flowers bloomed. Nature was his nurse and playfellow. For him she would let slip between the leaves golden shafts of sunlight that fell just within his grasp; she would send wandering breezes to visit him with the balm of bay and resinous gums; to him the tall red-woods nodded familiarly and sleepily, the bumble-bees buzzed, and the rooks cawed a slumbrous accompaniment.

Such was the golden summer of Roaring Camp. They were 'flush times' – and the Luck was with them. The claims had yielded enormously. The camp was jealous of its privileges and looked suspiciously on strangers. No encouragement was given to immigration, and, to make their seclusion more perfect, the land on either side of the mountain wall that surrounded the camp they duly pre-empted. This, and a reputation for singular proficiency with the revolver, kept the reserve of Roaring Camp inviolate. The expressman – their only connecting link with the surrounding world – sometimes told wonderful stories of the camp. He would say, 'They've a street up there in "Roaring", that would lay over any street in Red Dog. They've got vines and flowers round their houses, and they wash themselves twice a day. But they're mighty rough on strangers, and they worship an Ingin baby.'

With the prosperity of the camp came a desire for further improvement. It was proposed to build a hotel in the following spring, and to invite one or two decent families to reside there for the sake of 'The Luck' – who might perhaps profit by female companionship. The sacrifice that this concession to the sex cost these men, who were fiercely sceptical in regard to its general virtue and usefulness, can only be accounted for by their affection for Tommy. A few still held out. But the resolve could not be carried into effect for three months, and the minority meekly yielded in the hope that something might turn up to prevent it. And it did.

The winter of 1851 will long be remembered in the foothills. The snow lay deep on the Sierras, and every mountain creek became a river, and every river a lake. Each gorge and gulch was transformed into a tumultuous watercourse that descended the hillsides, tearing down giant trees and scattering its drift and debris along the plain. Red Dog had been twice under the water, and Roaring Camp had been forewarned. 'Water put the gold into them gulches,' said Stumpy. 'It's been here once and will be here again!' And that night the North Fork suddenly leaped over its banks, and swept up the triangular valley of Roaring Camp.

In the confusion of rushing water, crushing trees, and crackling timber, and the darkness which seemed to flow with the water and blot out the fair valley, but little could be done to collect the scattered camp. When the morning broke, the cabin of Stumpy nearest the river bank was gone. Higher up the gulch they found the body of its unlucky owner; but the pride, the hope, the joy, the Luck, of Roaring Camp had disappeared. They were returning with sad hearts, when a shout from the bank recalled them.

It was a relief-boat from down the river. They had picked up, they said, a man and an infant, nearly exhausted, about two miles below. Did anybody know them, and did they belong here?

It needed but a glance to show them Kentuck lying there, cruelly crushed and bruised, but still holding the Luck of Roaring Camp in his arms. As they bent over the strangely assorted pair, they saw that the child was cold and pulseless. 'He is dead,' said one. Kentuck opened his eyes. 'Dead?' he repeated, feebly. 'Yes, my man, and you are dying too.' A smile lit the eyes of the expiring Kentuck. 'Dying,' he repeated, 'he's a taking me with him – tell the boys I've got the Luck with me now'; and the strong man, clinging to the frail babe as a drowning man is said to cling to a straw, drifted away into the shadowy river that flows for ever to the unknown sea.

Bret Harte

The Cry of the Children

I

Do ye hear the children weeping, O my brothers,
   Ere the sorrow comes with years?
They are leaning their young heads against their mothers,
   And that cannot stop their tears.
The young lambs are bleating in the meadows,
   The young birds are chirping in the nest,
The young fawns are playing with the shadows,
   The young flowers are blowing toward the west –
But the young, young children, O my brothers,
   They are weeping bitterly!
They're weeping in the playtime of the others,
   In the country of the free.

II

Do you question the young children in the sorrow,
   Why their tears are falling so?
The old man may weep for his to-morrow
   Which is lost in Long Ago;
The old tree is leafless in the forest,
   The old year is ending in the frost,
The old wound, if stricken, is the sorest,
   The old hope is hardest to be lost.
But the young, young children, O my brothers,
   Do you ask them why they stand
Weeping sore before the bosoms of their mothers,
   In our happy Fatherland?

III

They look up with their pale and sunken faces,
   And their looks are sad to see,
For the man's hoary anguish draws and presses
   Down the cheeks of infancy.
'Your old earth,' they say, 'is very dreary,
   Our young feet,' they say, 'are very weak;

Few paces have we taken, yet are weary –
    Our grave-rest is very far to seek:
Ask the aged why they weep, and not the children,
    For the outside earth is cold,
And we young ones stand without, in our bewildering,
    And the graves are for the old.'

IV

'True,' say the children, 'it may happen
    That we die before our time:
Little Alice died last year, her grave is shapen
    Like a snowball, in the rime.
We looked into the pit prepared to take her:
    There was no room for any work in the close clay!
From the sleep wherein she lieth none will wake her,
    Crying, "Get up, little Alice! it is day."
If you listen by that grave, in sun and shower,
    With your ear down, little Alice never cries;
Could we see her face, be sure we should not know her,
    For the smile has time for growing in her eyes:
And merry go her moments, lulled and stilled in
    The shroud by the kirk-chime.
It is good when it happens,' say the children,
    'That we die before our time.'

V

Alas, alas, the children! they are seeking
    Death in life, as best to have:
They are binding up their hearts away from breaking,
    With a cerement from the grave.
Go out, children, from the mine and from the city,
    Sing out, children, as the little thrushes do;
Pluck your handfuls of the meadow-cowslips pretty,
    Laugh aloud, to feel your fingers let them slip through!
But they answer, 'Are your cowslips of the meadows
    Like our weeds anear the mine?
Leave us quiet in the dark of the coal-shadows,
    From your pleasures fair and fine!'

VI

'For oh,' say the children, 'we are weary,
        And we cannot run or leap;
If we cared for any meadows, it were merely
        To drop down in them and sleep.
Our knees tremble sorely in the stooping,
        We fall upon our faces, trying to go,
And, underneath our heavy eyelids drooping,
        The reddest flower would look as pale as snow.
For, all day, we drag our burden tiring
        Through the coal-dark underground;
Or, all day, we drive the wheels of iron
        In the factories, round and round.'

VII

'For, all day, the wheels are droning, turning;
        Their wind comes in our faces,
Till our hearts turn, our heads with pulses burning
        And the walls turn in their places:
Turns the sky in the high window, blank and reeling,
        Turns the long light that drops adown the wall,
Turn the black flies that crawl along the ceiling:
        All are turning, all the day, and we with all.
And all the day the iron wheels are droning,
        And sometimes we could pray,
"O ye wheels" (breaking out in a mad moaning)
        "Stop! be silent for to-day!" '

VIII

Ay, be silent! Let them hear each other breathing
        For a moment, mouth to mouth!
Let them touch each other's hands, in a fresh wreathing
        Of their tender human youth!
Let them feel that this cold metallic motion
        Is not all the life God fashions or reveals:
Let them prove their living souls against the notion
        That they live in you, or under you, O wheels!
Still, all day, the iron wheels go onward,

Grinding life down from its mark;
And the children's souls, which God is calling sunward,
    Spin on blindly in the dark.

IX

Now tell the poor young children, O my brothers,
    To look up to him and pray;
So the blessed One who blesseth all the others,
    Will bless them another day.
They answer, 'Who is God that He should hear us,
    While the rushing of the iron wheels is stirred?
When we sob aloud, the human creatures near us
    Pass by, hearing not, or answer not a word.
And *we* hear not (for the wheels in their resounding)
    Strangers speaking at the door:
Is it likely God, with angels singing round Him,
    Hears our weeping any more?'

X

'Two words, indeed, of praying we remember,
    And at midnight's hour of harm,
"Our Father," looking upward in the chamber,
    We say softly for a charm.
We know no other words except "Our Father,"
    And we think that, in some pause of angels' song,
God may pluck them with the silence sweet to gather,
    And hold both within His right hand which is strong.
"Our Father!" If He heard us, He would surely
    (For they call Him good and mild)
Answer, smiling down the steep world very purely,
    "Come and rest with me, my child." '

XI

'But, no!' say the children, weeping faster,
    'He is speechless as a stone:
And they tell us, of His image is the master
    Who commands us to work on.

Go to!' say the children, – 'up in Heaven,
    Dark, wheel-like, turning clouds are all we find.
Do not mock us; grief has made us unbelieving:
    We look up for God, but tears have made us blind.'
Do you hear the children weeping and disproving,
    O my brothers, what ye preach?
For God's possible is taught by His world's loving,
    And the children doubt of each.

XII

And well may the children weep before you!
    They are weary ere they run;
They have never seen the sunshine, nor the glory
    Which is brighter than the sun.
They know the grief of man, without its wisdom,
    They sink in man's despair, without its calm;
Are slaves, without the liberty in Christdom,
    Are martyrs, by the pang without the palm:
Are worn as if with age, yet unretrievingly
    The harvest of its memories cannot reap, –
Are orphans of the earthly love and heavenly.
    Let them weep! let them weep.

XIII

They look up with their pale and sunken faces,
    And their look is dread to see,
For they mind you of their angels in high places,
    With eyes turned on Deity.
'How long,' they say, 'how long, O cruel nation,
    Will you stand, to move the world on a child's heart, –
Stifle down with a mailed heel its palpitation,
    And treat onward to your throne amid the mart?
Our blood splashes upward, O gold-heaper,
    And your purple shows your path!
But the child's sob in the silence curses deeper
    Than the strong man in his wrath.'

Elizabeth Barrett Browning

The Babes in the Wood

It's a woeful bad tale I'm about to relate,
It happened years back, but I don't know the date;
It's a heart-rending tale of two babies so good,
Vot vos starved to death in a blackberry wood.
Ven they vos quite infants, they lost their mamma.
They vos both left alone in the vorld vith their pa,
To attend to his babbies was alvays his plan,

(Chorus)
But their nunky he vos such a vicked old man,
Their nunky he vos such a hard-hearted man.

In their daddy's last moments and on his death bed,
He sent for their nunky, and to him he said,
'I feel I am going, come, tip us your fin,
Look after my babbies, take care of their tin:
But should they both croak, vich I hope they vont do,
The whole of their ochre I give unto you.'
Says he, 'My dear brother I'll do all I can' –
But their nunky he vos a deceitful old man.
Their nunky he vos, etc.

He'd scarce laid his brother under the ground,
Vhen he sold all the things in the house vot vos found;
He took the two babbies home to his abode,
And he bought 'em some hard bake to eat on the road,
He bought 'em some apples – he bought 'em parched peas,
A new penny loaf, and a ha'porth of cheese;
He blowed out their bags vith all sorts of scran,
But their nunky he vos a deceitful old man,
Their nunky he vos, etc.

Vhen he looked at the kids, he longed for their gold
In damp sheets he laid 'em, 'cos he thought they'd catch cold:
They both caught the measles, and the whooping-cough,
And he prayed every night that it would take them off,
But they got over that, and all other disease

Vich kids mostly have – which it didn't him please;
So to cook the poor babbies, he thought on a plan,
For their nunky he vos a deceitful old man,
Their nunky he vos, etc.

He hired two barbers vot vos both out of vork,
To take the two babbies to Norwood to burk,[1]
Now ven they got there, they altered their minds –
They both cut their sticks – left their babbies behind.
They wandered about, did these infants so good,
They ate all the blackberries that growed in the wood,
Vith hips, haws, and sloes, their bellies did cram,
Through their nunky who vos such a vicked old man,
Their nunky he vos, etc.

They liv'd till next night ven they guv up the ghost,
They vos both on 'em freezed as stiff as a post;
A cock robin vos perched on a tree close by, –
He vept as he vitnessed those babbies die;
Then he kivered 'em over, as nice as could be,
Vith some cabbage leaves fresh, vot he picked off a tree,
And he hopped, and he twittered, and the song that he sang,
Vos 'Their nunky he must be a vicked old man.
Their nunky he vos, etc.'

Not a vink of sleep, after, nunky he got,
The whole of his body was seized vith the rot,
The whole of his toes dropped off his feet,
And teeth tumbled out of his mouth in the street.
The ghosts of the babbies, next night it is said,
They com'd and they tore all the hair off his head;
And vhen he valked out, the boys arter him ran,
Crying, cruel old nunky, you vicked old man.
Cried after their nunky, etc.

He dwindled away to a mere bag of bones,
Till the neighbours von night vos alarmed at his groans,
His house on that night vos burned down to the ground,
Not a remnant of nunky vos there to be found.

1 Murder – the word derives from the doings of the infamous Burke and Hare.

The ruins so strongly of brimstone did smell,
And the neighbours all round this story do tell;
That the devil that night avay vith him ran,
'Cos their nunky he vos such a vicked old man.
Cos their nunky he vos, etc.

Anon.

Lullaby

ONE SULTRY SUMMER NIGHT, in an out-of-the-way alley on the outskirts of the town, I saw a strange sight. A woman, standing in the middle of an enormous puddle, was stamping her feet, splashing the mud as little boys do – she was stamping and singing a bawdy song in a nasal voice.

During the day a storm had swept over the town. The heavy downpour had turned the clayey earth of the alley into mud. The puddle was deep. The woman was almost up to her knees in it. To judge by her voice, the singer was drunk. If, tired with dancing, she had dropped, she might easily have drowned in the liquid mud.

I pulled up my high boots, got into the puddle, grabbed her by the arms and dragged her to a dry spot. At first, apparently, she was frightened. She followed me obediently, without a word. But then with a vigorous movement of her whole body she wrenched her right arm free, struck me on the chest, and screamed, 'Help!' Then she resolutely made for the puddle again, dragging me with her.

'You devil!' she mumbled, 'I won't go! I'll get along without you . . . You get on without me . . . He-elp!'

The night-watchman emerged from the darkness, stopped five steps away from us and asked in a surly tone, 'Who's making that racket there?'

I told him that I was afraid the woman would drown in the mud, and that I wanted to pull her out. The watchman looked closely at the drunken woman, spat noisily, and commanded, 'Mashka, come on out.'

'I won't.'

'And I'm telling you, come on out!'

'I won't do it.'

'I'll give you a beating, you slut!' the watchman promised her without enmity, and turned to me affably. 'She lives around here – she picks oakum for a living. Mashka's her name. Got a smoke?'

We lit cigarettes. The woman was bravely striding through the puddle, shouting now and then, 'Bosses! I'm my own boss! I'll take a bath here, if I want to.'

'I'll give you a bath!' the watchman – a sturdy, bearded old man – warned her. 'That's the way she carried on almost every night, and she has a crippled son at home.'

'Does she live far from here?'

'She ought to be shot,' said the watchman, without answering me.

'She ought to be taken home,' I suggested.

The watchman sniggered in his beard, held his cigarette up to my face and clumped away on the soggy path. 'Take her but look at her mug first.'

Meanwhile the woman sat down in the mud, paddling it with her hands, and squawked fiercely in a nasal voice, 'Over the dee-eep sea-ea-ea . . .'

Not far from where she sat, a huge star was reflected from the black emptiness above us in the greasy muddy water. When a ripple ran across the puddle, the reflection vanished. Again I stepped into the puddle, took the singer by the armpits, lifted her, and shoving her with my knees, led her over to the fence. She held back, waved her arms, and challenged me, 'Well, hit me, hit me! Never mind! Hit me! Ah, you beast! Ah, you butcher! Go ahead, hit me!'

Propping her against the fence, I asked her where she lived. She lifted her drunken head and looked at me out of the dark spots that were her eyes. I noticed that her nose had caved in and what was left of it stuck out like a button, that her upper lip, pulled askew by a scar, bared small teeth, and that her little bloated face wore a repellent smile.

'All right, let's go,' she said.

We walked on, lurching against the fence. The wet hem of her skirt kept slapping across my legs.

'Come, dear,' she mumbled, as though sobering up. 'I'll let you in, I'll comfort you.'

She brought me into the courtyard of a large, two-storey house. Carefully, like one blind, she walked among the carts, barrels, boxes, and piles of firewood, stopped before a hole in the foundation, and invited me, 'Go in.'

Holding on to the slimy walls, grasping the woman by her waist, hardly able to keep her sprawling body together, I lowered myself down the slippery steps, found the felt strip and the latch of the door, opened it, and stood on the threshold of a black pit without having the courage to go further.

'Mammy, is it you?' a soft voice asked in the dark.

'It's me.'

A warm stench of decay and a smell of tar struck my nostrils. A match was lit and for a second the small flame illumined a pale childish face, and then went out.

'Who else would be coming to you? It's me,' said the woman, swaying against me.

Another match was struck, there was a clink of glass and a thin funny hand lit a small tin lamp.

'Darling,' said the woman, and swaying, tumbled into the corner. There, hardly raised above the brick floor, was a wide bed.

Watching the flame of the lamp closely, the child adjusted the wick as it began to smoke. He had a grave little face with a sharp nose and full lips like a girl's. It was a little face that looked as though it were painted with a fine brush, and it was startlingly out of place in this dark damp hole. Having taken care of the lamp, he looked at me with eyes so heavily fringed that they looked shaggy, and asked, 'She drunk?'

His mother, who lay across the bed, was hiccuping and snoring.

'She ought to be undressed,' I said.

'Undress her,' the boy replied, lowering his eyes. And when I began to pull the wet skirt off the woman, he asked quietly and in a business-like fashion, 'The lamp – shall I put it out?'

'What for?'

He did not answer. While I was handling his mother like a sack of flour, I was watching him. He sat on the floor in a box made of heavy boards on which there was an inscription in black letters: 'Handle with care. N.R. and Co.' The sill of the square window was flush with the boy's shoulder. Against the wall there were several narrow shelves, on which cigarette and matchboxes were piled. Next to the box in which the boy sat there was another one, covered with yellow paper, which apparently served as a table. His funny pitiful hands behind his neck, the boy was looking up at the dark window-panes.

Having undressed the woman, I threw her wet clothes on the stove. I washed my hands in the earthenware washbasin in the corner, and wiping them on a handkerchief, I said to the child, 'Well, now, good-bye.'

He looked at me, and, speaking with a slight lisp, asked, 'Now shall I put out the lamp?'

'If you like.'

'And you – are you going away? Aren't you going to bed?' With his little hand he pointed to his mother, 'With her.'

'What for?' I asked stupidly, surprised.

'You know, yourself,' he said with terrible simplicity, and, stretching himself, added, 'They all do it.'

Abashed, I looked about me. To the right, there was the mouth of an ugly stove, on the hearth were dirty dishes, in the corner behind the box – pieces of tarred rope and a pile of picked oakum, logs of firewood, kindling, and a yoke for carrying pails of water. At my feet stretched a snoring yellow form.

'May I sit with you awhile?' I asked the boy.

He looked at me from under his brows. 'But she won't wake up till morning.'

'But I don't need her.'

Squatting beside his box, I told him how I had come across his mother, trying to present the matter in a comic light. 'She was sitting in the mud, paddling with her hands and singing . . .'

He nodded his head, smiling a pale smile and scratching his narrow chest. 'She was drunk, that's why. Even when she's sober, she likes to carry on. Just like a child . . .'

Now I was able to see his eyes clearly. His eyelashes were astonishingly long, and his eyelids too were thickly covered with beautiful curved little hairs. The bluish shadows under his eyes added to the pallor of his bloodless skin; his high forehead with a wrinkle above the nose was surmounted by a shock of curly reddish hair. The expression of his eyes, which were both attentive and calm, was indescribable, and it was with difficulty that I bore this strange inhuman gaze.

'Your legs – what's wrong with them?'

He fumbled with the rags, disengaging a withered leg which looked like a cabbage-stalk, lifted it with his hand and placed it on the edge of the box.

'That's the sort they are. Both of them. Since I was born. They won't walk – they're not alive – that's how it is.'

'And what's in these boxes?'

'A menagerie,' he answered, lifted his leg in his hand as though it were a stick, stuck it into the rags on the bottom of the box, and with a serene, friendly smile, offered, 'Shall I show it to you? Well, make yourself comfortable. You've never seen anything like it.'

Manoeuvring adroitly with his extraordinarily long, thin arms, he hoisted himself up, and began to remove boxes from the shelves, handing them to me one after another.

'Take care, don't open them, or they'll run away. Put one to your ear and listen. well?'

'Something's moving.'

'Aha, a spider's sitting there, the scoundrel! His name is Drummer. He's a smart fellow!'

The boy's marvellous eyes grew lively and tender. A smile was playing over his livid face. With rapid movements of his nimble hands he was removing boxes from the shelves, putting them first to his ear, then to mine, and talking to me animatedly.

'And here is Anisim the cockroach, a show-off like a soldier. And this is a fly, an inspector's wife, a bad lot, the worst ever! She buzzes all day long, scolds everybody, she even pulled Mammy by the hair. Not a fly, but an inspector's wife, and her rooms have windows on the street. She only looks like a fly. And this is a black cockroach, a huge one: Master. He's all right. Only he's a drunk and has no shame. He'll get tight and crawl around the courtyard naked and as shaggy as a black dog. And here's a bug: Uncle Nikodim. I caught him in the courtyard. He is a pilgrim, one of the crooks – makes believe he collects for the church. Mammy calls him "Cheat". He is her lover too. She has more lovers than you can count, thick as flies, even if she has no nose.'

'She doesn't beat you?'

'She? You're crazy. She can't live without me. She has a good heart, only she drinks. But on our street everybody drinks. She's pretty, and jolly too . . . Only she drinks, the slut. I tell her, "Stop swilling vodka, you fool, then you'll get rich," and she laughs at me. A woman – foolish, of course. But she's a good egg. Well, she'll sleep it off and you'll see for yourself.'

He was smiling so enchantingly that you wanted to howl with unbearable burning pity for him, to cry out so that the whole town would hear you. His beautiful little head swayed on its thin neck like a strange flower, and his eyes blazed with growing animation, attracting me with irresistible power.

As I listened to his childish but terrible chatter, for a moment I forgot where I was sitting. Then suddenly I saw again the small prison window, spattered on the outside with mud, the black mouth of the stove, the heap of oakum in the corner and near the door on a pile of rags the body of the woman, the mother, yellow as butter.

'A good menagerie?' the boy asked proudly.

'Very good.'

'But I haven't one butterfly, nor any moths, either.'

'What's your name?'

'Lenka.'

'You're my namesake.'

'Really? And you – what kind of a man are you?'

'No kind.'

'Oh, you're lying. Everybody's something. I know that. You're a good chap.'

'Perhaps.'

'Oh, I can see. You're a 'fraidy-cat, too.'

'What makes you say that?'

'Oh, I know.' He smiled slyly and even winked at me.

'Why do you think so?'

'Well, you sit here with me, that means you're afraid to go home at night.'

'But it's already daybreak.'

'So you're going back?'

'I'll come back.'

He wouldn't believe me. He covered his dear shaggy eyes with his lashes and, after a pause, said, 'What for?'

'Why, just to see you. You're an interesting fellow. May I come?'

'Do come. And come to see me not Mammy, deuce take her. Let's you and I be friends, eh?'

'All right.'

'Very well. It doesn't matter that you're big. How old are you?'

'Twenty.'

'And I'm eleven. I haven't any chums. Only Katka, the water-carrier's daughter. Her mother beats her because she comes to see me . . . Are you a thief?'

'No. Why a thief?'

'Your mug, its terrible. Skinny. And you have a nose like a thief's. A couple of thieves come here. One, Sashka, is a fool, and nasty. The other, Vanichka, he's kind, he's kind as a dog. Have you got any little boxes?'

'I'll bring you some.'

'Do. I won't tell Mammy that you're coming.'

'Why not?'

'I just won't. She's always glad when men come. Why, she loves men, the bitch. It's simply awful. She's a funny girl, my Mammy. At fifteen she managed to have me, she herself doesn't know how it happened. When will you come?'

'Tomorrow evening.'

'In the evening? Then she'll be drunk. And what do you do, if you're not a thief?'

'I sell Bavarian kvas.'

'Yes? Bring me a bottle will you?'

'Sure. I'll bring one. Well, I must be going.'

'Run along. Will you come?'

'Positively.'

He stretched both his long hands out towards me, and I pressed and shook those thin chilly bones, and without looking back, I climbed out into the yard like one drunk.

Dawn was breaking. Over the damp pile of half-dilapidated buildings Venus was trembling as it faded away. From the dirty pit under the wall of the house the panes of the cellar window stared at me with their square eyes, murky and stained like the eyes of a drunkard. In a cart by the gate a red-faced peasant was asleep with his huge bare feet flung wide apart. His thick rough beard stuck up towards the sky, and white teeth glistened in it. It looked as though the peasant were laughing sarcastically with his eyes closed. An old dog with a bald spot on its back, apparently the result of a scald, ambled over to me, sniffed at my leg and howled gently and hungrily, filling my heart with futile pity for it. The morning sky, pale and pink, was reflected in the placid puddles, and these reflections lent the filthy puddles an unnecessary, insulting beauty which debauched the soul.

The following day I asked the boys on my block to catch some bugs and butterflies. I bought pretty little boxes at the apothecary's, and I went to see Lenka, taking along two bottles of kvas, some gingerbread, candy, and sweet rolls. Lenka received my gifts with vast amazement, opening his darling eyes wide. By daylight they were even more marvellous.

'Oh, oh, oh!' he cried out, in a low unchildlike voice. 'All the things you've brought! Are you rich? How's that – rich but badly dressed, and you say you're not a thief! And the little boxes! Oh, oh, oh! It's a shame to touch them. My hands aren't clean. Who's in here? Aha, a bug! Looks like a copper, green, even. Oh, you devil! And will they run out and fly away? Goodness me!'

And suddenly he shouted gaily, 'Mom! Climb down and wash my hands. And look, you goose, what he had brought me! It's the same fellow, the one who dragged you here last night, like a policeman, it's the same one. His name is Lenka, too.'

'You must thank him,' I heard a strange low voice behind me.

The boy nodded his head rapidly. 'Thank you. Thank you.'

A thick cloud of fibrous dust was floating through the cellar, and with difficulty I distinguished on the stove the dishevelled head, the disfigured face of the woman, the gleam of her teeth, the involuntary, indestructible smile.

'How do you do?'

'How do you do?' the woman repeated. Her nasal voice sounded muffled but jaunty, almost cheerful. She looked at me squinting and mockingly, as it were. Lenka, oblivious of me, munched the gingerbread and hummed, as he carefully opened the boxes. His eyelashes cast a shadow on his cheeks, emphasising the rings under his eyes. The sun, dull, like the face of an old man, peered through the dirty window-panes, and a mild light fell upon the boy's reddish hair. His shirt was unbuttoned, showing his chest, and I saw how the heart was beating behind the thin bones, lifting the skin and the barely perceptible nipple.

His mother climbed down from the stove, moistened a towel in the washbasin, and coming over to Lenka took his left hand.

'He's run away! Stop him! He's run away!' he shouted. And with his whole body he began to thresh about in the box, throwing the smelly rags around, baring his blue inert legs.

The woman burst out laughing, fumbling among the rags, and shouted too, 'Catch him!'

Having caught the bug, she placed him on her palm, examined him with her lively eyes, the colour of a cornflower, and said to me in the tone of an old acquaintance, 'There are lots of those.'

'Don't you crush it!' her son warned her sternly. 'Once when she was drunk she sat on my menagerie – and crushed a lot of them!'

'Try and forget it, darling.'

'I had to do a lot of burying . . .'

'But I caught some others for you afterwards.'

'Others! The ones you crushed were trained ones, sillybilly! The ones that croaked I buried under the stove. I'd crawl out and bury them – I have a cemetery there. You know, I once had a spider, Minka, he looked just like one of Mammy's lovers, the one who's in prison, the fat jolly one . . .'

'Oh, my precious darling,' said the woman, stroking her son's curls with a small, dark stumpy-fingered hand. Then, nudging me with her elbow, she asked, her eyes smiling, 'He's pretty, my little son? Look at those eyes, eh?'

'You can have one of my eyes, but give me legs,' suggested Lenka, smiling and examining a bug. 'He's an . . . iron one! So far! Mom, he looks like the monk, the one for whom you made the ladder – remember?'

'Sure I do.'

And laughingly she told me this, 'You see, a monk barged in here once, a bulky man, and says, "See here, you're an oakum-picker, can you make me a rope ladder?" And I, I'd never heard of such ladders. 'No," said I, "I can't." "Then I'll teach you," says he. He opened his cassock and there was a long strong thinnish rope all round his belly. He taught me. I twist it and twist it and think to myself, what does he want it for? Perhaps he wants to rob a church.'

She laughed aloud, hugging her son's shoulders, stroking him all the while. 'Oh, these cunning fellows! He came when he said he would, and I said to him, "Here, if this is to steal with, I won't have anything to do with it." And he laughs slyly. "No," he said, "that's for climbing over a wall. We have a great high wall, and we're sinful folk, and the sin is on the other side of the wall – understand?" Well, I understood. He needed it to go to women at night. He and I had a laugh together over it.'

'You certainly like to laugh,' the boy said, in the tone of an old person.

'You'd better heat the samovar.'

'But we haven't any sugar.'

'Go buy some.'

'But we haven't any money.'

'All because you're such a guzzler. Get some from him.' He turned to me. 'Got money?'

I gave the woman some money. She jumped to her feet, took from the stove a little battered tarnished samovar and disappeared behind the door, humming through her nose.

'Mom!' her son shouted after her. 'Wash the window. I can't see anything! A smart little baggage, I'm telling you,' he continued, carefully placing the boxes of insects on the shelves. They were of cardboard and suspended on strings from nails driven into the cracks between the bricks of the damp wall. 'A worker . . . when once she starts picking oakum, she raises such a dust that you almost choke. I shout: "Mammy, carry me out into the courtyard or I'll choke here." But she says, "Have patience. I'll be lonesome without you." She loves me, and that's all there is to it. She picks and sings. She knows a thousand songs."

Full of eagerness, his marvellous eyes flashing, he raised his thick eyebrows and sang in a hoarse alto, 'Arina lay on a featherbed . . .'

I listened for a while, then I said, 'A very dirty song.'

'They're all like that,' Lenka declared with assurance. Suddenly he started.

'Listen! There's the music! Quick, lift me up!'

I lifted his light little bones in their bag of thin grey skin. Eagerly he stuck his head out of the open window, and grew still, while his withered legs swung impotently, scraping against the wall. In the courtyard a barrel organ squeaked irritatedly, spitting out shreds of melody. A deep-voiced child cried merrily, and a dog howled. Lenka listened to this music and hummed gently through his teeth in time with it.

The dust in the cellar settled, and the place grew lighter. A cheap clock hung over his mother's bed; the pendulum, the size of a copper coin, crawled limpingly. The dishes on the hearth were dirty, a thick layer of dust rested on everything, particularly in the corners, where the cobwebs hung in dirty shreds. Lenka's home resembled a garbage pit, and the ugliness of poverty stared from every inch of it, wounding the senses.

The samovar began to drone gloomily, a hoarse voice roared, 'Get out!' and the barrel organ suddenly grew silent.

'Take me back,' said Lenka with a sigh, 'they have chased them off . . .'

I seated him in the box, and frowning and rubbing his chest with his hands, he coughed cautiously.

'My chest hurts me, it isn't good for me to breathe real air for long. Listen, have you ever seen devils?'

'No.'

'I haven't either. At night I keep looking under the stove – maybe one will show up. But they don't. There are devils in cemeteries, aren't there?'

'What do you want them for?'

'It's interesting. And what if one of them turns out to be kind? Katka, the water-carrier's girl, once saw a little devil in a cellar – only she got frightened. Me, I'm not afraid of scary things.'

He wrapped his legs up in the rags and continued pertly, 'I even like scary dreams, I do really. Once in my dream I saw a tree growing upside down: the leaves were on the ground, and the roots stuck up into the sky. I got into a sweat and woke up from fright. And once I saw Mammy: there she lies naked, and a dog is gnawing at her belly; the dog takes a bite, and spits it out, takes a bite, and spits it out. And once, our house suddenly shook itself and started to move down the street; it glided along banging the doors and windows, and behind it ran the cat of the inspector's wife . . .'

He hunched his sharp little shoulders as if he were chilly, took a candy, unfolded the coloured paper wrapper and carefully smoothing it out, placed it on the window-sill.

'I'll make something with these wrappers, something nice. Or I'll give them to Katka. She likes nice things too; pieces of glass, bits of crockery, paper, and things like that. And listen: if you kept on feeding a cockroach, would it grow to be the size of a horse?'

It was clear that he believed this to be true, so I said, 'If you feed it well, it will.'

'Of course!' he cried out joyfully. 'But Mammy, the silly, laughs at me.' And he added a bawdy word, insulting to a woman. 'She's foolish! And for a cat, you can feed it up so it gets to be the size of a horse in no time – isn't that so?'

'Why, yes, that's possible.'

'It's a pity, I haven't enough feed! That would be great!' He fairly shook with excitement, pressing his hand to his chest. 'There would be flies the size of a dog! And cockroaches could be used to cart bricks – if it's the size of a horse it must be strong, eh?'

'But you see they have whiskers.'

'There's nothing wrong with whiskers – they'd be like reins, the whiskers. Or else, you'd have a spider, as enormous as what? A spider the size of a kitten, even that would be frightful. If only I had legs I'd work real hard, and I'd feed up my whole menagerie. I'd go into business, and I'd buy a house for Mammy in the green fields. Have you ever been in the green fields?'

'Sure.'

'Tell me about it, will you?'

I began to tell him about fields and meadows. He listened eagerly without interrupting, his eyelashes dropped over his eyes and his little mouth opened slowly as though he were falling asleep. Seeing this, I began to speak more quietly. But his mother came in with the boiling samovar in her hands, a paper bag under her arm, and a bottle of vodka tucked in her breast.

'Here I am.'

'I liked that,' sighed the boy, opening his eyes wide. 'An empty place – just nothing but grass and flowers. Mammy, why don't you get a carriage and take me to the green fields? This way I'll croak, and I'll never see them. My word, Mammy, you're a bitch,' he concluded, in a sad abused tone.

His mother chided him tenderly, 'Don't you swear, you mustn't. You're still little . . .'

' "Don't swear!" It's all very well for you. You go where you please, just like a dog. You're a lucky one. Listen' – he turned to me – 'did God make the green fields?'

'Certainly.'

'Well, what for?'

'So people can go out on a jaunt.'

'Green fields,' said the boy, smiling pensively and sighing. 'I would take my menagerie there, and I would let them all loose – run along, brothers! Listen: where do they make God – at the poorhouse?'[1]

His mother shrieked and was literally bowled over with laughter. She fell upon the bed and shouted, kicking her legs, 'Good Lord! What a . . . darling! Why, the icon painters . . . It's side-splitting! He's the limit!'

Lenka looked at her with a smile, and swore at her tenderly in filthy language.

---

1 The translator of the Pyramid Books edition of 'Wine, Women and Vodka,' explains: 'The Russian word for a poorhouse contains a pun which might suggest this idea to an imaginative child.'

'She carries on like a child. Doesn't she love to laugh!' And he repeated the dirty word.

'Let her laugh,' I said. 'You don't mind.'

'No, I don't,' Lenka agreed. 'I'm only angry at her when she doesn't wash the window. I beg her and beg her: clean the windows, I can't see God's light. But she keeps on forgetting.'

The woman, chuckling now and then, washed the tea things, winked at me with her light blue eyes, and said, 'Haven't I a pretty darling? If it weren't for him, I'd have drowned myself long ago, I swear. I'd have strangled myself.' She said this with a smile.

Suddenly Lenka asked me, 'Are you a fool?'

'I don't know. Why?'

'Mammy says you're a fool.'

'But why do I say it?' the woman exclaimed, undaunted. 'He brings a drunken woman in from the street, puts her to bed, and goes off, there you have it. I didn't mean any harm. And you, you have to tell me. Oh, you're mean!' She too spoke like a child. Her manner of speech was that of a girl in her teens. And her eyes too had a girlish purity, which made her face, with its stump of a nose, its drawn lip and bared teeth, look all the more hideous. Her face showed a constant nightmarish sneer, but it was a jolly sneer.

'Well, let's have tea,' she offered solemnly.

The samovar stood on a box beside Lenka. A roguish jet of steam coming out from under the battered lid touched his shoulder. He put his little hand against it and when his palm grew moist, wiped it on his hair, screwing up his eyes dreamily.

'When I grow up,' he said, 'Mammy will make me a carriage. I'll crawl in the streets and beg alms. When they've given me enough, I'll crawl out into the green fields.'

'Ho-ho!' sighed his mother, and directly after, laughed gently. 'The country's paradise to him, the darling. But what do you find in the country? Camps, and beastly soldiers, and drunken peasants.'

'You're lying,' Lenka stopped her, frowning. 'Ask him what the country's like. He's seen it.'

'And I – haven't I seen it?'

'Yes, when you were drunk.'

They began to argue just like children, with as much heat and lack of logic. Meanwhile the warm evening had invaded the courtyard, a thick, dove-coloured cloud hung motionless in the reddened sky. It was getting dark in the cellar.

The boy drank a cup of tea, began to perspire, looked at me and at his mother, and said, 'I've eaten, I've drunk, now, by God, I'm sleepy.'

'Go to sleep,' his mother advised him.

'And he – he'll go. Will you go?'

'Don't worry, I won't let him go,' the woman said, nudging me with her knee.

'Don't you go,' Lenka begged, closed his eyes, and, stretching cosily, sank into the box. Then suddenly he lifted his head and said to his mother reproachfully, 'Why don't you marry him? And have a wedding like other women? This way you take up with all sorts . . . they only beat you . . . But he – he's good.'

'Hush, go to sleep,' the woman said quietly, bending over her cup of tea. 'He's rich.'

For a while the woman sat silent, sipping her tea from the saucer with clumsy lips. Then she turned to me as to an old acquaintance.

'That's the way we live, quietly, he and I, and nobody else. In the courtyard they scold me, call me a loose woman. Well, I'm not ashamed before anybody. Besides, you see what a mess I am, everyone sees right away what I'm good for. Yes. Sonny is asleep, the darling. I have a good child, eh?'

'Yes, very.'

'I can't look at him enough. And what a head he has!'

'Yes, he's a clever boy.'

'That's true. His father was a gentleman, an old man. He was a – what-do-you-call-'em? They have offices – God, I can't think . . . they're busy with papers . . .'

'You mean a notary public?'

'Yes, that's right! He was a dear old man. So kind. He loved me. I was a servant in the house.'

She covered her son's bare legs with the rags, straightened the dingy pillow under his head, and continued casually, 'And then he died suddenly. It was at night. I had just left him when he dropped to the floor, and that was the end of him. You sell kvas?'

'Yes.'

'In business for yourself?'

'No. I work for someone.'

She moved closer to me, saying, 'Don't turn up your nose at me, young man. You can't catch it from me any more. Ask anybody in the street. They all know.'

'I'm not turning up my nose at you.'

Placing on my knee her little hand, the skin of the fingers work-worn and the nails broken, she continued affectionately, 'I'm so grateful to you on Lenka's account. He's had a holiday today. It was good of you.'

'I have to go,' I said.

'Where to?' she asked in surprise.

'I've something to attend to.'

'Stay.'

'I can't.'

She looked at her son, at the window, at the sky, and said softly, 'Do stay. I'll cover my mug with a kerchief . . . I do so want to thank you on my son's account. I'll cover up, eh?'

She spoke persuasively, humanly, so affectionately, with such warm feeling. And her eyes, a child's eyes in a hideous face, shone with the smile not of a beggar, but of a person of wealth who can show gratitude in a substantial way.

'Mom,' the boy cried suddenly, starting, and hitching himself up. 'They're crawling! Mom, come!'

'He's dreaming,' she said to me, bending over him.

I went out into the courtyard, and stood there, thinking. A nasal voice was pouring from the open window of the cellar singing a song with a jolly tune. The mother was singing a strange lullaby to her son, uttering the words distinctly.

'The passions will come, and bring
Every unhappy thing,
Troubles that turn the wits
And tear the heart to bits,
Troubles and grief and care!
Where shall we hide, ah, where?'

I walked quickly out of the courtyard, gritting my teeth so as not to bawl.

Maxim Gorky

PETS
AND
PASTIMES

Gargantua on the Best Way to Wipe the Bottom

'THERE IS NO NEED of wiping one's tail,' said Gargantua, 'but when it is foul; foul it cannot be, unless one have been a-skiting; skite then we must before we wipe our tails.' 'Oh my pretty little waggish boy,' said Grangousier, 'what an excellent wit thou hast! I will make thee very shortly proceed doctor in the Belles Lettres, by G—, for thou hast more wit than age.

'Now, I prithee, go on in this bum-fodder discourse; and, by my beard I swear, for one puncheon thou shall have threescore pipes, I mean of the good Breton wine, not that which grows in Britain, but in the good country of Verron.'

'Afterwards I wiped my bum,' said Gargantua, 'with a kerchief, with a pillow, with a pantoufle, with a pouch, with a pannier, but that was a wicked and unpleasant wipe-breech; then with a hat; of hats, note that some are shorn, and others shaggy, some velveted, others covered with taffities, and others with satin; the best of all these is the shaggy hat, for it makes a very neat abstention of the faecal matter.

'Afterwards I wiped my tail with a hen, with a cock, with a pullet, with a calf's skin, with a hare, with a pigeon, with a cormorant, with an attorney's bag, with a montero, with a coif, with a falconer's lure; but to conclude, I say and maintain, that of all torcheculs, arse-wisps, bum-fodders, tail-napkins, bung-hole-cleansers and wipe-breeches, there is none in the world comparable to the neck of a goose, that is well downed, if you hold her head betwixt your legs: and believe me therein upon mine honour; for you will thereby feel in your nockhole a most wonderful pleasure, both in regard of the softness of the said down, and of the temperate heat of the goose; which is easily communicated to the bumgut and the rest of the intestines, in so far as to come even to the regions of the heart and brains.

'And think not, that the felicity of the heroes and demigods, in the Elysian fields, consisteth either in their Asphodele, Ambrosia or Nectar, as our old women here use to say; but in this (according to my judgment) that they wipe their tails with the neck of a goose, holding her head betwixt their legs, and such is the opinion of Master John of Scotland.'

François Rabelais, translated by Robert Urquhart and P. A. Motteux

Encomium on Flies

THE FLY HAS AS much the advantage in its size over the gnat and
suchlike insects, as it wants in competition with the bee. And as it
may be reckoned among the kingdom of birds, so the beauty and delicacy
of its wings as far excels those of other birds as linen or woollen is
inferior to silk. It is not covered with feathers, like other fowls, but has a
fine lawn, like the grasshopper; and when you see it in the sunshine,
there is as great a variety of curious colours as in a peacock's tail or a
pigeon's neck. It does not fly by the strength of its wings, as birds do, nor
by skips, as the grasshopper, but turns in a moment. The sound of its
flight is not so rough as that of wasps or drones, but bears the same
disproportion thereto as the pipe to the trumpet. Its eye is large, and
even with the head, which is hard and shines like horn; being not
fastened to the body as the grasshopper's is, but continued by a neck that
moves every way. Its body is joined together; its legs long – though the
wasp's are short; several shining divisions cover the belly like plates of a
coat of armour. It does not hurt, like bees, with a sting, but has a small
trunk that does the office of a mouth, having at the end of it a sort of
tooth; and it is with this that it wounds or draws up blood or milk, though
without any great pain. It has six legs in all; the two foremost supply the
want of hands. With these he scours and dresses himself, and feeds
himself besides. With the other four it executes the same offices as men
employ theirs to. Its original is base, being engendered by putrefaction; it
is at first but a worm, then, by little and little, it turns to a bird, shooting
out its legs and wings . . .

It is in man's company as long as it lives, and takes the freedom to taste
of all his food – oil only excepted, because it is poison to him. And
though its life is but short – for the fates have allowed him but a very
little line – it seems to live only in the light, and is seen flying about only
in that; for it rests all night, when it neither flies, nor sings, nor moves. I
might say that his prudence is not small, when he flies his ambushed
enemy, the spider. For he discovers him in ambuscade, and observes
him, declining his force, lest he be caught in his net, and fall into the
meshes of the little beast.

I need not say much as to his strength or courage: since Homer, the greatest
of all the poets, when he considered how he should praise the most excellent of
heroes, compares not the strength and vigour to a lion, pard, or boar, but to the
constant and intrepid mind and boldness of a fly. For he says that he is not rash,
but bold and confident; for though you remove and drive him away, he yet will

not be gone, but hovers about, seeking the means of giving his bite. But Homer is so large in the praise of the fly, and is so very fond of him, that he mentions him, not once or seldom, but frequently, and in many places, so much does the speaking of him adorn his verse. For here he describes his gregarious flight to the milk; and when he compares Minerva declining the dart from any mortal part of Menelaus to a mother careful of her sleeping child, a fly is again brought for an example. Besides, he adorns them with a very pretty epithet – calling them sweet, and their flock, nations.

But he is so strong, and of such force, that by his bite he inflicts a wound; not only in man's skin, but in that of an ox and a horse. They say that he is likewise troublesome to an elephant, when he gets into his wrinkles, and with his little proboscis, makes an incision in proportion to his bigness . . .

Though the fly be a sort of idle lazy creature, yet he reaps the fruit of the labour of others, and everywhere finds a full table. For him are goats milked, and the bees make honey for the flies as well as for men. For him do the confectioners make their sweetmeats, and he tastes them before the kings themselves, with whom he feasts, marching about the table and eating with them in all things.

He builds his nest or house not always in one place, but, taking a wandering flight, like the journey of the Scythians, he makes his house and his bed wherever night overtakes him. But in the dark, as I have already observed, he does nothing; for he will do nothing secretly; nor does he think anything done by him base, which done in the light would not be dishonour to him.

The fable tells us that the fly was originally a very beautiful but very loquacious woman, a perpetual tattler, and a singer into the bargain. She was rival to the Moon in her love for Endymion; and the Moon, being in a rage with her, turned her into a fly. And for this reason she still seems to envy everybody's sleep, especially the tender and young, retaining in her memory the sleep of Endymion. But her bites and thirst of blood proceed not from her cruelty, but humanity and love. For she enjoys beauty the way she is capable of, and crops some balmy particles from it.

There was besides a certain woman among the ancients whose name was Musca (i.e. a fly), a very learned and beautiful poetess. Nor did parents disdain to give their children this name. For this reason Tragedy itself has with a just praise mentioned the fly, to this purpose –

> That the fly may be with dreadful slaughter filled,
> She flies with wondrous force upon the body,
> And armed warriors fear her little dart.

I have a great deal to say of a fly from Pythagoras, were not that known to everybody. There are a sort of flies which the vulgar call militant, others dog flies, making a sharp sound with a swift wing. These flies are of a very long life, and subsist all the winter without food, contracting and hiding themselves, chiefly under the roofs of houses. I could say many more things on this head; but I will put an end to my oration, lest I should verify the old proverb, making an elephant of a fly.

Lucian of Samosata

Of English Dogs

Curs of the mongrel and rascal sort; and first of the dog; called, in Latin, Admonitor; *and of us in English,* Wap *or* Warner.

OF SUCH DOGS, as keep not their kind; of such as are mingled out of sundry sorts not imitating the conditions of some one certain species, because they resemble no notable shape, nor exercise any worthy property of the true perfect and gentle kind; it is not necessary that I write any more of them: but to banish them as unprofitable implements, out of the bounds of my book: unprofitable I say for any use that is commendable, except in entertaining strangers with their barking in the daytime, giving warning to them of the house, that such and such be newly come. Whereupon, we call them Admonishing Dogs; because, in that point, they perform their office.

Of the dog, called Turnspit; in Latin, Veruversator.

There is comprehended under the curs of the coarsest kind, a certain dog excellent in kitchen service. For when any meat is to be roasted, they go into a wheel; which they turning round with the weight of their bodies; and so diligently look to their business, that no drudge nor scullion can do the feat more cunningly. Whom the popular sort hereupon call, Turnspits; being the last of all those which we have first mentioned.

Of the dog, called the Dancer; in Latin, Saltator *or* Tympanista.

There be also dogs among us, of a mongrel kind, which are taught and exercised to dance in measure at the musical sound of an instrument; as, at the just stroke of the drum, at the sweet accent of the cithern, and tuned strings of the harmonious harp: showing many pretty tricks by the gesture of their bodies. As, to stand bolt upright, to lie flat upon the ground, to turn round as a ring holding their tails in their teeth, to beg for their meat and sundry such properties, which they learn of their vagabondical masters, whose instruments they are to gather gain withal in city, country, town, and village. As some which carry old apes on their shoulders in coloured jackets, to move men to laughter; for a little lucre.

From *Of English Dogs* by Dr Johannes Caius

The Love-Sick Frog

A frog he would a-wooing go,
    Heigho, said Rowly,
Whether his mother would let him or no,
    With a rowly, powly,
      Gammon and spinnage,
    Heigho, said Anthony Rowly.

Off he set with his opera hat,
    Heigho, said Rowly;
On the road he met with a Rat,
    With a rowly, powly, &c.

They soon arrived at the Mouse's hall,
    Heigho, said Rowly;
They gave a loud tap, and they gave a loud call,
    With a rowly, powly, &c.

Pray, Mrs Mouse, are you within?
    Heigho, said Rowly;
Yes, kind sirs, I'm sitting to spin,
    With a rowly, powly, &c.

Come, Mrs Mouse, now give us some beer,
    Heigho, said Rowly;
That Froggy and I may have some cheer,
    With a rowly, powly, &c.

Pray, Mr Frog, will you give us a song?
    Heigho, said Rowly;
Let the subject be something that's not very long,
    With a rowly, powly, &c.

Indeed, Mrs Mouse, replied the Frog,
    Heigho, said Rowly;
A cold has made me as hoarse as a hog,
    With a rowly, powly, &c.

Since you have caught cold, Mr Frog, Mousey said,
    Heigho, said Rowley,
I'll sing you a song that I have just made,
    With a rowly, powly, &c.

As they were in glee and merry-making,
    Heigho, said Rowly,
A Cat and her Kittens came tumbling in.
    With a rowly, powly, &c.

The Cat she seized the Rat by the crown,
    Heigho, said Rowley;
The Kittens they pulled the little Mouse down.
    With a rowly, powly, &c.

This put Mr Frog in a terrible fright,
    Heigho, said Rowly;
He took up his hat and he wish'd 'em good night.
    With a rowly, powly, &c.

As Froggy was crossing it over a brook,
    Heigho, said Rowly,
A lily-white duck came and gobbled him up,
    With a rowly, powly, &c.

So here's an end to one, two, and three,
    Heigho, said Rowly,
The Rat, the Mouse, and the little Froggy,
    With a rowly, powly, &c.

                                            Anon.

The Grey Cat

The grey cat's kittled in Charlie's wig,
The grey cat's kittled in Charlie's wig;
There's one of them living and two of them dead,
The grey cat's kittled in Charlie's wig.

Anon.

Of the Secrets of Angling

But every fish loves not each bait alike,
Although sometimes they feed upon the same;
But some do one, and some another seek,
As best unto their appetite doth frame;
The roach, the bream, the carp, the chub, and bleek,
With paste or corn their greedy hunger tame;
 The dace, the ruff, the gudgeon and the rest,
 The smaller sort of crawling worms love best.

The chavender and chub do more delight
To feed on tender cheese or cherries red;
Black snails, their bellies slit to show their white;
Or grasshoppers that skip in every mead:
The perch, the tench and eel do rather bite
At great red worms, in field or garden bred;
 That have been scoured in moss or fennel rough,
 To rid their filth, and make them hard and tough.

And with this bait hath often taken bin
The salmon fair, of river fish the best;
The shad that in the springtime cometh in;
The suant swift, that is not set by least;
The bocher sweet, the pleasant flounder thin;
The peel, the tweat, the botling, and the rest,
 With many more, that in the deep doth lie
 Of Avon, Usk, of Severn and of Wye.

Alike they bite, alike they pull down low
The sinking cork that strives to rise again;
And when they feel the sudden deadly blow,
Alike they shun the danger and the pain;
And as an arrow from the Scythian bow,
All flee alike into the stream amain;
   Until the angler by his wary skill,
   There tires them out, and brings them up at will.

From 'Of the Secrets of Angling' by John Dennis

Cock-Fighting in Scottish Schools

THE SCHOOL, like almost all the other grammar-schools of the period in Scotland, had its yearly cock-fight, preceded by two holidays and a half, during which the boys occupied themselves in collecting and bringing up their cocks. And such always was the array of fighting birds mustered on the occasion, that the day of the festival, from morning till night, used to be spent in fighting out the battle. For weeks after it had passed, the school-floor would continue to retain its deeply-stained blotches of blood, and the boys would be full of exciting narratives regarding the glories of gallant birds, who had continued to fight until both their eyes had been picked out, or who, in the moment of victory, had dropped dead in the middle of the cock-pit. The yearly fight was the relic of a barbarous age; and, in at least one of its provisions, there seemed evidence that it was that of an intolerant age also: every pupil at school, without exemption, had his name entered on the subscription list, as a cock-fighter, and was obliged to pay the master at the rate of twopence per head, ostensibly for leave to bring his birds to the pit; but, amid the growing humanities of a better time, though two pences continued to be exacted, it was no longer imperative to bring the birds.

From *My Schools and Schoolmasters* by Hugh Miller

Suzi the Cat and a Bird Called Hope

IT WASN'T A REAL DOVE, just an albino pigeon with pure white feathers. Hussein and Murat, two teenage soldiers, trapped the bird and brought it to the foreigners' block. The exercise yard, roughly the size of a tennis court, was littered with prisoners soaking up the sunshine when the soldiers appeared carrying the bird which was locked in a hand-carved wooden cage. Bashfully, unsettled by the presence of so many half-naked men, they presented their gift to Sayed Ahmed.

Sayed was overjoyed. He cooed and whistled softly at the pink-eyed creature while the soldiers looked on, grinning with reflected pleasure. Then, to their utter astonishment, Sayed opened the cage door, took the bird out and threw it into the air.

'It's wrong to lock anybody in a cage, even a bird,' Sayed explained gently.

At the same time, no one talked about it and I thought I was the only foreigner to be moved. Prison is no place to confess such sentiments. And to empathise openly with Sayed, a Pakistani who flaunted his gayness, would have been doubly unwise.

Homosexuality was forbidden in the prison. Enforcement of the ruling was left to the lifers and long-sentence men. Punishment was usually swift and brutal. Once, as the senior European in the block, I was delegated to beat Charlie, a young German who had been too open about his affair with Sayed. In the event, I only explained the dangers to him. Charlie spent the rest of his short sentence lying on a bunk, reading travel books.

No one ever thought of punishing Sayed. It was too dangerous. He was a lifer convicted of one murder who had already stabbed two men behind bars. But his charm was an even more effective deterrent. The balding, middle-aged Pakistani was always elegantly dressed in brightly coloured silk pyjamas. His generosity, refined manners and sensitive tact gave the whole block class. And Sayed, more than any other foreigner, had the friendship and respect of the Turkish officials, guards and soldiers. The albino pigeon was one of many gifts he was always receiving.

If only that bird had seized its freedom and flown off into the blue. Instead, it joined Oscar's flock of pigeons, sparrows and starlings waiting on the roof for their daily meals.

Oscar's devotion to his feathered friends was absolute. The plump German, convicted of raping his daughter, spent at least two hours a day crumbling bread, washing water bowls and sweeping away stale left-overs. The birds were all he ever talked about. Every morning, he rose at dawn to scatter their breakfast through a window. The birds fed in peace before the gate was opened and the courtyard became crowded with prisoners. And every evening, come rain or shine, Oscar lingered until lock-up to throw the birds their dinner, the corn kernels he scrounged from the kitchen.

There was nothing unique about Sayed's white bird, yet all the prisoners gave it a special value. It was attractive and distinctive; something bright and alive amidst the greyness.

We looked upon it as a symbol. Many of us interpreted its decision to join Oscar's flock as gratitude to Sayed. As if the bird had opted to hang around to console him. As if it shared our passionate belief that nothing was more precious than freedom. I can't remember who first dubbed it *Umit*, Hope, but the name stuck.

To be fair, it was inspiring to watch Hope soar heavenward, float down gracefully and perch on a chimney-stack. On countless occasions when despair and misery threatened to overwhelm us, someone would sigh, 'At least Hope is still with us; everything will work out.'

The summer of 1983 was long, hot and deathly boring. Turkey was in the tight grip of the military. The prisons were packed and a shortage of everything from toothpaste to cigarettes nagged and irritated. The opposite block was stuffed with children; barefoot, undernourished and perpetually squalling.

If I had to sum up the wretched conditions in one word, it would be 'RATS'. Hundreds of them. Swarming out from drains and cracks at night, scampering around the courtyard, flitting under bunks and crawling through pipes to enter the cells. Grey, greasy and ugly, some were as big as cats, others were so tiny they could squeeze through keyholes to reach edibles. There was no way to fight them. Sometimes the children trapped a real monster and burned it alive. But that hardly diminished their numbers.

Because of the overcrowding, many children slept on the floor. We were woken frequently in the night by their terrified screams when the rats nipped their fingers or toes. The administration, worried that a child might contract rabies, decided to shift all the kids to the clinic. In effect, the block was surrendered to the rats.

Lacking any alternative, we adapted to the rats. We stored all our belongings and food in sacks hanging on the walls. Prisoners on the vulnerable bottom bunks slept in tightly fastened sleeping bags. We swept each cell daily to deny the animals the smallest morsel of food or crumb of bread. We survived, but we hated those rats.

Throughout the bitterly cold winter, Hope stayed with us. In the spring, it was reassuring to watch her preening in the sunshine. Then, Mohammed found the chewed-up remnants of a rat in the courtyard. He picked the gruesome object up by the tail and gleefully paraded it around the block.

I was one of the prisoners who had suggested getting a cat to combat the rats but the idea had been vetoed by the Arab majority in the block. Cats carried disease, left droppings and were lazy. Mustafa was allergic to cats.

Another claimed a friend had been smothered by one settling on his face. Claudio was the first actually to see her. The young Italian, who spent most nights moon-gazing, shook me awake, whispering excitedly, 'Come and see our new friend.'

Grumbling, angry at being disturbed, I climbed from my bunk and joined him by the window. My eyes had to adjust to the darkness before I saw the cat. She was a motionless shadow in one corner of the courtyard. It wasn't until she slid along a window-ledge and was illuminated by a light that I saw her properly. As cats go, she was far from appealing; small, with a long out-of-proportion body, greyish-white fur with black and brown blotches and mean, squinty, green eyes. Watching out for her became a sudden passion of the block. Each night, a dozen foreigners sat silently by the top-floor windows, urging her on. As she stalked a rodent, we pinched each other to control our excitement, hissing fervently, 'Kill it, kill it.' The satisfaction of seeing her pounce on rats as big as herself was so intense, we shouted and clapped, disturbing the sleeping men.

Weeks after her arrival, the sight of a single rat was rare. They were still there, lurking under the foundations, but the cat put an end to their carefree rampage.

She was certainly wild. Unlike domesticated cats, she kept well away from humans, passing the day snoozing in the vacant block. It was a month before she deigned to make our acquaintance. We lured her out into the open with saucers of milk, which she lapped cautiously, her ears pricked to sense any danger. Only when the empty block was filled with informers and high-security prisoners did she consent to live with us. Even then she was wary. Razor-sharp claws deterred our attempts to pet her and she always preferred a diet of rats to any food we offered.

The more she disdained our company, the more she appealed to us. Some Arabs continued to deny any feelings for her yet were the first to notice her absence when she disappeared for days on end. Despite their prejudices, she quickly won their admiration, if not their hearts. She went under a number of names: *Kdei* (Cat), *Aslan* (Lion) and *Kaplan* (Tiger) were the most common. When her pregnancy became obvious, some of the men began calling her *Herospor* (Whore), and other derogatory names but most settled on Suzi, after the literary prostitute Suzi Wong.

Suzi's condition was generally frowned upon. Her job in the block was to catch rats, not to have kittens. Tolerating our celibate lives was hard enough, but Suzi's promiscuity rubbed salt into the wound and tarnished her image as an honest, hard-working friend of the block. However, we began to have long discussions on how to cope with the situation.

It was the plans for her confinement that raised emotions and triggered arguments.

With three qualified doctors in the block and my own experience in general nursing, there was no shortage of medical advice. As if that wasn't enough, it seemed as if every prisoner in the block had witnessed the birth of a baby, foal, puppy or calf and had strong ideas as to how Suzi should be treated.

A score of men squeezed into a cell and more stood in the doorway to join in the discussion. The doctors ridiculed the opinions of us lesser-educated men with their medical jargon. But the controversy didn't end there.

The height of absurdity was reached when Dr Zeki, the 'fresh air' advocate, punched Dr Abdul Aziz, the 'closed, calm corner' advocate, smack on the nose to settle the argument over the site of Suzi's confinement. Naturally, Suzi displayed her complete lack of respect for human expertise by choosing her own time, place and technique to give birth.

Her four cuddly kittens smoothed away our friction and even seduced the dedicated cat-haters. Only a few die-hards continued to grumble that the kittens would get under our feet and cause mess. Suzi's fame as a ratter solved the problem. Waiting for the doctor, riding in the bus to court, we boasted of her skills to Turkish friends. Desperate to de-rat their own blocks, the Turkish prisoners offered considerable sums of money for the kittens, in the belief that they would inherit Suzi's killer instinct.

Suspecting trickery, hawk-eyed foreigners watched possessively as a string of block chiefs paid us visits and handled the minute bundles of fur with awed longing.

The chiefs had been elected by fellow prisoners to represent and protect the interests of each block. Strength, size and notoriety were prime considerations. Honesty and honour were also important but there was one quality the Turks respected above all – guile.

Ibrahim, the chief of a Kurdish block, spoke of lavish sums as he drank tea and fondled the kittens. Scratching the stubble of his outsized, fleshy chin, he haggled convincingly. Nobody saw him slip a kitten into the pouch of his baggy *shalvas*. Fortunately it mewed just as Ibrahim was leaving, otherwise he would have been the laughing stock of the prison.

It was six weeks before we reluctantly handed over the kittens to the four carefully-chosen block chiefs. In fact, none of the kittens grew up to become successful ratters, but Suzi quickly returned to the fray with a vengeance.

Apart from the usual prison dramas, life continued normally until one morning Oscar rushed in from the courtyard and raced up and down the narrow corridor outside the cells wailing, 'Murder. Bloody murder.'

We started up from our bunks, expecting the worst. Whose control had snapped? Who was the victim? And there was Oscar, waving a handful of blood-smeared feathers and sobbing, 'Suzi's eaten Hope.'

Minutes later, Suzi strolled into sight, white feathers trailing from her mouth. Stepping daintily over our toes, her tail erect, she rubbed herself lightly against our shins. We glared down at her with horror and dismay as she looked back with nothing less than smug pride.

For any other crime she would have been forgiven, but killing Hope went beyond the pale. We had to decide her punishment.

Grim and resolute, we squeezed into a cell to talk it over but all our attempts at reaching a democratic decision failed. Hardliners demanded an eye for an eye and voted for drowning. Moderates wanted the short sharp shock of a couple of slaps across her snout. Dr Zeki argued successfully against leniency with a long speech on the need to uphold biblical values. I preached my liberal, modern views and swung the vote back again. After a long day of solid discussion, we reached a compromise. Suzi's sentence was exile to a political block on the other side of the prison.

Katil (Killer), an immense tomcat, was Suzi's first replacement. About as much help as a scarecrow, he spent hours on the window-ledge watching the rats. Even when starved, it never occurred to him to eat any.

Katil was followed by *Gul*, named after a notorious murderer featured in all the newspapers. She was equally ineffectual. One cat we tested had its name changed from *Korkmaz* (Fearless) to *Korkluk* (Fearful). She hid under a bunk at the mere glimpse of a rat.

The last cat was Eve who chased and actually caught rats but, when the game was over, let them go. Watching her was so frustrating, we swallowed our pride and I was sent off to buy back Suzi.

No Sale.

Tefik, the political chief, refused to consider any deals. The lanky Marxist sneered at my offer. 'You English think money will buy anything.' He smirked, 'You can have first pick from Suzi's next litter.'

Belongings and food bags were hoisted back onto the walls. Bottom-bunk dwellers unrolled their sleeping bags. We resigned ourselves to co-existing with the rats.

Standing at a window, watching the hateful creatures flitting around the courtyard, Osama lamented, 'Everything's gone wrong since Suzi ate Hope.'

Arif took the words out of my mouth. 'You're crazy. We're all crazy! Hope was just a dumb bird.'

From *Under the Crescent Moon* by Daniel de Souza

Of the Rats in the Sewers

T HE SEWER RAT is the common brown or Hanoverian rat, said by the
Jacobites to have come in with the first George, and established itself
after the fashion of his royal family; and undoubtedly such was the era of
their appearance. One man, who had worked twelve years in the sewers
before flushing was general, told me he had never seen but *two* black (or old
English) rats; another man of ten years' experience, had seen but one;
others had noted no difference in the rats. I may observe that in my
inquiries as to the sale of rats (as a part of the live animals dealt in by a class
in the metropolis), I ascertained that in the older granaries, where there
were series of floors, there were black as well as brown rats. 'Great black
fellows,' said one man who managed a Bermondsey granary, 'as would
frighten a lady into asterisks to see of a sudden.'

From *London Labour and the London Poor* by Henry Mayhew

A Seller of Bird's Nests, Hedgehogs and Other Creatures

' T HE HEDGEHOGS IS 1*s.* each; I gets them mostly in Essex. I've took one
hedgehog with three young ones, and sold the lot for 2*s.* 6*d.* People in
the streets bought them of me – they're wanted to kill the black-beetles;
they're fed on bread and milk, and they'll suck a cow quite dry in their wild
state. They eat adders, and can't be poisoned, at least it says so in a book
I've got about 'em at home.

'The effects I get orders for in the streets. Gentlemen gives me their cards,
and tells me to bring them one; they're 2*d.* apiece. I get them at Hampstead
and Highgate, from the ponds. They're wanted for cur'osity.

'The snails and frogs I sell to Frenchmen. I don't know what part they eat
of the frog, but I know they buy them, and the dandelion root. The frogs is
6*d.* and 1*s.* a dozen. They like the yellow-bellied ones, the others they're
afraid is toads. They always pick out the yellow-bellied first; I don't know
how to feed 'em, or else I might fatten them. Many people swallows young
frogs, they're reckoned very good things to clear the inside. The frogs I
catch in ponds and ditches up at Hampstead and Highgate, but I only get
them when I've a order. I've had a order for as many as six dozen, but that
was for the French hotel in Leicester-square; but I *have* sold three dozen a

week to one man, a Frenchman, as keeps a cigar shop in R—r's-court.

'The snails I sell by the pailful – at 2*s*. 6*d*. the pail. There is some hundreds in a pail. The wet weather is the best times for catching 'em; the French people eats 'em. They boils 'em first to get 'em out of the shell and get rid of the green froth; then they boils them again, and after that in vinegar. They eats 'em hot, but some of the foreigners likes 'em cold. They say they're better, if possible, than whelks. I used to sell a great many to a lady and gentleman in Soho-square, and to many of the French I sell 1*s*.'s worth, that's about three or four quarts. Some persons buys snails for birds, and some to strengthen a sickly child's back; they rub the back all over with the snails, and a very good thing they tell me it is. I used to take 2*s*.'s worth a week to one woman, it's the green froth that does the greatest good. There are two more birds'-nest sellers besides myself, they don't do as many as me the two of 'em. They're very naked, their things is all to ribbins; they only go into the country once in a fortnight. They was never nothing, no trade – they never was in place – from what I've heard – either of them. I reckon I sell about 20 nesties a week take one week with another, and that I do four months in the year. (This altogether makes 320 nests). Yes, I should say, I do sell about 300 birds'-nests every year, and the other two, I'm sure, don't sell half that. Indeed they don't want to sell; they does better by what they gets give to them. I can't say what they takes, they're Irish, and I never was in conversation with them. I get about 4*s*. to 5*s*. for the 20 nests, that's between 2*d*. and 3*d*. apiece. I sell about a couple of snakes every week, and for some of them I get 1*s*, and for the big ones 2*s*. 6*d*.; but them I seldom find. I've only had three hedgehogs this season, and I've done a little in snails and frogs, perhaps about 1*s*. The many foreigners in London this season hasn't done me no good. I haven't been to Leicester-square lately, or perhaps I might have got a large order or two for frogs.'

From *London Labour and the London Poor* by Henry Mayhew

Toads

THE TOAD TRADE is amost a nonentity. One man, who was confident he had as good a trade in that line as any of his fellows, told me that last year he only supplied one toad; in one year, he had forgot the precise time, he collected ten. He was confident that from 12 to 24 a year was now the extent of the toad trade, perhaps 20. There was no regular price, and the men only 'work to order', 'It's just what the shopkeeper, mostly a herbalist, likes to give.' I was told from 1*d*. to 6*d*. according to size. 'I don't know what they're wanted for, something about the doctors, I believe. But if you wants any toads, sir, for anything, I know a place between Hampstead and Willesden, where there's real stunners.'

From *London Labour and the Poor* by Henry Mayhew

Whelks

'THEY NEVER KICKS as they boils, like lobsters or crabs,' said one whelk dealer, 'they takes it quiet. A missionary cove said to me, "Why don't you kill them first? It's murder." They doesn't suffer; I've suffered more with a toothache than the whole measure of whelks has in a boiling, that I'm clear upon.'

From *London Labour and the London Poor* by Henry Mayhew

Elegy on the Death of a Mad Dog

Good people all, of every sort,
　　Give ear unto my song;
And if you find it wondrous short,
　　It cannot hold you long.

In Islington there was a Man,
　　Of whom the world might say,
That still a godly race he ran,
　　Whene'er he went to pray.

A kind and gentle heart he had,
　　To comfort friends and foes,
The naked every day he clad,
　　When he put on his clothes.

And in that town a Dog was found,
　　As many dogs there be,
Both mongrel, puppy, whelp, and hound,
And curs of low degree.

This Dog and Man at first were friends;
　　But when a pique began,
The Dog, to gain some private ends,
　　Went mad and bit the Man.

Around from all the neighbouring streets
　　The wond'ring neighbours ran,
And swore the Dog had lost his wits,
　　To bite so good a Man.

This wound it seem'd both sore and sad
　　To every Christian eye;
And while they swore the Dog was mad,
　　They swore the Man would die.

But soon a wonder came to light,
　　That show'd the rogues they lied:
The Man recover'd of the bite,
　　The Dog it was that died.

　　　　　　　　　　　　Oliver Goldsmith

To Smoke, or Not to Smoke

To smoke, or not to smoke – that is the question!
Whether 'tis better to abjure the habit,
And trust the warnings of a scribbling doctor,
Or buy at once a box of best Havanas,
And ten a day consume them? To smoke, to puff,
Nay more, to waste the tender fabric of the lungs
And risk consumption and its thousand ills
The practice leads to – 'tis a consummation
Discreetly to be shunned. To smoke, to puff—
To puff, perhaps to doze – ay, there's the rub;
For in that dozing state we thirsty grow,
And, having burned the tube up to a stump,
We must have drink, and that's one cause
We modern youth are destined to short life;
For who can bear to feel his mouth parched up,

His throat like whalebone and his chest exhausted,
His head turned giddy, and his nerves unstrung,
When he himself might drench these ills away
With wine or brandy? Who could live in smoke,
And pine and sicken with a secret poison;
But that the dread of breaking e'er a rule
Prescribed by fashion, whose controlling will
None disobey, puzzles ambitious youth,
And makes us rather bear the ills we feel
Than others that the doctor warns us of.
Thus custom does make spectres of us all,
And thus the native hue of our complexion
If sicklied o'er with a consumptive cast;
The appetite, a loss of greater moment,
Palled by the weed, and the digestive powers
Lose all their action.

John W. Farrell

My Hookah

What is it, that affords such joys
On Indian shores and never cloys,
But makes that pretty, bubbling noise?
My Hookah.

What is it, that a party if in
At breakfast, dinner, or at Tiffin,
Surprises and delights the Griffin?
My Hookah.

What is it to Cadets gives pleasure?
What is it occupies their leisure?
What do they deem the greatest treasure?
My Hookah.

Say – what makes Decency wear sable?
What makes each would-be nabob able
To cock his legs upon the table?
My Hookah.

What is it (trust me, I'm not joking,
'Tis truth – altho', I own provoking)
That sets e'en Indian *belles* a smoking?
My Hookah.

What is it – wheresoe'er we search
In ev'ry place; – *except the Church*,
That leaves sweet converse in the lurch?
My Hookah.

But hold my Muse – for shame for shame—
One question ere you smoking blame—
What is it gives your book a name?
My Hookah.

My fault I own – my censure ends,
Nay more – I'll try to make amends,
Who is the safest of all friends?
My Hookah.

Say who? or what retains the power,
When fickle Fortune 'gins to lour,
To solace many a lonely hour?
My Hookah.

When death-like dews and fogs prevailing
In pinnace or in Budg'row sailing,
What is it that prevents our ailing?
My Hookah.

When we're our skins with claret soaking,
And heedless wits their friends are joking,
Which friend will stand the *greatest smoking*?
My Hookah.

By what – (nay, answer at your ease,
While pocketing your six rupees) –
By what d'ye mean the town to please?
My Hookah.

From *My Hookah; or The Stranger in Calcutta*,
a collection of poems by an officer

His First Cigar

A small boy puffed at a big cigar
  His eyes bulged out and his cheeks sank in:
He gulped rank fumes with his lips ajar,
  While muscles shook in his youthful chin.
His gills were green, but he smole a smile;
He sat high up on the farmyard stile,
And cocked his hat o'er his glassy eye,
Then wunk a wink at a cow near by.

The earth swam round, but the stile stood still,
  The trees rose up and the kid crawled down
He groaned aloud for he felt so ill,
  And knew that cigar had 'done him brown'.
His head was light, and his feet like lead,
His cheeks grew white as a linen spread,
While he weakly gasped, as he gazed afar,
'If I live, this here's my last cigar.'

From *Nicotiana* by Henry James Meller

The Song of Nicotine

  Should you ask me why this meerschaum,
  Why these clay-pipes and churchwardens,
  With the odours of tobacco,
  With the oile and fume of 'mixture',
  With the curling smoke of 'bird's-eye',
  With the gurgling of rank juices,
  With renewed expectorations
  As of sickness on the fore-deck?
    I should answer, I should tell you,
  From the cabbage, and the dust-heaps,
  From the old leeks of the Welshland,
  From the soil of kitchen gardens,
  From the mud of London sewers,
  From the garden-plots and churchyards,
  Where the linnet and cocksparrow

Feed upon the weeds and groundsel,
I receive them as I buy them
From the boxes of Havana,
The concoctor, the weird wizard.
   Should you ask how this Havana
Made cigars so strong and soothing,
Made the 'bird's-eye' and 'York river'
I should answer, I should tell you,
In the purlieus of the cities,
In the cellars of the warehouse,
In the dampness of the dungeon,
Lie the rotten weeds that serve him
In the gutters and the sewers,
In the melancholy alleys,
Half-clad Arab boys collect them,
Crossing-sweepers bring them to him,
Costermongers keep them for him,
And he turns them by his magic
Into 'cavendish' and 'bird's eye',
For those clay-pipes and churchwardens,
For this meerschaum, or he folds them,
And 'cigars' he duly labels
On the box in which he sells them.

From *Figaro*, October 1874

Sneezing

What a moment, what a doubt!
All my nose is inside out,—
All my thrilling, tickling caustic
Pyramid rhinocerostic,
Wants to sneeze and cannot do it!
How it yearns me, thrills me, stings me,
How with rapturous torment wrings me!
Now says, 'Sneeze, you fool – get through it.'
Shee-shee oh! 'tis most del-ishi-
Ishi-ishi-most del-ishi!
(Hang it, I shall sneeze till Spring!)
Snuff is a delicious thing.

Leigh Hunt

Train Journey in the Age of Steam

The travellers are returning after a pleasant day out in Hastings.

WE REACHED THE STATION at about half-past six, before the thunder was overhead, but not before Ellen had got wet, despite all my efforts to protect her. She was also very hot from hurrying, and yet there was nothing to be done but to sit in a kind of covered shed till the train came up. The thunder and lightning were, however, so tremendous, that we thought of nothing else. When they were at their worst, the lightning looked like the upset of a cauldron of white glowing metal – with such strength, breadth, and volume did it descend. Just as the train arrived, the roar began to abate, and in about half-an-hour it had passed over to the north, leaving behind the rain, cold and continuous, which fell all round us from a dark, heavy, grey sky. The carriage in which we were was a third-class, with seats arranged parallel to the sides. It was crowded, and we were obliged to sit in the middle, exposed to the draught which the tobacco smoke made necessary. Some of the company were noisy, and before we got to Red Hill became noisier, as the brandy-flasks which had been well filled at Hastings began to work. Many were drenched, and this was an excuse for much of the drinking; although for that matter, any excuse or none is generally sufficient. At

Red Hill we were stopped by other trains, and before we came to Croydon we were an hour late. We had now become intolerably weary. The songs were disgusting, and some of the women who were with the men had also been drinking, and behaved in a manner which it was not pleasant that Ellen and Marie should see. The carriage was lighted fortunately by one dim lamp only which hung in the middle, and I succeeded at last in getting seats at the further end, where there was a knot of more decent persons who had huddled up there away from the others. All the glory of the morning was forgotten. Instead of three happy, exalted creatures, we were three dejected, shivering mortals, half-poisoned with foul air and the smell of spirits. We crawled up to London Bridge at the slowest pace, and finally, the railway company discharged us on the platform at ten minutes past eleven. Not a place in any omnibus could be secured, and we therefore walked for a mile or so till I saw a cab, which – unheard-of expense for me – I engaged, and we were landed at our own house exactly at half-past twelve.

From *Deliverance* by Mark Rutherford

Tam O' Shanter

When chapman billies leave the street,
And drouthy neebors, neebors meet,
As market days are wearing late,
An' folk begin to take the gate;
While we sit bousing at the nappy,
An' getting fou and unco happy,
We think na on the lang Scots miles,
The mosses, waters, slaps, and styles,
That lie between us and our hame,
Whare sits our sulky sullen dame,
Gathering her brows like gathering storm,
Nursing her wrath to keep it warm.
   This truth fand honest Tam o' Shanter,
As he frae Ayr ae night did canter
(Auld Ayr, wham ne'er a town surpasses,
For honest men and bonnie lasses).
   O Tam! hadst thou but been sae wise,
As ta'en thy ain wife Kate's advice!

She tauld thee weel thou wast a skellum,
A blethering, blustering, drunken blellum;
That frae November till October,
Ae market day thou was na sober;
That ilka medler, wi' the miller,
Thou sat as lang as thou had siller;
That ev'ry naig was ca'd a shoe on,
The smith and thee gat roaring fou on;
That at the Lord's house, ev'n on Sunday,
Thou drank wi' Kirton Jean till Monday.
She prophesied that, late or soon,
Thou would be found deep drowned in Doon;
Or catched wi' warlocks in the mirk,
By Alloway's auld haunted kirk.

   Ah, gentle dames! it gars me greet,
To think how monie counsels sweet,
How mony lengthened, sage advices,
The husband frae the wife despises!

   But to our tale: Ae market night,
Tam had got planted unco right;
Fast by an ingle, bleezing finely,
Wi' reaming swats, that drank divinely;
And at his elbow, Souter Johnny,
His ancient, trusty, droughty crony;
Tam lo'ed him like a vera brither;
They had been fou for weeks thegither.
The night drave in wi' sangs and clatter;
And ay the ale was growing better:
The landlady and Tam grew gracious,
Wi favours, secret, sweet, and precious:
The souter tauld his queerest stories;
The landlord's laugh was ready chorus:
The storm without might rair and rustle,
Tam did na mind the storm a whistle.

   Care, mad to see a man sae happy,
E'en drowned himsel amang the nappy:
As bees flee hame wi' lades o' treasure,
The minutes winged their way wi' pleasure;
Kings may be blest, but Tam was glorious,
O'er a' the ills o' life victorious!

But pleasures are like poppies spread,
You seize the flow'r, its bloom is shed;
Or like the snow falls in the river,
A moment white – then melts forever;
Or like the borealis race,
That flit ere you can point their place;
Or like the rainbow's lovely form
Evanishing amid the storm –
Nae man can tether time or tide; –
The hour approaches Tam maun ride;
That hour o' night's black arch the keystane,
That dreary hour he mounts his beast in;
And sic a night he taks the road in,
As ne'er poor sinner was abroad in.

The wind blew as 'twad blawn its last;
The rattling show'rs rose on the blast;
The speedy gleams the darkness swallowed;
Loud, deep, and lang, the thunder bellowed:
That night, a child might understand,
The deil had business on his hand.

Weel mounted on his gray mare, Meg,
A better never lifted leg,
Tam skelpit on thro' dub and mire,
Despising wind, and rain, and fire;
Whiles holding fast his gude blue bonnet;
Whiles crooning o'er some auld Scots sonnet:
Whiles glow'ring round wi' prudent cares,
Lest bogles catch him unawares;
Kirk-Alloway was drawing nigh,
Whare ghaists and houlets nightly cry. –

By this time he was cross the ford,
Whare in the snaw, the chapman smoored;
And past the birks and meikle stane,
Whare drunken Charlie brak's neck-bane;
And thro' the whins, and by the cairn,
Whare hunters fand the murdered bairn;
And near the thorn, aboon the well,
Whare Mungo's mither hanged hersel. –
Before him Doon pours all his floods;
The doubling storm roars thro' the woods;

The lightnings flash from pole to pole;
Near and more near the thunders roll:
When, glimmering thro' the groaning trees,
Kirk-Alloway seemed in a bleeze;
Thro' ilka bore the beams were glancing;
And loud resounded mirth and dancing. –
  Inspiring bold John Barleycorn!
What dangers thou canst make us scorn!
Wi' tippenny, we fear nae evil;
Wi' usquebae, we'll face the devil! –
The swats sae ream'd in Tammie's noddle,
Fair play, he cared na deils a boddle.
But Maggie stood right sair astonished,
Till, by the heel and hand admonished,
She ventured forward on the light;
And, vow! Tam saw an unco sight!
Warlocks and witches in a dance;
Nae cotillion brent new frae France,
But hornpipes, jigs, strathspeys, and reels,
Put life and mettle in their heels.
A winnock bunker in the east,
There sat auld Nick, in shape o' beast;
A towzie tyke, black, grim, and large,
To gie them music was his charge:
He screwed the pipes and gart them skirl,
Till roof and rafters a' did dirl. –
Coffins stood round like open presses,
That shawed the dead in their last dresses;
And by some devilish cantraip slight
Each in its cauld hand held a light, –
By which heroic Tam was able
To note upon the haly table,
A murderer's banes in gibbet airns;
Twa span-lang, wee, unchristened bairns;
A thief, new-cutted frae the rape,
Wi' his last gasp his gab did gape;
Five tomahawks, wi' blude red-rusted;
Five scimitars, wi' murder crusted;
A garter, which a babe had strangled;
A knife, a father's throat had mangled,

Whom his ain son o' life bereft,
The gray hairs yet stack to the heft;
Wi' mair o' horrible and awfu',
Which ev'n to name wad be unlawfu'.
   As Tammie glowred, amazed and curious,
The mirth and fun grew fast and furious:
The piper loud and louder blew;
The dancers quick and quicker flew;
They reeled, they set, they crossed, they cleekit,
Till ilka carlin swat and reekit,
And coost her duddies to the wark,
And linket at it in her sark!
   Now Tam, O Tam! had thae been queans,
A' plump and strapping in their teens;
Their sarks, instead o' creeshie flannen,
Been snaw-white seventeen hunder linen!
Thir breeks o' mine, my only pair,
That ance were plush, o' gude blue hair,
I wad hae gi'en them off my hurdies,
For ae blink o' the bonie burdies!
   But withered beldams, auld and droll,
Rigwoodie hags wad spean a foal,
Lowping and flinging on a crummock,
I wonder didna turn thy stomach.
   But Tam kend what was what fu' brawlie,
There was ae winsome wench and walie,
That night enlisted in the core,
Lang after kend on Carrick shore
(For mony a beast to dead she shot,
And perished mony a bonie boat,
And shook baith meikle corn and bear,
And kept the country side in fear),
Her cutty sark, o' Paisley harn,
That while a lassie she had worn,
In longitude tho' sorely scanty,
It was her best, and she was vauntie. –
Ah! little kend thy reverend grannie,
That sark she coft for her wee Nannie,
Wi' twa pund Scots ('twas a' her riches),
Wad ever graced a dance of witches!

But here my muse her wing maun cour;
Sic flights are far beyond her power;
To sing how Nannie lap and flang,
(A souple jade she was, and strang),
And how Tam stood, like ane betwitched,
And thought his very een enriched;
Even Satan glowred, and fidged fu' fain,
And hotched and blew wi' might and main:
Till first ae caper, syne anither,
Tam tint his reason a' thegither,
And roars out, 'Weel done, Cutty-sark!'
And in an instant all was dark:
And scarcely had he Maggie rallied,
When out the hellish legion sallied.

   As bees bizz out wi' angry fyke,
When plundering herds assail their byke;
As open pussie's mortal foes,
When, pop! she starts before their nose;
As eager runs the market crowd,
When 'Catch the thief!' resounds aloud,
So Maggie runs, the witches follow,
Wi' monie an eldritch skreech and hollow.

   Ah, Tam! ah, Tam! thou'll ge' thy fairin!
In hell they'll roast thee like a herrin!
In vain thy Kate awaits thy comin!
Kate soon will be a woefu' woman!
Now, do thy speedy utmost, Meg,
And win the keystane of the brig:
There at them thou thy tail may toss,
A running stream they darena cross.
But ere the keystane she could make,
The fient a tail she had to shake!
For Nannie, far before the rest,
Hard upon noble Maggie prest,
And flew at Tam wi' furious ettle;
But little wist she Maggie's mettle –
Ae spring brought off her master hale,
But left behind her ain gray tail:
The carlin claught her by the rump,
And left poor Maggie scarce a stump.

Now, what this tale o' truth shall read,
Ilk man and mother's son, take heed,
Whene'er to drink you are inclined,
Or cutty-sarks run in your mind,
Think, ye may buy the joys o'er dear,
Remember Tam o' Shanter's mare.

Robert Burns

POOR
BUT
HONEST

A Tea Party

In which Mrs Harris, assisted by a teapot, is the cause of a division between friends.

MRS GAMP'S APARTMENT in Kingsgate Street, High Holborn, wore, metaphorically speaking, a robe of state. It was swept and garnished for the reception of a visitor. That visitor was Betsey Prig: Mrs Prig of Bartlemy's; or as some said Barklemy's, or as some said Bardlemy's: for by all these endearing and familiar appellations, had the hospital of Saint Bartholomew become a household word among the sisterhood which Betsey Prig adorned.

Mrs Gamp's apartment was not a spacious one, but, to a contented mind, a closet is a palace; and the first-floor front of Mr Sweedlepipe's may have been, in the imagination of Mrs Gamp, a stately pile. If it were not exactly that, to restless intellects, it at least comprised as much accommodation as any person, not sanguine to insanity, could have looked for in a room of its dimensions. For only keep the bedstead always in your mind; and you were safe. That was the grand secret. Remembering the bedstead, you might even stoop to look under the little round table for anything you had dropped, without hurting yourself much against the chest of drawers, or qualifying as a patient of Saint Bartholomew, by falling into the fire.

Visitors were much assisted in their cautious efforts to preserve an unflagging recollection of this piece of furniture, by its size: which was great. It was not a turn-up bedstead, nor yet a French bedstead, nor yet a four-post bedstead, but what is poetically called a tent: the sacking whereof, was low and bulgy, insomuch that Mrs Gamp's box would not go under it, but stopped halfway, in a manner which while it did violence to the reason, likewise endangered the legs, of a stranger. The frame too, which would have supported the canopy and hangings if there had been any, was ornamented with divers pippins carved in timber, which on the slightest provocation, and frequently on none at all, came tumbling down; harassing the peaceful guest with inexplicable terrors.

The bed itself was decorated with a patchwork quilt of great antiquity; and at the upper end, upon the side nearest to the door, hung a scanty curtain of blue check, which prevented the Zephyrs that were abroad in Kingsgate Street, from visiting Mrs Gamp's head too roughly. Some rusty gowns and other articles of that lady's wardrobe depended from the post; and these had so adapted themselves by long usage to her figure, that more than one impatient husband coming in precipitately, at about the time of twilight, had been for an instant stricken dumb by the supposed discovery that Mrs Gamp had hanged herself. One gentleman, coming on the usual hasty errand, had said indeed, that they looked like guardian angels 'watching of her in her sleep'. But that, as Mrs Gamp said, 'was his first', and he never repeated the sentiment, though he often repeated his visit.

The chairs in Mrs Gamp's apartment were extremely large and broad-backed, which was more than a sufficient reason for there being but two in number. They were both elbow-chairs, of ancient mahogany; and were chiefly valuable for the slippery nature of their seats, which had been originally horsehair, but were now covered with a shiny substance of a bluish tint, from which the visitor began to slide away with a dismayed countenance, immediately after sitting down. What Mrs Gamp wanted in chairs she made up in bandboxes; of which she had a great collection, devoted to the reception of various miscellaneous valuables, which were not, however, as well protected as the good woman, by a pleasant fiction, seemed to think; for, though every bandbox had a carefully closed lid, not one among them had a bottom; owing to which cause, the property within was merely, as it were, extinguished. The chest of drawers having been originally made to stand upon the top of another chest, had a dwarfish, elfin look, alone; but, in regard of its security it had a great advantage over the bandboxes, for as all the handles had been long ago pulled off, it was very difficult to get at its contents. This indeed was only to be done by one of two devices; either by tilting the whole structure forward until all the drawers fell out together, or by opening them singly with knives, like oysters.

Mrs Gamp stored all her household matters in a little cupboard by the fire-place; beginning below the surface (as in nature) with the coals, and mounting gradually upwards to the spirits, which, from motives of delicacy, she kept in a tea-pot. The chimney-piece was ornamented with a small almanack, marked here and there in Mrs Gamp's own hand, with a memorandum of the date at which some lady was expected to fall due. It was also embellished with three profiles: one, in colours, of Mrs Gamp herself in early life; one, in bronze, of a lady in feathers, supposed to be Mrs Harris, as she appeared when dressed for a ball; and one, in black, of Mr Gamp, deceased. The last was a full length, in order that the likeness might be rendered more obvious and forcible, by the introduction of the wooden leg.

A pair of bellows, a pair of pattens, a toasting-fork, a kettle, a pap-boat, a spoon for the administration of medicine to the refractory, and lastly, Mrs Gamp's umbrella, which as something of great price and rarity was displayed with particular ostentation, completed the decorations of the chimney-piece and adjacent wall. Towards these objects, Mrs Gamp raised her eyes in satisfaction when she had arranged the tea-board, and had concluded her arrangements for the reception of Betsey Prig, even unto the setting forth of two pounds of Newcastle salmon, intensely pickled.

'There! Now drat you, Betsey, don't be long!' said Mrs Gamp, apostrophising her absent friend. 'For I can't abear to wait, I do assure you. To wotever place I goes, I sticks to this one mortar, "I'm easy pleased; it is but little as I wants; but I must have that little of the best, and to the minute when the clock strikes, else we do not part as I could wish, but bearin' malice in our arts." '

Her own preparations were of the best, for they comprehended a delicate new loaf, a plate of fresh butter, a basin of fine white sugar, and other arrangements on the same scale. Even the snuff with which she now refreshed herself, was so choice in quality, that she took a second pinch.

'There's the little bell a ringing now,' said Mrs Gamp, hurrying to the stair-head and looking over. 'Betsey Prig, my – why it's that there disapintin' Sweedlepipes, I do believe.'

'Yes, it's me,' said the barber in a faint voice; 'I've just come in.' 'You're always a comin' in, I think,' muttered Mrs Gamp to herself, 'except wen you're a-going out. I ha'n't no patience with that man!'

'Mrs Gamp,' said the barber. 'I say! Mrs Gamp!'

'Well,' cried Mrs Gamp, impatiently, as she descended the stairs. 'What is it? Is the Thames a-fire, a cooking its own fish, Mr Sweedlepipes? Why wot's the man gone and been a-doin' of to himself? He's as white as chalk!'

She added the latter clause of inquiry, when she got down stairs, and found him seated in the shaving-chair, pale and disconsolate.

'You recollect,' said Poll. 'You recollect young – '

'Not young Wilkins!' cried Mrs Gamp. 'Don't say young Wilkins, wotever you do. If young Wilkins' wife is took – '

'It isn't anybody's wife,' exclaimed the little barber. 'Bailey, young Bailey!'

'Why, wot do you mean to say that chit's been a-doin' of?' retorted Mrs Gamp, sharply. 'Stuff and nonsense, Mr Sweedlepipes!'

'He hasn't been a-doing anything!' exclaimed poor Poll, quite desperate.

'What do you catch me up so short for, when you see me put out, to that extent, that I can hardly speak? He'll never do anything again. He's done for. He's killed. The first time I ever see that boy,' said Poll, 'I charged him too much for a red-poll. I asked him three-halfpence for a penny one, because I was afraid he'd beat me down. But he didn't. And now he's dead; and if you was to crowd all the steam-engines and electric fluids that ever was, into this shop, and set 'em every one to work their hardest, they couldn't square the account, though it's only a ha'penny!'

Mr Sweedlepipe turned aside to the towel, and wiped his eyes with it.

'And what a clever boy he was!' he said. 'What a surprising young chap he was! How he talked! and what a deal he know'd! Shaved in this very chair he was; only for fun; it was all his fun; he was full of it. Ah! to think that he'll never be shaved in earnest! The birds might every one have died, and welcome,' cried the little barber, looking round him at the cages, and again applying to the towel, 'sooner than I'd have heard this news!'

'How did you ever come to hear it?' said Mrs Gamp. 'Who told you?'

'I went out,' returned the little barber, 'into the City, to meet a sporting Gent, upon the Stock Exchange, that wanted a few slow pigeons to practise at; and when I'd done with him, I went to get a little drop of beer, and there I heard everybody a-talking about it. It's in the papers.'

'You are in a nice state of confugion, Mr Sweedlepipes, you are!' said Mrs Gamp, shaking her head; 'and my opinion is, as half-a-dudgeon fresh young lively leeches on your temples, wouldn't be too much to clear your mind, which so I tell you. Wot were they a-talkin' on, and wot was in the papers?'

'All about it!' cried the barber. 'What else do you suppose? Him and his master were upset on a journey, and he was carried to Salisbury, and was breathing his last when the account came away. He never spoke afterwards. Not a single word. That's the worst of it to me; but that ain't all. His master can't be found. The other manager of their office in the city: Crimple, David Crimple: has gone off with the money, and is advertised for, with a reward, upon the walls. Mr Montague, poor young Bailey's master (what a boy he was!) is advertised for, too. Some say he's slipped off, to join his friend abroad; some say he mayn't have got away yet; and they're looking for him high and low. Their office is a smash; a swindle altogether. But what's a Life Assurance Office to a Life! And what a Life Young Bailey's was!'

'He was born into a wale,' said Mrs Gamp, with philosophical coolness, 'and he lived in a wale; and he must take the consequences of sech a sitivation. But don't you hear nothink of Mr Chuzzlewit in all this?'

'No,' said Poll, 'nothing to speak of. His name wasn't printed as one of the board, though some people say it was just going to be. Some believe he was took in, and some believe he was one of the takers-in; but however that may be, they can't prove nothing against him. This morning he went up of his own accord afore the Lord Mayor or some of them City big-wigs, and complained that he'd been swindled, and that these two persons had gone off and cheated him, and that he had just found out that Montague's name wasn't even Montague, but something else. And they do say that he looked like Death, owing to his losses. But, Lord forgive me,' cried the barber, coming back again to the subject of his individual grief, 'what's his looks to me! He might have died and welcome, fifty times, and not been such a loss as Bailey!'

At this juncture the little bell rang, and the deep voice of Mrs Prig struck into the conversation.

'Oh! You're a-talkin' about it, are you!' observed that lady. 'Well, I hope you've got it over, for I ain't interested in it myself.'

'My precious Betsey,' said Mrs Gamp, 'how late you are!'

The worthy Mrs Prig replied, with some asperity, 'that if perwerse people went off dead, when they was least expected, it warn't no fault of her'n'. And further, 'that it was quite aggrawation enough to be made late when one was dropping for one's tea, without hearing on it again'.

Mrs Gamp, deriving from this exhibition of repartee some clue to the state of Mrs Prig's feelings, instantly conducted her up stairs: deeming that the sight of pickled salmon might work a softening change.

But Betsey Prig expected pickled salmon. It was obvious that she did; for her first words, after glancing at the table, were:

'I know'd she wouldn't have a coucumber!'

Mrs Gamp changed colour, and sat down upon the bedstead.

'Lord bless you, Betsey Prig, your words is true. I quite forgot it!'

Mrs Prig, looking steadfastly at her friend, put her hand in her pocket, and with an air of surly triumph drew forth either the oldest of lettuces or youngest of cabbages, but at any rate, a green vegetable of an expansive nature, and of such magnificent proportions that she was obliged to shut it up like an umbrella before she could pull it out. She also produced a handful of mustard and cress, a trifle of the herb called dandelion, three bunches of radishes, an onion rather larger than an average turnip, three substantial slices of beetroot, and a short prong of antler of celery; the whole of this garden-stuff having been publicly exhibited, but a short time before, as a twopenny salad, and purchased by Mrs Prig, on condition that the vendor could get it all into her pocket. Which had been happily accomplished, in High Holborn, to the breathless interest of a hackney-coach stand. And she laid so little stress on this surprising forethought that she did not even smile, but returning her pocket into its accustomed sphere merely recommended that these products of nature should be sliced up, for immediate consumption, in plenty of vinegar.

'And don't go a dropping none of your snuff in it,' said Mrs Prig. 'In gruel, barley-water, apple-tea, mutton-broth, and that, it don't signify. It stimilates a patient. But I don't relish it myself.'

'Why, Betsey Prig!' cried Mrs Gamp; 'how *can* you talk so!'

'Why, ain't your patients, wotever their diseases is, always a sneezin' their wery heads off, along of your snuff?' said Mrs Prig.

'And wot if they are!' said Mrs Gamp.

'Nothing if they are,' said Mrs Prig. 'But don't deny it, Sairah.'

'Who deniges of it?' Mrs Gamp inquired.

'Mrs Prig returned no answer.

'WHO deniges of it, Betsey?' Mrs Gamp inquired again. Then Mrs Gamp, by reversing the question, imparted a deeper and more awful character of solemnity to the same. 'Betsey, who deniges of it?'

It was the nearest possible approach to a very decided difference of opinion between these ladies; but Mrs Prig's impatience for the meal being greater at the moment than her impatience of contradiction, she replied, for the present, 'Nobody, if you don't, Sairah,' and prepared herself for tea. For a quarrel can be taken up at any time, but a limited quantity of salmon cannot.

Her toilet was simple. She had merely to 'chuck' her bonnet and shawl upon the bed; give her hair two pulls, one upon the right side and one upon the left, as if she were ringing a couple of bells; and all was done. The tea was already made, Mrs Gamp was not long over the salad and they were soon at the height of their repast.

The temper of both parties was improved, for the time being, by the enjoyments of the table. When the meal came to a termination (which it was pretty long in doing), and Mrs Gamp having cleared away, produced the tea-pot from the top-shelf, simultaneously with a couple of wine-glasses, they were quite amiable.

'Betsey,' said Mrs Gamp, filling her own glass, and passing the tea-pot, 'I will now propoge a toast. My frequent pardner, Betsey Prig!'

'Which, altering the name to Sairah Gamp; I drink,' said Mrs Prig, 'with love and tenderness.'

From this moment symptoms of inflammation began to lurk in the nose of each lady; and perhaps, notwithstanding all appearances to the contrary, in the temper also.

'Now, Sairah,' said Mrs Prig, 'joining business with pleasure, wot is this case in which you wants me?'

Mrs Gamp betraying in her face some intention of returning an evasive answer, Betsey added:

'*Is* it Mrs Harris!'

'No, Betsey Prig, it ain't,' was Mrs Gamp's reply.

'Well!' said Mrs Prig, with a short laugh. 'I'm glad of that, at any rate.'

'Why should you be glad of that, Betsey?' Mrs Gamp retorted, warmly. 'She is unbeknown to you except by hearsay, why should you be glad? If you have anythink to say contrairy to the character of Mrs Harris, which well I knows behind her back, afore her face, or anywheres, is not to be impeaged, out with it, Betsey. I have know'd that sweetest and best of women,' said Mrs Gamp, shaking her head, and shedding tears, 'ever since afore her First, which Mr Harris who was dreadful timid went and stopped his ears in a empty dog-kennel, and never took his hands away or come out once till he was showed the baby, wen bein' took with fits, the doctor collared him and laid him on his back upon the airy stones, and she was told to ease her mind, his owls was organs. And I have know'd her, Betsey Prig, when he has hurt her feelin' art by sayin' of his Ninth that it was one too many, if not two, while that dear innocent was cooin' in his face, which thrive it did though bandy, but I have never know'd as you had occagion to be glad, Betsey, on accounts of Mrs Harris not requiring you. Require she never will, depend upon it, for her constant words in sickness is, and will be, "Send for Sairey!" '

During this touching address, Mrs Prig adroitly feigning to be the victim of that absence of mind which has its origin in excessive attention to one topic, helped herself from the tea-pot without appearing to observe it. Mrs Gamp observed it, however, and came to a premature close in consequence.

'Well it ain't her, it seems,' said Mrs Prig, coldly: 'who is it then?'

'You have heerd me mention, Betsey,' Mrs Gamp replied, after glancing in an expressive and marked manner at the tea-pot, 'a person as I took care on at the time as you and me was pardners off and on, in that there fever at the Bull?'

'Old Snuffey,' Mrs Prig observed.

Sarah Gamp looked at her with an eye of fire, for she saw in this mistake of Mrs Prig, another wilful and malignant stab at that same weakness or custom of hers, an ungenerous allusion to which, on the part of Betsey, had first disturbed their harmony that evening. And she saw it still more clearly, when, politely but firmly correcting that lady by the distinct enunciation of the word 'Chuffey', Mrs Prig received the correction with a diabolical laugh.

The best among us have their failings, and it must be conceded of Mrs Prig, that if there were a blemish in the goodness of her disposition, it was a habit she had of not bestowing all its sharp and acid properties upon her patients (as a thoroughly amiable woman would have done), but of keeping a considerable remainder for the service of her friends. Highly pickled salmon, and lettuces chopped up in vinegar, may, as viands possessing some acidity of their own, have encouraged and increased this failing in Mrs Prig; and every application to the tea-pot, certainly did; for it was often remarked of her by her friends, that she was most contradictory when most elevated. It is certain that her countenance became about this time derisive and defiant, and that she sat with her arms folded, and one eye shut up, in a somewhat offensive, because obtrusively intelligent, manner.

Mrs Gamp observing this, felt it the more necessary that Mrs Prig should know her place, and be made sensible of her exact station in society, as well as of her obligations to herself. She therefore assumed an air of greater patronage and importance, as she went on to answer Mrs Prig a little more in detail.

'Mr Chuffey, Betsey,' said Mrs Gamp, 'is weak in his mind. Excuge me if I makes remark, that he may neither be so weak as people thinks, nor people may not think he is so weak as they pretends, and what I knows, I knows; and what you don't, you don't; so do not ask me, Betsey. But Mr Chuffey's friends has made propojals for his bein' took care on, and has said to me "Mrs Gamp, *will* you undertake it? We couldn't think," they says, "of trusting him to nobody but you, for, Sairey, you are gold as has passed the furnage. Will you undertake it, at your own price, day and night, and by your own self?" "No," I says, "I will not. Do not reckon on it. There is," I says, "but one creetur in the world as I would undertake on sech terms, and her name is Harris. But," I says, "I am acquainted with a friend, whose name is Betsey Prig, that I can recommend, and will assist me. Betsey," I says, "is always to be trusted, under me, and will be guided as I could desire".'

Here Mrs Prig, without any abatement of her offensive manner, again counterfeited abstraction of mind, and stretched out her hand to the tea-pot. It was more than Mrs Gamp could bear. She stopped the hand of Mrs Prig with her own, and said, with great feeling:

'No, Betsey! Drink fair, wotever you do!'

Mrs Prig, thus baffled, threw herself back in her chair, and closing the same eye more emphatically, and folding her arms tighter, suffered her head to roll slowly from side to side, while she surveyed her friend with a contemptuous smile.

Mrs Gamp resumed:

'Mrs Harris, Betsey' –

'Bother Mrs Harris!' said Betsey Prig.

Mrs Gamp looked at her with amazement, incredulity, and indignation; when Mrs Prig, shutting her eye still closer, and folding her arms still tighter, uttered these memorable and tremendous words:

'I don't believe there's no sich a person!'

After the utterance of which expressions, she leaned forward, and snapped her fingers once, twice, thrice; each time nearer to the face of Mrs Gamp, and then rose to put on her bonnet, as one who felt that there was now a gulf between them, which nothing could ever bridge across.

The shock of this blow was so violent and sudden, that Mrs Gamp sat staring at nothing with uplifted eyes, and her mouth open as if she were gasping for breath, until Betsey Prig had put on her bonnet and her shawl, and was gathering the latter about her throat. Then Mrs Gamp rose – morally and physically rose – and denounced her.

'What!' said Mrs Gamp, 'you bage creetur, have I know'd Mrs Harris five and thirty year, to be told at last that there ain't no sech a person livin'! Have I stood her friend in all her troubles, great and small, for it to come at last to sech a end as this, which her own sweet picter hanging up afore you all the time, to shame your bragian words! But well you mayn't believe there's no sech a creetur, for she wouldn't demean herself to look at you, and often has she said, when I have made mention of your name, which, to my sinful sorrow, I have done, "What, Sairey Gamp! debage yourself to *her!*" Go along with you.'

'I'm a goin', ma'am, ain't I?' said Mrs Prig, stopping as she said it.

'You had better, ma'am,' said Mrs Gamp.

'Do you know who you're talking to, ma'am?' inquired her visitor.

'Aperiently,' said Mrs Gamp, surveying her with scorn from head to foot, 'to Betsey Prig. Aperiently so. *I* know her. No one better. Go along with you!'

'And *you* was a going to take me under you!' cried Mrs Prig, surveying Mrs Gamp from head to foot in her turn. '*You* was, was you? Oh, how kind! Why, deuce take your imperence,' said Mrs Prig, with a rapid change from banter to ferocity, 'what do you mean?'

'Go along with you!' said Mrs Gamp. 'I blush for you.'

'You had better blush a little for yourself, while you *are* about it!' said Mrs

Prig. 'You and your Chuffeys! What, the poor old creetur isn't mad enough, isn't he? Aha!'

'He'd very soon be mad enough, if you had anything to do with him,' said Mrs Gamp.

'And that's what I was wanted for, is it?' cried Mrs Prig, triumphantly. 'Yes. But you'll find yourself deceived. I won't go near him. We shall see how you get on without me. I won't have nothink to do with him.'

'You never spoke a truer word than that!' said Mrs Gamp. 'Go along with you!'

She was prevented from witnessing the actual retirement of Mrs Prig from the room, notwithstanding the great desire she had expressed to behold it, by that lady, in her angry withdrawal, coming into contact with the bedstead, and bringing down the previously mentioned pippins; three or four of which came rattling on the head of Mrs Gamp so smartly, that when she recovered from this wooden shower-bath, Mrs Prig was gone.

She had the satisfaction, however, of hearing the deep voice of Betsey, proclaiming her injuries and her determination to have nothing to do with Mr Chuffey, down the stairs, and along the passage, and even out in Kingsgate Street. Likewise of seeing in her own apartment, in the place of Mrs Prig, Mr Sweedlepipe and two gentlemen.

'Why, bless my life!' exclaimed the little barber, 'what's amiss? The noise you ladies have been making, Mrs Gamp! Why, these two gentlemen have been standing on the stairs, outside the door, nearly all the time, trying to make you hear, while you were pelting away, hammer and tongs! It'll be the death of the little bullfinch in the shop, that draws his own water. In his fright, he's been a straining himself all to bits, drawing more water than he could drink in a twelvemonth. He must have thought it was Fire!'

Mrs Gamp had in the meanwhile sunk into her chair, from whence, turning up her overflowing eyes, and clasping her hands, she delivered the following lamentation:

'Oh, Mr Sweedlepipes, which Mr Westlock also, if my eyes do not deceive, and a friend not havin' the pleasure of bein' beknown, wot I have took from Betsey Prig this blessed night, no mortial creetur knows! If she had abuged me, bein' in liquor, which I thought I smelt her wen she come, but could not be believe, not bein' used myself' – Mrs Gamp, by the way, was pretty far gone, and the fragrance of the tea-pot was strong in the room – 'I could have bore it with a thankful art. But the words she spoke of Mrs Harris, lambs could not forgive. No, Betsey!' said Mrs Gamp, in a violent burst of feeling, 'nor worms forget!'

The little barber scratched his head, and shook it, and looked at the tea-pot and gradually got out of the room. John Westlock, taking a chair, sat down on one side of Mrs Gamp. Martin, taking the foot of the bed, supported her on the other.

'You wonder what we want, I dare say,' observed John. 'I'll tell you presently, when you have recovered. It's not pressing, for a few minutes or so. How do you find yourself? Better?'

Mrs Gamp shed more tears, shook her head and feebly pronounced Mrs Harris's name.

'Have a little – ' John was at a loss what to call it.

'Tea,' suggested Martin.

'It ain't tea,' said Mrs Gamp.

'Physic of some sort, I support,' cried John. 'Have a little.'

Mrs Gamp was prevailed upon to take a glassful. 'On condition,' she passionately observed, 'as Betsey never has another stroke of work from me.'

'Certainly not,' said John. 'She shall never help to nurse *me*.'

'To think,' said Mrs Gamp, 'as she should ever have helped to nuss that friend of yourn, and been so near of hearing things that – Ah!'

John looked at Martin.

'Yes,' he said. 'That was a narrow escape, Mrs Gamp.'

'Narrer, in-deed!' she returned. 'It was only my having the night, and hearin' of him in his wanderins; and her the day, that saved it. Wot would she have said and done, if she had know'd what *I* know; that perfeejus wretch! Yet, oh good gracious me!' cried Mrs Gamp, trampling on the floor, in the absence of Mrs Prig, 'that I should hear from that same woman's lips what I have heerd her speak to Mrs Harris!'

'Never mind,' said John. 'You know it is not true.'

'Isn't true!' cried Mrs Gamp. 'True! Don't I know as that dear woman is expecting of me at this minnit, Mr Westlock, and is a lookin' out of window down the street, with little Tommy Harris in her arms, as calls me his own Gammy, and truly calls, for bless the mottled little legs of that there precious child (like Canterbury Brawn his own dear father says, which so they are) his own I have been, ever since I found him, Mr Westlock, with his small red worsted shoc a gurglin' in his throat, where he had put it in his play, a chick, wile they was leavin' of him on the floor a looking for it through the ouse and him a choakin' sweetly in the parlour! Oh, Betsey Prig, what wickedness you've showed this night, but never shall you darken Sairey's doors agen, you twining serpiant!'

'You were always so kind to her, too!' said John, consolingly.

'That's the cutting part. That's where it hurts me, Mr Westlock,' Mrs

Gamp replied; holding out her glass unconsciously, while Martin filled it.

'Chosen to help you with Mr Lewsome!' said John. 'Chosen to help you with Mr Chuffey!'

'Chose once, but chose no more,' cried Mrs Gamp. 'No pardnership with Betsey Prig, agen, sir!'

'No, no,' said John. 'That would never do.'

'I don't know as it ever would have done, sir,' Mrs Gamp replied, with the solemnity peculiar to a certain stage of intoxication. 'Now that the marks,' by which Mrs Gamp is supposed to have meant mask, 'is off that creetur's face. I do not think it ever would have done. There are reagions in families for keeping things a secret, Mr Westlock, and havin' only them about you as you knows you can repoge in. Who could repoge in Betsey Prig, arter her words of Mrs Harris, setting in that chair afore my eyes!'

'Quite true,' said John; 'quite. I hope you have time to find another assistant, Mrs Gamp?'

Between her indignation and the tea-pot, her powers of comprehending what was said to her began to fail. She looked at John with tearful eyes, and murmuring the well-remembered name which Mrs Prig had challenged – as if it were a talisman against all earthly sorrows – seemed to wander in her mind.

'I hope,' repeated John, 'that you have time to find another assistant?'

'Which short it is, indeed,' cried Mrs Gamp, turning up her languid eyes, and clasping Mr Westlock's wrist with matronly affection. 'To-morrow evenin', sir, I waits upon his friends. Mr Chuzzlewit apinted it from nine to ten.'

'From nine to ten,' said John, with a significant glance at Martin; 'and then Mr Chuffey retires into safe keeping, does he?'

'He needs to be kep safe, I do assure you,' Mrs Gamp replied, with a mysterious air. 'Other people besides me has had a happy deliverance from Betsey Prig. I little know'd that woman. She'd have let it out!'

'Let *him* out, you mean,' said John.

'Do I!' retorted Mrs Gamp. 'Oh!'

The severely ironical character of this reply was strengthened by a very slow nod, and a still slower drawing down of the corners of Mrs Gamp's mouth. She added with extreme stateliness of manner, after indulging in a short doze:

'But I am a keepin' of you gentlemen, and time is precious.'

Mingling with that delusion of the tea-pot which inspired her with the belief that they wanted her to go somewhere immediately, a shrewd avoidance of any further reference to the topics into which she had lately strayed, Mrs Gamp rose; and putting away the tea-pot in its accustomed place, and locking the cupboard with much gravity, proceeded to attire herself for a professional visit.

This preparation was easily made, as it required nothing more than the snuffy black bonnet, the snuffy black shawl, the pattens, and the indispensable umbrella, without which neither a lying-in nor a laying-out could by any possibility be attempted. When Mrs Gamp had invested herself with these appendages she returned to her chair, and sitting down again, declared herself quite ready.

'It's a appiness to know as one can benefit the poor sweet creetur,' she observed, 'I'm sure. It isn't all as can. The torters Betsey Prig inflicts is frightful!'

Closing her eyes as she made this remark, in the acuteness of her commiseration for Betsey's patients, she forgot to open them again until she dropped a patten. Her nap was also broken at intervals, like the fabled slumbers of Friar Bacon, by the dropping of the other patten, and of the umbrella. But when she had got rid of those incumbrances, her sleep was peaceful.

The two young men looked at each other, ludicrously enough; and Martin, stifling his disposition to laugh, whispered in John Westlock's ear:

'What shall we do now?'

'Stay here,' he replied.

Mrs Gamp was heard to murmur 'Mrs Harris' in her sleep.

'Rely upon it,' whispered John, looking cautiously towards her, 'that you shall question this old clerk, though you go as Mrs Harris yerself. We know quite enough to carry her our own way now, at all events; thanks to this quarrel, which confirms the old saying that when rogues fall out, honest people get what they want. Let Jonas Chuzzlewit look to himself; and let her sleep as long as she likes. We shall gain our end in good time.'

From *Martin Chuzzlewit* by Charles Dickens

The Joiner's Apprentices

First.
'Tis a shuddering work, 'tis a work of dread;
Between the boards shall be laid the dead.

Second.
How now! What makes thy tears run fast?
Child of the stranger, a weak heart thou hast.

First.
Nay, do not so quickly grow angry, I pray;
I ne'er made a coffin, in truth, till to-day.

Second.
Be it first time, or last time, now pledge me in wine;
Then to work; and never let faint heart be thine.

First cut up the boards as the length may decide,
Then plane the curling-up shavings aside.

Board unto board next mortise them tight,
Then polish the narrow bed black and bright.

Next, the varnish-perfumed coffin within,
Lay the down-fallen shavings so white and thin;

For, on shavings must slumber the perishing clay:
With all undertakers 'tis ever the way.

Then carry the coffin to th' house of grief;
Corpse within, lid screwed down, and the work is Brief.

First.
I cut the boards; and, with accurate ell,
Above and below I have measured it well.

I plane the rough boards so smooth; but yet
My arm is weak, and my eye is wet.

I mortise the boards above and below;
Yet my heart is full, and my heart is woe.

'Tis a shuddering work, and a work of dread;
For between the boards must be laid the dead.

Translation from the German by Mary Howitt

The Sea-Fowler

The baron hath the landward park, the fisher hath the sea;
But the rocky haunts of the sea-fowl belong alone to me.

The baron hunts the running deer, the fisher nets the brine;
But every bird that builds a nest on ocean-cliffs is mine.

Come on then, Jock and Alick, let's to the sea-rocks bold:
I was trained to take the sea-fowl ere I was five years old.

The wild sea roars, and lashes the granite crags below;
And round the misty islets the loud strong tempest blow.

And let them blow! Roar wind and wave, they shall not me dismay;
I've faced the eagle in her nest and snatched her young away.

The eagle shall not build her nest, proud bird although she be,
Nor yet the strong-winged cormorant, without the leave of me.

The eider-duck has laid her eggs, the tern doth hatch her young,
And the merry gull screams o'er her brood; but all to me belong.

Away, then, in the daylight, and back again ere eve;
The eagle could not rear her young, unless I gave her leave.

The baron hath the landward park, the fisher hath the sea;
The the rocky haunts of the sea-fowl belong alone to me.

Mary Howitt

The Courting

Zekle crep' up, quite unbeknown,
  An' peeked in thru the winder,
An' there sot Huldy all alone
  'Ith no one nigh to hender.

Agin' the chimbly crooknecks hung,
  An' in amongst 'em rusted
The old queen's arm thet Gran'ther Young
  Fetched back frum Concord busted.

The wannut logs shot sparkles out
  Towards the pootiest, bless her!
An' leetle fires danced all about
  The chiny on the dresser.

The very room, coz she wuz in,
  Looked warm frum floor to ceilin',
An' she looked full ez rosy agin
  Ez th' apples she wuz peelin'.

She heerd a foot an' knowed it, tu,
  A raspin' on the scraper, –
All ways to once her feelins flew
  Like sparks in burnt-up paper.

He kin' o' l'itered on the mat,
  Some doubtfle o' the seekle;
His heart kep' goin' pitypat,
  But hern went pity Zekle.

An' yet she gin her cheer a jerk
  Ez though she wished him furder,
An' on her apples ke' to work
  Ez ef a wager spurred her.

'You want to see my Pa, I spose?'
  'Wal, no; I come designin' – '

'To see my Ma? She's sprinklin' clo'es
  Agin to-morrow's i'nin'.'

He stood a spell on one foot fust
  Then stood a spell on t'other,
An' on which one he felt the wust
  He couldn't ha' told ye, nuther.

Sez he, 'I'd better call agin';
  Sez she, 'Think likely, Mister';
The last word pricked him like a pin,
  An' – wal, he up and kist her.

When Ma bimeby upon 'em slips,
  Huldy sot pale ez ashes,
All kind o' smily round the lips
  An' teary round the lashes.

Her blood riz quick, though, like the tide
  Down to the Bay o' Fundy,
An' all I know is they wuz cried
  In meetin', come nex' Sunday.

James Russell Lowell

Sally in Our Alley

Of all the girls that are so smart
  There's none like pretty Sally;
She is the darling of my heart
  And she lives in our alley.
There is no lady in the land
  Is half so sweet as Sally;
She is the darling of my heart,
  And she lives in our alley.

Her father he makes cabbage nets
  And through the streets does cry 'em
Her mother she sells laces long

To such as please to buy 'em:
But sure such folks could ne'er beget
   So sweet a girl as Sally!
She is the darling of my heart,
   And she lives in our alley.

When she is by, I leave my work,
   I love her so sincerely;
My master comes like any Turk,
   And bangs me most severely –
But let him bang his bellyful,
   I'll bear it all for Sally –
She is the darling of my heart,
   And she lives in our alley.

Of all the days that's in the week
   I dearly love but one day –
And that's the day that comes betwixt
   A Saturday and Monday;
For then I'm drest all in my best
   To walk abroad with Sally;
She is the darling of my heart,
   And she lives in our alley.

My master carries me to church,
   And often am I blamed
Because I leave him in the lurch
   As soon as text is named;
I leave the church in sermon time
   And slink away to Sally;
She is the darling of my heart,
   And she lives in our alley.

When Christmas comes about again
   O then I shall have money;
I'll hoard it up, and box it all,
   I'll give it to my honey;
I would it were ten thousand pounds,
   I'd give it all to Sally;
She is the darling of my heart,
   And she lives in our alley.

My master and the neighbours all
  Make game of me and Sally,
And, but for her, I'd better be
  A slave and row a galley;
But when my seven long years are out
  O then I'll marry Sally, –
O then we'll wed, and then we'll bed,
  But not in our alley!

Henry Carey

The Oath of Scavagers, or Scavengers, of the Ward

'YE SHAL SWEAR, that ye shal wel and diligently oversee that the pavements in every ward be wel and rightfully repaired, and not haunsed[1] to the noyaunce of the neighbours; and that the ways, streets, and lanes, be kept clean from donge and other filth, for the honesty of the city. And that all the chimneys, redosses,[2] and furnaces, be made of stone for defence of fire. And if ye know any such ye shall shew it to the Alderman, that he may make due redress therefore. And this ye shall not lene.[3] So help you God.'

To aid the scavengers in their execution of the duties of the office, the following among others were the injunctions of the civic law. They indicate the former state of the streets of London better than any description. A 'goung (or dung) fermour' appears to be a nightman, a dung-carrier or bearer, the servant of the master or ward scavenger.

'No goungfermour shall spill any ordure in the street, under pain of thirteen shillings and fourpence.

'No goungfermour shall carry any ordure till after nine of the clock in the night, under pain of thirteen shillings and fourpence. No man shall cast any urine boles, or ordure boles, into the streets by day or night, afore the hour of nine in the night. And also he shall not cast it out, but bring it down and lay it in the canal, under pain of three shillings and fourpence. And if he do so cast it upon any person's head, the person to have a lawful recompense, if he have hurt thereby.

1 *haunsed* – made too high.
2 *Redosses* – reredos, i.e. back-flues.
3 *Lene* – let or lease.

'No man shall bury any dung, or goung, within the liberties of this city, under pain of forty shillings.'

From *London Labour and the London Poor* by Henry Mayhew, quoting from the laws in the time of Henry VIII

Directions to the Housemaid

IF YOUR MASTER and lady go into the country for a week or more, never wash the bedchamber or dining-room until just the hour before you expect them to return: thus the rooms will be perfectly clean to receive them, and you will not be at the trouble to wash them so soon again.

I am very much offended with those ladies who are so proud and lazy, that they will not be at the pains of stepping into the garden to pluck a rose, but keep an odious implement; sometimes in the bedchamber itself, or at least in a dark closet adjoining, which they make use of to ease their worst necessities: and you are the usual carriers away of the pan; which makes not only the chamber, but even their clothes, offensive to all who come near. Now to cure them of this odious practice, let me advise you, on whom the office lies to convey away this utensil, that you will do it openly down the great stairs, and in the presence of the footmen; and if anybody knocks, to open the street door while you have the vessel filled in your hands; this, if any thing can, will make your lady take the pains of evacuating her person in the proper place, rather than expose her filthiness to all the men-servants in the house.

Leave a pail of dirty water with a mop in it, a coal-box, a bottle, a broom, a chamberpot, and such other unsightly things, either in a blind entry, or upon the darkest part of the back-stairs, that they may not be seen: and if people break their shins by trampling on them, it is their own fault.

Never empty the chamberpots until they are quite full: if that happens in the night, empty them into the street; if in the morning, into the garden; for it would be an endless work to go a dozen times from the garret and upper rooms down to the backside; but never wash them in any other liquor except their own: what cleanly girl would be dabbling in other folk's urine? and besides, the smell of stale, as I observed before, is admirable against the vapours; which a hundred to one, may be your lady's case.

Brush down the cobwebs with a broom that is wet and dirty, which will make them stick the faster to it, and bring them down more effectually.

When you rid up the parlour hearth in a morning, throw the last night's ashes into a sieve, and what falls through, as you carry it down, will serve instead of sand for the rooms and the stairs.

When you have scoured the brasses and irons in the parlour chimney, lay the foul wet clout upon the next chair, that your lady may see you have not neglected your work: observe the same rule when you clean the brass locks, only with this addition, to leave the marks of your fingers on the doors, to show you have not forgot.

Leave your lady's chamberpot in her bedchamber window all day to air.

Bring up none but large coals to the dining-room and your lady's chamber; they make the best fires, and if you find them too big, it is easy to break them on the marble hearth.

When you go to bed, be sure take care of fire; and therefore blow the candle out with your breath, and then thrust it under your bed. Note, the smell of the snuff is very good against vapours.

Persuade the footman, who got you with child, to marry you before you are six months gone: and if your lady asks you why you would take a fellow who was not worth a groat? let your answer be, That service is no inheritance.

When your lady's bed is made, put the chamberpot under it, but in such a manner as to thrust the valance along with it, that it may be full in sight, and ready for your lady when she has occasion to use it.

Lock up a cat or a dog in some room or closet so as to make such a noise all over the house as may frighten away the thieves, if any should attempt to break or steal in.

When you wash any of the rooms toward the street over night, throw the foul water out of the street door but be sure not to look before you, for fear those on whom the water lights might think you uncivil, and that you did it on purpose. If he who suffers, breaks the windows in revenge, and your lady chides you, and gives positive orders that you should carry the pail down, and empty it in the sink, you have an easy remedy: when you wash an upper room, carry down the pail so as to let the water dribble on the stairs all the way down to the kitchen; by which not only your load will be lighter, but you will convince your lady, that it is better to throw the water out of the windows, or down the street-door steps, besides, this latter practice will be very diverting to you and the family in a frosty night, to see a hundred people on their noses or backsides before your door, when the water is frozen.

Polish and brighten the marble hearths and chimney pieces with a clout dipped in grease; nothing makes them shine so well; and it is the business of the ladies to take care of their petticoats.

If your lady be so nice that she will have the room scoured with freestone, be sure to leave the marks of the freestone six inches deep round the bottom of the wainscot, that your lady may see your obedience to her orders.

From *Directions to Servants* by Jonathan Swift

Kitchens

IT IS NOT a figure of speech, it is a mere statement of fact to say that a French cook will spit in the soup – that is, if he is not going to drink it himself. He is an artist, but his art is not cleanliness. To a certain extent he is even dirty because he is an artist, for food, to look smart, needs dirty treatment. When a steak, for instance, is brought up for the head cook's inspection, he does not handle it with a fork. He picks it up in his fingers and slaps it down, runs his thumb round the dish and licks it to taste the gravy, runs it round and licks it again, then steps back and contemplates the piece of meat like an artist judging a picture, then presses it lovingly into place with his fat, pink fingers, every one of which he has licked a hundred times that morning. When he is satisfied, he takes a cloth and wipes his fingerprints from the dish, and hands it to the waiter. And the waiter, of course, dips *his* fingers into the gravy – his nasty, greasy fingers which he is for ever running through his brilliantined hair. Whenever one pays more than, say, ten francs for a dish of meat in Paris, one may be certain that it has been fingered in this manner. In very cheap restaurants it is different; there, the same trouble is not taken over the food, and it is just forked out of the pan and flung onto a plate, without handling. Roughly speaking, the more one pays for food, the more sweat and spittle one is obliged to eat with it.

Dirtiness is inherent in hotels and restaurants, because sound food is sacrificed to punctuality and smartness. The hotel employee is too busy getting food ready to remember that it is meant to be eaten. A meal is simply '*une commande*' to him, just as a man dying of cancer is simply 'a case' to the doctor. A customer orders, for example, a piece of toast. Somebody, pressed with work in a cellar deep underground, has to prepare it. How can he stop and say to himself, 'This toast is to be eaten – I must make it eatable'? All he knows is that it must look right and must be ready in three minutes. Some large drops of sweat fall from his forehead onto the toast. Why should he worry? Presently the toast falls among the filthy sawdust on the floor. Why trouble to make a new piece? It is much quicker to wipe the sawdust off.

From *Down and Out in Paris and London* by George Orwell

How to Start a Low Lodging-House

T O 'START' a low lodging-house is not a very costly matter. Furniture which will not be saleable in the ordinary course of auction, or of any traffic, is bought by a lodging-house 'start'. A man possessed of some money, who took an interest in a bricklayer, purchased for 20*l*., when the Small Pox Hospital, by King's-cross, was pulled down, a sufficiency of furniture for four lodging-houses, in which he 'started' the man in question. None others would buy this furniture, from a dread of infection.

It was the same at Marlborough-house, Peckham, after the cholera had broken out there. The furniture was sold to a lodging-house keeper, at 9*d*. each article. 'Big and little, sir,' I was told; 'a penny pot and a bedstead – all the same; each 9*d*. Nobody else would buy.'

From *London Labour and the London Poor* by Henry Mayhew

A Doss-House

I T WAS a tall, battered-looking house, with dim lights in all the windows, some of which were patched with brown paper. I entered a stone passage-way, and a little etiolated boy with sleepy eyes appeared from a door leading to a cellar. Murmurous sounds came from the cellar, and a wave of hot air and cheese. The boy yawned and held out his hand.

'Want a kip? That'll be a 'og, guv'nor.'

I paid the shilling, and the boy led me up a rickety unlighted staircase to a bedroom. It had a sweetish reek of paregoric and foul linen; the windows seemed to be tight shut, and the air was almost suffocating at first. There was a candle burning, and I saw that the room measured fifteen feet square by eight high, and had eight beds in it. Already six lodgers were in bed, queer lumpy shapes with all their own clothes, even their boots, piled on top of them. Someone was coughing in a loathsome manner in one corner.

When I got into the bed I found that it was as hard as a board, and as for the pillow, it was a mere hard cylinder like a block of wood. It was rather worse than sleeping on a table, because the bed was not six feet long, and very narrow, and the mattress was convex, so that one had to hold on to avoid falling out. The sheets stank so horribly of sweat that I could not bear them near my nose. Also, the bedclothes only consisted of the sheets and a cotton counterpane, so that though stuffy it was none too warm. Several noises recurred throughout the night. About once in an hour the man on my left – a sailor, I think – woke up, swore vilely, and lighted a cigarette. Another man, victim of bladder disease, got up and noisily used his chamber-pot half a dozen times during the night. The man in the corner had a coughing fit once in every twenty minutes, so regularly that one came to listen for it as one listens for the next yap when a dog is baying the moon. It was an unspeakably repellent sound; a foul bubbling and retching, as though the man's bowels were being churned up within him. Once when he struck a match I saw that he was a very old man, with a grey, sunken face like that of a corpse, and he was wearing his trousers wrapped round his head as a nightcap, a thing which for some reason disgusted me very much. Every time he coughed or the other man swore, a sleepy voice from one of the other beds cried out:

'Shut up! Oh, for Christ's – *sake* shut up!'

I had about an hour's sleep in all. In the morning I was woken by a dim impression of some large brown thing coming towards me. I opened my eyes and saw that it was one of the sailor's feet, sticking out of bed close to my face. It was dark brown, quite dark brown like an Indian's, with dirt. The walls were leprous, and the sheets, three weeks from the wash, were almost raw umber colour. I got up, dressed and went downstairs. In the cellar were a row of basins and two slippery roller towels. I had a piece of soap in my pocket, and I was going to wash, when I noticed that every basin was streaked with grime – solid, sticky filth as black as boot-blacking. I went out unwashed. Altogether, the lodging-house had not come up to its description as cheap *and* clean. It was however, as I found later, a fairly representative lodging-house.

From *Down and Out in Paris and London* by George Orwell

The House

Hugh Miller has inherited a house which proves more of a liability than a blessing.

IT FORMED the lowermost floor of an old black building, four stories in height, flanked by a damp narrow court along one of its sides, and that turned to the street its sharp-peaked, many-windowed gable. The lower windows were covered up by dilapidated, weather-bleached shutters; in the upper, the comparatively fresh appearance of the rags that stuffed up holes where panes ought to have been, and a few very pale-coloured petticoats and very dark-coloured shirts fluttering in the wind, gave evident signs of habitation. It cost my conductor's one hand an arduous wrench to lay open the lock of the outer door, in front of which he had first to dislodge a very dingy female, attired in an earth-coloured gown, that seemed as if starched with ashes; and as the rusty hinges creaked, and the door fell against the wall, we became sensible of a damp, unwholesome smell, like the breath of a charnel-house, which issued from the interior. The place had been shut up for nearly two years; and so foul had the stagnant atmosphere become, that the candle which we brought with us to explore burned dim and yellow like a miner's lamp. The floors, broken up in fifty different places, were littered with rotten straw; and in one of the corners there lay a damp heap, gathered up like the lair of some wild beast, on which some one seemed to have slept, mayhap months before. The partitions were crazed and tottering; the walls blackened with smoke; broad patches of plaster had fallen from the ceilings, or still dangled from them, suspended by single hairs; and the bars of the grates, crusted with rust, had become red as foxtails. Mr M'Craw nodded his head over the gathered heap of straw. 'Ah,' he said – 'got in again, I see! The shutters must be looked to.' 'I daresay,' I remarked, looking disconsolately around me, 'you don't find it very easy to get tenants for houses of this kind.' 'Very easy!' said Mr M'Craw, with somewhat of a Highland twang, and, as I thought, with also a good deal of Highland hauteur – as was of course quite natural in so shrewd and extensive a house-agent, when dealing with the owner of a domicile that would not let, and who made foolish remarks – 'No, nor easy at all, or it would not be locked up in this way: but if we took off the shutters you would soon get tenants enough.' 'Oh, I suppose so; and I daresay it is as difficult to see as to let such houses.' 'Ay, and more,' said Mr M'Craw: 'it's all sellers, and no buyers, when we get this low.'

The past history of the house . . .

It had been let as a public-house and tap-room, and had been the scene of a somewhat rough, and, I daresay, not very respectable, but yet profitable trade; but no sooner had it become mine than, in consequence of some alterations in the harbour, the greater part of the shipping that used to lie at the Coal-hill removed to a lower reach; the tap-room business suddenly fell off; and the rent sank, during the course of one twelve-month, from twenty-four to twelve pounds. And then in its sere and wintry state, the unhappy house came to be inhabited by a series of miserable tenants, who, though they sanguinely engaged to pay the twelve pounds, never paid them. I still remember the brief, curt letters from our agent, the late Mr Veitch, town-clerk of Leith, that never failed to fill my mother with terror and dismay, and very much resembled, in at least the narrative parts, jottings by the poet Crabbe, for some projected poem on the profligate poor. Two of our tenants made moonlight flittings just on the eve of the term; and though the little furniture which they left behind them was duly rouped at the cross, such was the inevitable expense of the transaction, that none of the proceeds of the sale reached Cromarty. The house was next inhabited by a stout female, who kept a certain description of lady-lodgers; and for the first half-year she paid the rent most conscientiously; but the authorities interfering, there was another house found for her and her ladies in the neighbour-hood of the Carlton, and the rent of the second half-year remained unpaid. And as the house lost, in consequence of her occupation, the modicum of character which it had previously retained, it lay for five years wholly untenanted, save by a mischievous spirit – the ghost, it was said, of a murdered gentleman, whose throat had been cut in an inner apartment by the ladies, and his body flung by night into the deep mud of the harbour. The ghost was, however, at length detected by the police, couching in the form of one of the ladies themselves, on a lair of straw in the corner of one of the rooms, and exorcised into Bridewell; and then the house came to be inhabited by a tenant who had both the will and the ability to pay. One year's rent, however, had to be expended in repairs; and ere the next year passed, the heritors of the parish were rated for the erection of the magnificent parish church of North Leith, then in course of building, with its tall and graceful spire and classic portico; and as we had no one to state our case, our house was rated, not according to its reduced, but according to its original value. And so the entire rental of the second year, with several pounds additional which I had to subtract from my hard-earned savings as a mason, were appropriated in behalf of the ecclesiastical Establishment of the country, by the builders of the church and spire. I had attained my majority when lodging in the fragment of a salt storehouse in Gairloch; and, competent in the eye of the law to dispose of the house on the Coal-hill, I now hoped to find, if not a purchaser, at least some one foolish enough to take it off my hands for nothing.

From *My Schools and Schoolmasters* by Hugh Miller

Drury Lane

M'KAY had found a room near Parker Street, Drury Lane, in which he proposed to begin, and that night, as we trod the pavement of Portland Place, he propounded his plans to me, I listening without much confidence, but loth nevertheless to take the office of Time upon myself, and to disprove what experience would disprove more effectually. His object was nothing less than gradually to attract Drury Lane to come and be saved. The first Sunday I went with him to the room. As we walked over the Drury Lane gratings of the cellars a most foul stench came up, and one in particular I remember to this day. A man half dressed pushed open a broken window beneath us, just as we passed by, and there issued such a blast of corruption, made up of gases bred by filth, air breathed and rebreathed a hundred times, charged with odours of unnameable personal uncleanness and disease, that I staggered to the gutter with a qualm which I could scarcely conquer. At the doors of the houses stood grimy women with their arms folded and their hair disordered. Grimier boys and girls had tied a rope to broken railings, and were swinging on it. The common door to a score of lodgings stood ever open, and the children swarmed up and down the stairs carrying with them patches of mud every time they came in from the street. The wholesome practice which amongst the decent poor marks off at least one day in the week as a day on which there is to be a change; when there is to be some attempt to procure order and cleanliness; a day to be preceded by soap and water, by shaving, and by as many clean clothes as can be procured, was unknown here. There was no break in the uniformity of squalor; nor was it even possible for any single family to emerge amidst such altogether suppressive surroundings. All self-respect, all effort to do anything more than to satisfy somehow the grossest wants, had departed. The shops were open; most of them exhibiting a most miscellaneous collection of goods, such as bacon cut in slices, fire-wood, a few loaves of bread, and sweetmeats in dirty bottles. Fowls, strange to say, black as the flagstones, walked in and out of these shops, or descended into the dark areas. The undertaker had not put up his shutters. He had drawn down a yellow blind, on which was painted a picture of a suburban cemetery. Two funerals, the loftiest effort of his craft, were depicted approaching the gates. When the gas was alight behind the blind, an effect was produced which was doubtless much admired.

From *Deliverance* by Mark Rutherford

Epigram

You blot upon a Summer's Quarter Day,
Vacerra, you and yours are now away,
With two years' rent unpaid, at last ejected,
Taking the traps the landlord, even, rejected.
First came your wife, with her seven reddish curls –
She did the carrying – then the other girls,
Your white-haired mother, and, last, to assist her,
The hulking creature that you call your sister.
I thought them Furies, risen from Down Below!
They forged ahead, you followed after, slow,
Cold, hungry, shrivelled, of faded boxwood-grain –
The beggar, Irus, come to life again!
Aricia's hill, where beggars daily stand,
One would have thought was moving from the land!
A three-legg'd bed was first to greet the morn,
Then an oil-lamp, a mixing-bowl of horn,
Beside a table, with two legs gone missing;
A cracked old chamber-pot, that came out pissing;
Under a brazier, green with verdigris
A wry-necked flagon lay dejectedly;
Then there were pilchards, salt-fish too, I think,
A jug betrayed them by the filthy stink,
A powerful smell that even reeked beyond
The brackish water in a fishy pond.
What else? Cheese from Toulouse its presence told,
A blackened wreath of flea-bane, four years old,
And onion-ropes – but only ropes were left –
And garlic-strings – of garlic all bereft;
A pot of resin, from your mother's lair,
That Jezebels use to strip themselves of hair.
But say, why seek new lodgings for your crew
To taunt the rent-collectors yet anew,
When you could lodge yourself and baggage free
Upon the Bridge – with all your company?

        Marcus Valerius Martialis, translated by Olive Pitt-Kethley

Strolling Players

Drawn by the annual call, we now behold
Our Troop Dramatic, heroes known of old,
And those, since last they marched, enlisted and enrolled:
Mounted on hacks or borne in wagons some,
The rest on foot (the humbler brethren) come.
Three favoured places, an unequal time,
Join to support the company sublime:
Ours for the longer period – see how light
Yon parties move, their former friends in sight,
Whose claims are all allowed, and friendship glads the night.
Now public rooms shall sound with words divine,
And private lodgings hear how heroes shine;
No talk of pay shall yet on pleasure steal,
But kindest welcome bless the friendly meal;
While o'er the social jug and decent cheer,
Shall be described the fortunes of the year.
    Peruse these bills, and see what each can do, –
Behold the prince, the slave, the monk, the Jew;
Change but the garment, and they'll all engage
To take each part, and act in every age:
Culled from all houses, what a house are they!
Swept from all barns, our Borough critics say;
But with some portion of a critic's ire,
We all endure them; there are some admire;
They might have praise confined to farce alone;
Full well they grin, they should not try to groan;
But then our servants' and our seamen's wives
Love all that rant and rapture as their lives:
He who Squire Richard's part could well sustain,
Finds as King Richard he must roar amain –
'My horse! my horse!' – Lo! now to their abodes,
Come lords and lovers, empresses and gods.
The master mover of these scenes has made
No trifling gain in this adventurous trade;
Trade we may term it, for he duly buys
Arms out of use and undirected eyes;
These he instructs, and guides them as he can,

And vends each night the manufactured man:
Long as our custom lasts they gladly stay,
Then strike their tents, like Tartars! and away.
The place grows bare where they too long remain,
But grass will rise ere they return again.
    Children of Thespes, welcome! knights and queens!
Counts! barons! beauties! when before your scenes,
And mighty monarchs thund'ring from your throne;
Then step behind, and all your glory's gone:
Of crown and palace, throne and guards bereft,
The pomp is vanished and the care is left.
Yet strong and lively is the joy they feel,
When the full house secures the plenteous meal;
Flatt'ring and flattered, each attempts to raise
A brother's merits for a brother's praise:
For never hero shows a prouder heart,
Than he who proudly acts a hero's part;
Nor without cause; the boards, we know, can yield
Place for fierce contest, like the tented field.
    Graceful to tread the stage, to be in turn
The prince we honour, and the knave we spurn;
Bravely to bear the tumult of the crowd,
The hiss tremendous, and the censure loud:
These are their parts, – and he who these sustains
Deserves some praise and profit for his pains.
Heroes at least of gentler kind are they,
Against whose swords no weeping widows pray,
No blood their fury sheds, nor havoc marks their way.
    Sad happy race! soon raised and soon depressed;
Your days all passed in jeopardy and jest;
Poor without prudence, with afflictions vain,
Not warned by misery, not enriched by gain:
Whom justice, pitying, chides from place to place,
A wandering, careless, wretched, merry race,
Who cheerful looks assume, and play the parts
Of happy rovers with repining hearts;
Then cast off care, and in the mimic pain
Of tragic woe feel spirits light and vain,
Distress and hope – the mind's the body's wear,
The man's affliction, and the actor's tear:

Alternate times of fasting and excess
Are yours, ye smiling children of distress.
   Slaves though ye be, your wand'ring freedom seems,
And with your varying views and restless schemes,
Your griefs are transient, as your joys are dreams.
   Yet keen those griefs – ah! what avail thy charms,
Fair Juliet! with that infant in thine arms;
What those heroic lines thy patience learns,
What all the aid thy present Romeo earns,
Whilst thou art crowded in that lumbering wain
With all thy plaintive sisters to complain?
Nor is their lack of labour – To rehearse,
Day after day, poor scraps of prose and verse;
To bear each other's spirit, pride, and spite;
To hide in rant the heartache of the night;
To dress in gaudy patchwork, and to force
The mind to think on the appointed course; –
This is laborious, and may be defined
The bootless labour of the thriftless mind.
   There is a veteran dame: I see her stand
Intent and pensive with her book in hand;
Awhile her thoughts she forces on her part,
Then dwells on objects nearer to the heart;
Across the room she paces, gets her tone,
And fits her features for the Danish throne;
Tonight a queen – I mark her motion slow,
I hear her speech, and Hamlet's mother I know.
   Methinks 'tis pitiful to see her try
For strength of arms and energy of eye;
With vigour lost, and spirits worn away,
Her pomp and pride she labours to display;
And when awhile she's tried her part to act,
To find her thoughts arrested by some fact;
When struggles more and more severe are seen,
In the plain actress than the Danish queen, –
At length she feels her part, she finds delight,
And fancies all the plaudits of the night;
Old as she is, she smiles at every speech,
And thinks no youthful part beyond her reach.
But as the mist of vanity again

Is blown away, by press of present pain,
Sad and in doubt she to her purse applies
For cause of comfort, where no comfort lies:
Then to her task she sighing turns again –
'Oh! Hamlet, thou hast cleft my heart in twain!'
   And who that poor, consumptive, withered thing,
Who strains her slender throat and strives to sing?
Panting for breath, and forced her voice to drop,
And far unlike the inmate of the shop,
Where she, in youth and health, alert and gay,
Laughed off at night the labours of the day;
With novels, verses, fancy's fertile powers,
And sister converse passed the evening hours;
But Cynthia's soul was soft, her wishes strong,
Her judgement weak, and her conclusions wrong;
The morning call and counter were her dread,
And her contempt the needle and the thread;
But when she read a gentle damsel's part,
Her woe, her wish! she had them all by heart.
   At length the hero of the boards drew nigh,
Who spake of love till sigh re-echoed sigh;
He told in honeyed words his deathless flame,
And she his own by tender vows became;
Nor ring nor licence needed souls so fond,
Alfonso's passion was his Cynthia's bond:
And thus the simple girl, to shame betrayed,
Sinks to the grave forsaken and dismayed.
   Sick without pity, sorrowing without hope,
See her! the grief and scandal of the troop;
A wretched martyr to a childish pride,
Her woe insulted, and her praise denied;
Her humble talents, though derided, used;
Her prospects lost, her confidence abused;
All that remains – for she not long can brave
Increase of evils – is an early grave.
   Ye gentle Cynthias of the shop, take heed
What dreams ye cherish, and what books ye read.

George Crabbe

POOR
AND
DISHONEST

The Bug-Trap

A patterer – a profession halfway between a tramp and a salesman – told the following tale to Henry Mayhew after staying at the 'Bug-trap' in Sheffield.

AFTER A SOMEWHAT tedious ramble, we arrived at Water-lane; at the 'Bug-trap', which from time immemorial has been the name of the most renowned lodging-house in that or perhaps any locality. Water-lane is a dark narrow street, crowded with human beings of the most degraded sort – the chosen atmosphere of cholera and the stronghold of theft and prostitution. In less than half an hour, my fair companion and myself were sipping our tea, and eating Yorkshire cake in this same lodging-house.

'God bless every happy couple!' was echoed from a rude stentorian voice, while a still ruder hand bumped down upon our tea-table a red earthen dish of no small dimensions, into which was poured, from the mouth of a capacious bag, fragments of fish, flesh, and fowl, viands and vegetables of every sort, intermingled with bits of cheese and dollops of Yorkshire pudding. The man to whom this heterogeneous mass belonged, appeared anything but satisfied with his lot. 'Well,' said he, 'I don't know what this 'ere monkry will come to, after a bit. Three bob and a tanner, and that there dish o' scran' (enough to feed two families for a fortnight) 'is all I got this blessed day since seven o'clock in the morning, and now it's nine at night.' I ventured to say something, but a remark, too base for repetition, 'put the stunners on me,' and I held my peace.

I was here surprised, on conversing with my young female companion, to find that she went to church, said her prayers night and morning, and knew many of the collects, some of which she repeated, besides a pleasing variety of Dr Watts's hymns. At the death of her mother, her father had given up housekeeping; and, being too fond of a wandering life, had led his only child into habits like his own.

As the night advanced, the party at the 'Bug-trap' more than doubled. High-flyers, shallow-coves, turnpike-sailors, and swells out of luck, made up an assembly of fourscore human beings, more than half of whom were doomed to sleep on a 'make-shift' – in other words, on a platform, raised just ten inches above the floor of the garret, which it nearly equalled in dimensions. Here were to be huddled together, with very little covering, old men and women, young men and children, with no regard to age, sex, or propensities.

The 'mot' of the 'ken' (nickname for 'matron of the establishment') had discovered that I was a 'more bettermost' sort of person, and hinted that, if I would 'come down with twopence more' (threepence was the regular nightly charge), I, 'and the young gal as I was with', might have a little 'crib' to ourselves in a little room, along with another woman wot was married and had a 'kid', and whose husband had got a month for 'griddling in the main drag' (singing in the high street), and being 'cheekish' (saucy) to the beadle.

From *London Labour and the London Poor* by Henry Mayhew

Georgy Barnwell

In Cheapside there liv'd a merchant
A man he vas of wery great fame,
And he had a handsome prentice,
Georgy Barnwell vas his name.

This youth he vas both good and pious,
Dutiful beyond all doubt,
And he always staid vithin doors
'Cause his master vouldn't let him out.

And much his master's darter lov'd him,
She slept in next room to him, 'tis said,
And she bored a hole right through the wainscoat,
To look at Georgy going to bed.

A vicked voman of the town, sirs,
Hon him cast a vishful eye;
And she came to the shop, one morning,
A flannel petticoat to buy.

When she paid him down the money,
She gave his hand a wery hard squeeze,
Which so frightened Georgy Barnwell,
That together, he knocked his knees.

Then she left her card, vereon vas written
Mary Millwood does entreat,
That Mister Barnwell vould call and see her,
At Cummins's in Dyot Street.

Now as soon as he'd shut the shop up,
He vent to this naughty dicky bird,
And ven he vent home the next morning,
Blow me if he could speak a vord.

Now soon this woman did persuade him,
Vith her fascinating pipes,
To go down into the country,
And let loose his uncle's tripes.

There he found his uncle in the grove,
Studying hard at his good books,
And Georgy Barnwell vent and struck him,
All among the crows and rooks.

Ven Millwood found he'd got no money,
Not so much as to buy a jewel,
She vent that wery day and peached him,
Now vas not that 'ere werry cruel?

The Judge put his three-cornered cap on,
And said – vich Barnwell much surprized,
You must hang until you dead are,
Then you must be a-nat-o-mized.

Now Georgy was hung upon a gibbet,
Molly Millwood died in prison,
At her fate no one lamented,
But every body pitied his'n.

The merchant's darter died soon arter,
Tears she shed, but spoke no vords,
So all young men, I pray take varning,
Don't go with naughty dicky birds.

Anon.

The Canters Dictionarie

Autem, a church.
Autem-mort, a married woman.
Boung, a purse.
Borde, a shilling.
Half a Borde, sixpence.
Bowse, drinke.
Bowsing Ken, an ale-house.
Bene, good.
Beneship, very good.
Buse, a Dogge.
Bing a wast, get you hence.
Caster, a cloake.
Commission, a shirt.
Chates, the gallowes.
To cly the Ierke, to be whipped.
To cutt, to speake.
To cutt bene, to speake gently.
To cutt bene whiddes, to speake good wordes.
To cutt quier whiddes, to give evill language.
To Cant, to speake.
To couch a Hogshead, to lye downe a sleepe.
Drawers, hosen.
Dudes, clothes.
Darkemans, the night.
Dewse-a-vile, the country.
Dup the Giger, open the dore.
Fambles, hands.
Fambling Chete, a ring.
Flag, a Goat.
Glasiers, eyes.
Gan, a mouth.
Gage, a quart pott.
Grannam, corne.
Gybe, a writing.
Glymmer, fire.
Gigger, a doore.
Gentry Mort, a gentlewoman.

Gentry coses Ken, a Noble mans house.

Warman bek, a constable.

Harmans, the stockes.

Heave a bough, rob a boothe.

Iarke, a seale.

Ken, a house.

Lage of Dudes, a bucke of clothes.

Libbege, a bed.

Lowre, money.

Lap, butter, milke, or whaye.

Libken, a house to lye in.

Lage, water.

Light-mans, the day.

Mynt, golde.

A Make, a halfe-penny.

Margery Prater, a henne.

Mawnding, asking.

To Mill, to steale.

Mill a Ken, rob a house.

Nosegent, a Nunne.

Niggling, companying with a woman.

Pratt, a buttock.

Peck, meate.

Poplars, pottage.

Prancer, a horse.

Prigging, riding.

Patrico, a priest.

Pad, a way.

Quaromes, a body.

Ruffpeck, bacon.

Roger, or Tib of the Buttry, a goose.

Rome-vile, London.

Rome-bowse, wine.

Rome-mort, a queene.

Ruffmans, the woodes, or bushes.

Ruffian, the divell.

Stampes; legges.

Stampers, shooes.

Slate, a sheete.

Skew, a cup.

Salomon, the masse.
Stuling ken, a house to receive stolen goods.
Skipper, a barne.
Strommel, straw.
Smelling chete, an orchard or garden.
To scowre the Cramp-ring, to weare boults.
Stalling, making or ordeyning.
Tryning, hanging.
To twore, to see.
Wyn, a penny.
Yarum, milke.

From *Lanthorne and Candle-light* by Thomas Dekker

London Slang

I WANT TO put in some notes, as short as possible, on London slang and swearing. These (omitting the ones that everyone knows) are some of the cant words now used in London:

A gagger – a beggar or street performer of any kind. A moocher – one who begs outright, without pretence of doing a trade. A nobber – one who collects pennies for a beggar. A chanter – a street singer. A clodhopper – a street dancer. A mugfaker – a street photographer. A glimmer – one who watches vacant motor-cars. A gee (or jee – it is pronounced jee) – the accomplice of a cheapjack, who stimulates trade by pretending to buy something. A split – a detective. A flattie – a policeman. A didecai – a gypsy. A toby – a tramp.

A drop – money given to a beggar. Funkum – lavender or other perfume sold in envelopes. A boozer – a public-house. A slang – a hawker's licence. A kip – a place to sleep in, or a night's lodging. Smoke – London. A judy – a woman. The spike – the casual ward. The lump – the casual ward. A tosheroon – a half-crown. A deaner – a shilling. A hog – a shilling. A sprowsie – a sixpence. Clods – coppers. A drum – a billy can. Shackles – soup. A chat – a louse. Hard-up – tobacco made from cigarette ends. A stick or cane – a burglar's jemmy. A peter – a safe. A bly – a burglar's oxy-acetylene blowlamp.

To bawl – to suck or swallow. To knock off – to steal. To skipper – to sleep in the open.

From *Down and Out In Paris and London* by George Orwell

London

I wander through each chartered street,
    Near where the chartered Thames does flow,
And mark in every face I meet
    Marks of weakness, marks of woe.

In every cry of every man,
    In every infant's cry of fear,
In every voice, in every ban,
    The mind-forged manacles I hear:

How the chimney-sweeper's cry
    Every blackening church appalls,
And the hapless soldier's sigh
    Runs in blood down palace-walls.

But most, through midnight streets I hear
    How the youthful harlot's curse
Blasts the new-born infant's tear,
    And blights with plagues the marriage-hearse.

William Blake

A Prostitute's Story

THE NARRATIVE which follows – that of a prostitute, sleeping in the low lodging-houses, where boys and girls are all huddled promiscuously together, discloses a system of depravity, atrocity, and enormity, which certainly cannot be paralleled in any nation, however barbarous, nor in any age however 'dark'. The facts detailed it will be seen are gross enough to make us all blush for the land in which such scenes can be daily perpetrated. The circumstances, which it is impossible to publish, are of the most loathsome and revolting nature.

A good-looking girl of sixteen gave me the following awful statement: –

'I am an orphan. When I was ten I was sent to service as maid of all-work, in a small tradesman's family. It was a hard place, and my mistress used me very cruelly, beating me often. When I had been in place three weeks, my mother died, my father having died twelve years before. I stood my mistress's ill-treatment for about six months. She beat me with sticks as well as with her hands. I was black and blue, and at last I ran away. I got to Mrs—, a low lodging-house. I didn't know before that there was such a place. I heard of it from some girls at the Glasshouse (baths and washhouses), where I went for shelter. I went with them to have a halfpenny worth of coffee, and they took me to the lodging-house. I then had three shillings, and stayed about a month, and did nothing wrong, living on the three shillings and what I pawned my clothes for, as I got some pretty good things away with me. In the lodging-house I saw nothing but what was bad, and heard nothing but what was bad. I was laughed at, and was told to swear. They said, "Look at her for a d— modest fool"— sometimes worse than that, until by degrees I got to be as bad as they were. During this time I used to see boys and girls from ten and twelve years old sleeping together, but understood nothing wrong. I had never heard of such places before I ran away. I can neither read nor write. My mother was a good woman, and I wish I'd had her to run away to. I saw things between almost children that I can't describe to you – very often I saw them, and that shocked me. At the month's end, when I was beat out, I met with a young man of fifteen – I myself was going on to twelve years old – and he persuaded me to take up with him. I stayed with him three months in the same lodging-house, living with him as his wife, though we were mere children, and being true to him. At the three months' end he was taken up for picking pockets, and got six months. I was sorry, for he was kind to me; though I was made ill through him, so I broke some windows in St Paul's-churchyard to get into prison to get cured. I had a month in the Compter, and came out well. I was scolded very much in the Compter, on account of the state I was in, being so young. I had 2s. 6d. given to me when I came out, and was forced to go into the streets for a living. I continued walking the streets for three years, sometimes making a good deal of money, sometimes none, feasting one day and starving the next. The bigger girls could persuade me to do anything they liked with my money. I was never happy all the time, but I could get no character and could not get out of the life. I lodged all this time at a lodging-house in Kent-street. They were all thieves and bad girls. I have known between three and four dozen boys and girls sleep in one room. The beds were horrid filthy and full of vermin. There was very wicked carryings on. The boys, if any difference, was the worst. We lay packed on a full night, a dozen boys and girls squeedged into one bed. That was very often the case – some at the foot and some at the top – boys and girls all mixed. I can't go into all the particulars, but whatever could take place in words or acts between boys and girls did take place, and in the midst of the others. I am sorry to say I took part in these bad ways myself, but I wasn't so bad as some of the others. There was only a candle burning all night, but in summer it was light great part of the night. Some boys and girls slept without any clothes and would dance about the room that way. I have seen them, and, wicked as I was, felt ashamed. I have seen two dozen capering about the room that way; some mere children, the boys generally the youngest.

'There were no men or women present. There was often fights. The deputy never interfered. This is carried on just the same as ever to this day, and is the same every night. I have heard young girls shout out to one another how often they had been obliged to go to the hospital, or the infirmary or the workhouse. There was a great deal of boasting about what the boys and girls had stolen during the day. I have known boys and girls change their "partners" just for a night. At three years' end I stole a piece of beef from a butcher. I did it to get into prison. I was sick of the life I was leading, and didn't know how to get out of it. I had a month for stealing. When I got out I passed two days and a night in the streets doing nothing wrong, and then went and threatened to break Messrs – windows again. I did that to get into prison again; for when I lay quiet of a night in prison I thought things over, and considered what a shocking life I was leading, and how my health might be ruined completely, and I thought I would stick to prison rather than go back to such a life. I got six months for threatening. When I got out I broke a lamp next morning for the same purpose, and had a fortnight. That was the last time I was in prison. I have since been leading the same life as I told you of for the three years, and lodging at the same houses, and seeing the same goings on. I hate such a life now more than ever. I am willing to do any work that I can in washing and cleaning. I can do a little at my needle. I could do hard work, for I have good health. I used to wash and clean in prison, and always behaved myself there. At the house where I am it is 3*d*. a night; but at Mrs— 's it is 1*d*. and 2*d*. a night, and just the same goings on. Many a girl – nearly all of them – goes out into the streets from this penny and twopenny house, to get money for their favourite boys by prostitution. If the girl cannot get money she must steal something, or will be beaten by her "chap" when she comes home. I have seen them beaten, often kicked and beaten until they were blind from bloodshot, and their teeth knocked out with kicks from boots as the girl lays on the ground. The boys, in their turn, are out thieving all day, and the lodging-housekeeper will buy any stolen provisions of them, and sell them to the lodgers. I never saw the police in the house. If a boy comes to the house on a night without money or sawney,[1] or something to sell to the lodgers, a handkerchief or something of that kind, he is not admitted, but told very plainly, "Go thieve it, then." Girls are treated just the same. Anybody may call in the daytime at this house and have a halfpenny-worth of coffee and sit any length of time until evening. I have seen three dozen sitting there that way, all thieves and bad girls. There are no chairs, and only one form in front of the fire, on which a dozen can sit. The others sit on the floor all about the room, as near the fire as they can. Bad language goes on during the day, as I have told you it did during the night, and indecencies too, but nothing like so bad as at night. They talk about where there is good places to go and thieve. The missioners call sometimes, but they're laughed at often when they're talking, and always before the door's closed on them. If a decent girl goes there to get a ha'porth of coffee, seeing the board over the door, she is always shocked. Many a poor girl has been ruined in this house since I was, and boys have boasted about it. I never knew boy or girl do good, once get used there. Get used there, indeed, and you are life-ruined. I was an only child, and haven't a friend in the world. I have heard several girls say how they would like to get out of the life, and out of the place. From those I know, I think that cruel parents and mistresses cause many to be driven there. One lodging-house keeper, Mrs—, goes out dressed respectable, and pawns any stolen property, or sells it at public-houses.'

From *London Labour and the London Poor* by Henry Mayhew

Katusha Maslova

THE STORY of the prisoner Maslova's life was a very common one. Maslova's mother was the unmarried daughter of a village woman employed on a dairy-farm belonging to two maiden ladies who were landowners. This unmarried woman had a baby every year, and, as often happens among the village people, each one of these undesired babies, after being carefully baptised, was neglected by its mother, whom it hindered at her work, and was left to starve. Five children had died in this way. They had all been baptised and then not sufficiently fed, and just allowed to die. The sixth baby, whose father was a gipsy tramp, would have shared the same fate, had it not so happened that one of the maiden ladies came into the farmyard to scold the dairymaids for sending up cream that smelt of the

1 *Sawney* – stolen meat.

cow. The young woman was lying in the cowshed with a fine, healthy, new-born baby. The old maiden lady scolded the maids again, for allowing the woman (who had just been confined) to lie in the cowshed, and was about to go away; but seeing the baby, her heart was touched, and she offered to stand godmother to the little girl. Pity for her little goddaughter induced her to give milk and a little money to the mother, so that she should feed the baby; and the child lived. The old ladies spoke of her as 'the saved one'. When the child was three years old her mother fell ill and died, and the maiden ladies took the child from the old grandmother, to whom she was only a burden.

The little black-eyed maiden grew to be extremely pretty, and so full of spirits that the ladies found her very entertaining.

The younger of the ladies, Sophia Ivanovna, who had stood godmother to the girl, had the kinder heart of the two sisters; Mary Ivanovna, the elder, was rather hard. Sophia Ivanovna dressed the little girl in nice clothes and taught her to read and write, meaning to educate her like a lady. Mary Ivanovna thought the child should be brought up to work, and trained to be a good servant. She was exacting; she punished, and, when in a bad temper, even struck, the little girl. Growing up under these two different influences, the girl turned out half servant, half young lady. They called her Katusha, which sounds less refined than Katinka, but is not quite so common at Katka. She used to sew, tidy up the rooms, polish the metal cases of the icons with chalk, and do other light work, and sometimes she sat and read to the ladies.

Though she had more than one offer she would not marry. She felt that life as the wife of any of the working men who were courting her would be too hard for her, spoilt as she was by an easy life.

She lived in this way till she was sixteen, when the nephew of the old ladies, a rich young Prince and a university student, came to stay with his aunts; and Katusha, not daring to acknowledge it even to herself, fell in love with him.

Two years later this same nephew stayed four days with his aunts before proceeding to join his regiment, and the night before he left he seduced Katusha, and, after giving her a one hundred rouble note, went away. Five months later she knew for certain that she was pregnant. After that, everything seemed repugnant to her, her only thought being how to escape from the shame awaiting her; and she not only began to serve the ladies in a half-hearted and negligent way, but once, without knowing how it happened, she was very rude to them, though she repented afterwards, and asked them to let her leave. They let her go, very dissatisfied with her. Then she got a housemaid's place in a police-officer's house, but stayed there only three months, for the police-officer, a man of fifty, began to molest her, and once, when he was in a specially enterprising mood, she fired up, called him 'fool' and 'old devil', and gave him such a push on his chest that he fell. She was turned out for her rudeness. It was useless to look for another situation, for the time of her confinement was drawing near, so she went to the house of a village midwife and illicit retailer of spirits. The confinement was easy; but the midwife, who had a case of fever in the village, infected Katusha, and her baby boy had to be sent to the foundlings' hospital, where, according to the old woman who took him there, he died at once. When Katusha went to the midwife she had a hundred and twenty-seven roubles in all, twenty-seven she had earned and the hundred given her by her seducer. When she left she had but six roubles; she did not know how to keep money, but spent it on herself and gave to all who asked. The midwife took forty roubles for two months' keep and attendance, twenty-five went to get the baby into the foundlings' hospital, and forty the midwife borrowed to buy a cow with. Some twenty roubles went just for clothes and dainties. Having nothing left to live on, Katusha had to look out for a place again, and found one in the house of a forester. The forester was a married man, but he, too, began to beset her from the first day. She disliked him and tried to avoid him. But he, besides being her master who could send her wherever he liked, was more experienced and cunning, and managed to violate her. His wife found it out, and catching Katusha and her husband in a room all by themselves began beating her. Katusha defended herself and they had a fight, and Katusha was turned out of the house without being paid her wages.

Then she went to live with her aunt in town. Her uncle, a bookbinder, had once been comfortably off, but he had lost all his customers and taken to drink, and spent all he could lay hands on at the public-house. The aunt kept a small laundry and managed to support herself, her children, and her wretched husband. She offered Katusha a place as assistant laundress; but, seeing what a life of misery and hardship her aunt's assistants led, Katusha hesitated, and applied to a registry office. A place was found for her with a lady who lived with her two sons, pupils at a public day-school. A week after Katusha had entered the house, the elder, a big fellow with moustaches, threw up his studies and gave her no peace, continually following her about. His mother laid all the blame on Katusha, and gave her notice.

It so happened that after many fruitless attempts to find a situation Katusha again went to the registry office, and there met a woman with bracelets on her bare, plump arms and rings on most of her fingers. Hearing that Katusha was badly in want of a place, the woman gave her her address and invited her to come to her house. Katusha went. The woman received her very kindly, set cake and sweet wine before her, then wrote a note and gave it to a servant to take to somebody. In the evening a tall man, with long, grey hair and white beard, entered the room and sat down at once near Katusha, smiling and gazing at her with glistening eyes. He began joking with her. The hostess called him away into the next room, and Katusha heard her say, 'A fresh one from the country.' Then the hostess called Katusha away and told her that the man was an author, and that he had a geat deal of money, and that if he liked her he would not grudge her anything. He did like her, and gave her twenty-five roubles, promising to see her often. The twenty-five roubles soon went; some she paid to her aunt for board and lodging, the rest was spent on a hat, ribbons, and such like. A few days later the author sent for her and she went. He gave her another twenty-five roubles and offered her a separate lodging.

Next door to the lodging rented for her by the author there lived a jolly young shopman, with whom Katusha soon fell in love. She told the author, and moved to a small lodging of her own. The shopman, who had promised to marry her, went off to Nijni on business without mentioning it to her, having evidently thrown her up, and Katusha remained alone. She meant to continue living in the lodging by herself, but was informed by the police that in that case she would have to get a yellow (prostitute's) passport and be subjected to medical examinations. She returned to her aunt. Seeing her fine dress, her hat, and mantle, her aunt no longer offered her laundry work. As she understood things, her niece had risen above that. The question as to whether she was to become a laundress or not did not occur to Katusha either. She looked with pity at the thin, hard-worked laundresses, some already in consumption, who stood washing or ironing with their thin arms in the fearfully hot front room, which was always full of soapy steam and draughts from the windows; and she thought with horror that she might have shared the same fate. It was just at this time, when Katusha was in very narrow straits, no 'protector' appearing upon the scene, that a procuress found her out.

Katusha had begun to smoke some time before, and since the young shopman had thrown her up she was getting more and more into the habit of drinking. It was not so much the flavour of wine that attracted her, as the fact that it gave her a chance of forgetting the misery she suffered, making her feel unrestrained and more confident of her own worth, which she was not when quite sober: without wine she felt sad and ashamed. The procuress brought all sorts of dainties, to which she treated the aunt, and also wine, and while Katusha drank she offered to place her in one of the largest establishments in the city, explaining all the advantages and benefits of the situation. Katusha had the choice before her of either going into service to be humiliated, probably annoyed by the attentions of the men and having occasional secret sexual connection; or accepting an easy, secure position sanctioned by law, and open, well-paid, regular sexual connection – and she chose the latter. Besides, it seemed to her as though she could, in this way, revenge herself on her seducer, and the shopman, and all those who had injured her. One of the things that tempted her and influenced her decision, was the procuress telling her she might order her own dresses: velvet, silk, satin, low-necked ball dresses – anything she liked. A mental picture of herself in a bright yellow silk trimmed with black velvet, with low neck and short sleeves, conquered her, and she handed over her passport. That same evening the procuress took an *izvoztchik* and drove her to the notorious house kept by Caroline Albertovna Kitaeva.

From that day a life of chronic sin against human and divine laws commenced for Katusha Maslova, a life which is led by hundreds of thousands of women, and which is not merely tolerated but sanctioned by the Government, anxious for the welfare of its subjects; a life which for nine women out of ten ends in painful disease, premature decrepitude, and death.

Heavy sleep until late in the afternoon followed the orgies of the night. Between three and four o'clock came the weary getting up from a dirty bed, soda water, coffee, listless pacing up and down the room in bedgowns and dressing-jackets, lazy gazing out of the windows from behind the drawn curtains, indolent disputes with one another; then washing, perfuming and anointing the body and hair, trying on dresses, disputes about them with the mistress of the house, surveying one's self in looking-glasses, painting the face, the eyebrows; fat, sweet food; then dressing in gaudy silks, exposing much of the body, and coming down into the ornamented and brilliantly illuminated drawing-room; then the arrival of visitors, music, dancing, sexual connection with old and young and middle-aged, with lads and decrepit old men, bachelors, married men, merchants, clerks, Armenians, Jews, Tartars; rich and poor, sick and healthy, tipsy and sober, rough and tender, military men and civilians, students and mere school-boys – of all classes, ages, and characters. And shouts and jokes, and brawls and music, and tobacco and wine, and wine and tobacco, from evening until daylight, no relief till morning, and then heavy sleep; the same every day and all the week. Then at the end of the week came the visit to the police station, as instituted by the Government, where doctors – men in the service of the Government – sometimes seriously and strictly, sometimes with playful levity, examined these women, completely destroying the modesty given as a protection not only to human beings but also to animals, and gave them written permissions to continue in the sins they and their accomplices had been committing all the week. Then followed another week of the same kind: always the same every night, summer and winter, work days and holidays.

And in this manner Katusha Maslova lived seven years. During this time she had changed houses backwards and forwards once or twice, and had once been to the hospital. In the seventh year of her life in the brothel, when she was twenty-eight years old, happened that for which she was put in prison and for which she was now being taken to be tried, and after more than three months' confinement with thieves and murderers in the stifling air of a prison.

From *Resurrection* by Leo Tolstoy, translated by Louise Maude

The Ruined Maid

'O 'Melia, my dear, this does everything crown!
Who could have supposed I should meet you in Town?
And whence such fair garments, such prosperi-ty?' –
'O didn't you know I'd been ruined?' said she.

-'You left us in tatters, without shoes or socks,
Tired of digging potatoes, and spudding up docks;
And now you've gay bracelets and bright feathers three!' –
'Yes: that's how we dress when we're ruined,' said she.

-'At home in the barton you said "thee" and "thou",
And "thik oon", and "theäs oon", and "t'other"; but now
Your talking quite fits 'ee for high compa-ny!' –
'Some polish is gained with one's ruin,' said she.

-'Your hands were like paws then, your face blue and bleak
But now I'm bewitched by your delicate cheek,
And your little gloves fit as on any la-dy!' –
'We never do work when we're ruined,' said she.

-'You used to call home-life a hag-ridden dream,
And you'd sigh, and you'd sock; but at present you seem
To know not of megrims or melancho-ly!' –
'True. One's pretty lively when ruined,' said she.

-'I wish I had feathers, a fine sweeping gown,
And a delicate face, and could strut about Town!' –
'My dear – a raw country girl, such as you be,
Cannot quite expect that. You ain't ruined,' said she.

Thomas Hardy

The Sacking Law

THE COMPANION of a theefe is commonly a whore; it is not amisse therefore, pinneon them together: for what the theefe gets the strumpet spends. The trade of these *tale-bearers* goes under the name of the *Sacking-law*; and rightly may it be called sacking, for as in the sacking of a city, all the villanies in the world are set abroach, so when a Harlot comes to the sacking of a mans wealth and reputation (for she besiegeth both together) she leaves no stratagem unpractised to bring him to confusion. Westminster and Holborn have chambers full of these students of the *Sacking-law*. In Clerken-well, they had wont & are still well cliented: White Friers is famous for their meeting: The Spittle flourishes with the yong fry, that are put to it to learne it. Sacks come to these milles every houre, but the Sacking-lawe empties them faster then a Miller grindes his bushels of corne. He that hath a lust to practise this law, must bee furnished with these five bookes, viz.

The *Baud*, who if she be a woman is called a *Pandaresse*.

The *Apple-Squire*, who is to fetch in wine.

The *Whore*, who is called the *Commodity*.

The *Whore-house*, which is called a *Trugging-place*.

These five Authors are so well knowne, and have bin so turned over leafe by leafe, that every man (almost) that lives in sight of the smoake of the Citie, hath them at his fingers ends; or if he cannot, it is an easie matter to finde them by a Table. I will onely refer you to the suburbs. But there is a second part of this Sacking-law, and that instructs Punckes to attire themselves neatly in summer evenings, and about ten or eleven of the clock at night to walke up and downe the most peopled streetes of the citie, very soberly and gingerly, til ye wine (by one Gull or other) be offered, which with a little intreaty he takes; but being in the midst of their bowles, or perhaps the silly cony being trayned home to a lodging, where he falles to *Nibling*; in comes a Ruffian with a drawne rapier, calles the Punck (as she is) damned whore, askes what Rogue that is, and what he does with his wife. The conclusion of all this counterfeit swaggering being a plot betwixt this panderly ruffian and the whore to geld the silly foole of all the money hee hath in his purse, and sometimes to make him (rather than his credit should be called into question) to seale a bill or bond for other sums of money at such and such daies, and so send him packing, when he hath paide too deare for a bad dish of meate which he never tasted: the base Apple-squire and his yong mistresse, laughing to see what a woodcocke they puld, and sharing the feathers betweene them. But when such comedies (of the *Sacking-law* as these, are played, then the Actors have other names than are set downe before, and these they be:

The whore is then called the *Traffick*.
The man that is brought in, is the *Simpler*.
The Ruffian that takes him napping, is the *Crosbiter*.

From *The Belman of London* by Thomas Dekker

The Unfortunate Traveller

During his travels in Europe, Jack Wilton has been mistaken for a robber. According to the law in Rome, the householder may take him as his bondman or hang him. The doctor outside whose house he was found decides to fatten him up to use as an anatomy specimen.

BUT FIRST Ile tell you what betided mee after I was brought to Doctor Zacharies. The purblind Doctor put on his spectacles and lookt upon me: and when he had throughly viewd my face, he caused me to be stript naked, to feele and grope whether each lim wer sound & my skin not infected. Then he picrst my armc to see how my blood ran: which assayes and searchings ended, he gaue Zadoch his full price and sent him away, then lockt me up in a darke chamber till the day of anatomie.

O, the colde sweating cares which I conceived after I knewe I should be cut like a French summer dublet. Me thought already the blood began to gush out at my nose: if a flea on the arme had but bit me, I deemed the instrument had prickt me. Wel, I may scoffe at a shrowd turne, but theres no such readie way to make a man a true Christian, as to perswade himselfe he is taken up for an anatomie. Ile depose I praid then more than I did in seven yeare before. Not a drop of sweate trickled downe my breast and my sides, but I dreamt it was a smooth edged razer tenderly slicing downe my breast and sides. If anie knockt at doore, I supposd it was the Bedle of surgeons hal come for me. In the night I dreamd of nothing but phlebotomie, bloudie fluxes, incarnatives, running ulcers. I durst not let out a wheale for feare through it I should bleede to death. For meat in this distance, I had plumporredge of purgations ministred me one after another to clarifie my blood, that it should not lye cloddered in the flesh. Nor did he it so much for clarifying Phisicke, as to save charges. Miserable is that Mouse that lives in a Phisitions house, *Tantalus* lives not so hunger starved in hell, as she doth there. Not the verie crums that fall from his table, but Zacharie sweepes together, and of them moulds up a Manna. Of the ashie parings of his bread, he would make conserve of chippings. Out of bones after the meate was eaten off, hee would alchumize an oyle, that hee sold for a shilling a dram. His snot and spittle a hundred times hee hath put ouer to his Apothecarie for snow water. Anie spider hee would temper to perfect Mithridate. His rumaticke eies when hee went in the winde, or rose early in a morning, dropt as coole allome water as you would request. He was dame Niggardize sole heire & executor. A number of old books had he eaten with the moaths and wormes, now all day would not he studie a dodkin, but picke those wormes and moaths out of his librarie, and of their mixture make a preseruative against the plague. The licour out of his shooes hee would wring to make a sacred Balsamum against barrennes.

From *The Unfortunate Traveller* by Thomas Nashe

Mary Young, ALIAS Jenny Diver (the Head of a Numerous Gang of Thieves, of Every Description, and May Be Called the Female Macheath), Executed at Tyburn, March 18, 1740

A CHARACTER more skilled in the various arts of imposition and robbery we cannot expect to present to our readers than that of Mary Young. Her depredations, executed with the courage of a man, and the softer deceptions of an artful female surpass any thing which we have, as yet, come to in our researches into crimes and punishments.

Mary Young was born in the north of Ireland; her parents were in indigent circumstances; and dying while she was in a state of infancy, she had no recollection of them.

At about ten years of age she was taken into the family of an ancient gentlewoman, who had known her father and mother, and who caused her to be instructed in reading, writing, and needle-work; and in the latter she attained to a proficiency unusual to girls of her age.

Soon after she had arrived to her fifteenth year, a young man, servant to a gentleman who lived in the same neighbourhood, made pretensions of love to her; but the old lady being apprized of his views, declared that she would not consent to their marriage, and positively forbad him to repeat his visits at her house.

Notwithstanding the great care and tenderness with which she was treated, Mary formed the resolution of deserting her generous benefactor, and of directing her course towards the metropolis of England; and the only obstacle to this design was, the want of money for her support till she could follow some honest means of earning a subsistence.

She had no strong prepossession in favor of the young man who had made a declaration of love to her; but she, determining to make his passion subservient to the purpose she had conceived, promised to marry him on condition of his taking her to London. He joyfully embraced this proposal, and immediately engaged for a passage in a vessel bound for Liverpool.

A short time before the vessel was to sail, the young man robbed his master of a gold watch and eighty guineas, and then joined the companion of his flight, who was already on board the ship, vainly imagining that his infamously acquired booty would contribute to the happiness he should enjoy with his expected bride. The ship arrived at the destined port in two days: and Mary being indisposed in consequence of her voyage, her companion hired a lodging in the least frequented part of the town, where they lived a short time in the character of man and wife, but avoiding all intercourse with their neighbours; the man being apprehensive that measures would be pursued for rendering him amenable to justice.

Mary being restored to health, they agreed for a passage in a waggon that was to set out for London in a few days. On the day preceding that fixed for their departure, they accidentally called at a public-house, and the man being observed by a messenger, dispatched in pursuit of him from Ireland, he was immediately taken into custody. Mary, who, a few hours before his apprehension, had received ten guineas from him, voluntarily accompanied him to the mayor's house, where he acknowledged himself guilty of the crime alleged against him, but without giving the least intimation that she was an accessory in his guilt. He being committed to prison, Mary sent him all his clothes, and part of the money she had received from him and the next day took her place in the waggon for London. In a short time her companion was sent to Ireland where he was tried, and condemned to suffer death; but his sentence was changed to that of transportation.

Soon after her arrival in London, Mary contracted an acquaintance with one of her country-women, named Anne Murphy, by whom she was invited to partake of a lodging in Long-acre. Here she endeavoured to obtain a livelihood by her needle; but not being able to procure sufficient employment, in a little time her situation became truly deplorable.

Murphy intimated to her, that she could introduce her to a mode of life that would prove exceedingly lucrative; adding that the most profound secrecy was required. The other expressed an anxious desire of learning the means of extricating herself from the difficulties under which she laboured, and made a solemn declaration that she would never divulge what Murphy should communicate. In the evening, Murphy introduced her to a number of men and women, assembled in a kind of club, near St Giles's. These people gained their living by cutting off women's pockets, and stealing watches, etc. from men in the avenues of the theatres, and at other places of public resort; and, on the recommendation of Murphy, they admitted Mary a member of the society.

After Mary's admission, they dispersed, in order to pursue their illegal occupation; and the booty obtained that night consisted of eighty pounds in cash, and a valuable gold watch. As Mary was not yet acquainted with the art of thieving, she was not admitted to an equal share of the night's produce; but it was agreed that she should have ten guineas. She now regularly applied two hours every day in qualifying herself for an expert thief, by attending to the instructions of experienced practitioners; and, in a short time, she was distinguished as the most ingenious and successful adventurer of the whole gang.

A young fellow of genteel appearance who was a member of the club, was singled out by Mary as the partner of her bed; and they cohabited for a considerable time as husband and wife.

In a few months our heroine became so expert in her profession, as to acquire great consequence among her associates, who, as we conceive, distinguished her by the appellation of Jenny Diver, on account of her remarkable dexterity; and by that name we shall call her in the succeeding pages of this narrative.

Jenny, accompanied by one of her female accomplices, joined the crowd at the entrance of a place of worship in the Old Jewry, where a popular divine was to preach, and observing a young gentleman with a diamond ring on his finger, she held out her hand, which he kindly received in order to assist her; and at this juncture she contrived to get possession of the ring, without the knowledge of the owner; after which she slipped behind her companion, and heard the gentleman say, that as there was no probability of gaining admittance, he would return. Upon his leaving the meeting he missed his ring, and mentioned his loss to the persons who were near him, adding, that he suspected it to be stolen by a woman whom he had endeavoured to assist in the crowd: but, as the thief was unknown, she escaped.

The above robbery was considered as such an extraordinary proof of Jenny's superior address, that her associates determined to allow her an equal share of all their booties, even though she was not present when they were obtained. In a short time after the above exploit, she procured a pair of false hands and arms to be made; and concealing her real ones under her clothes, she then put something beneath her stays, to make herself appear as if in a state of pregnancy, she repaired on a Sunday evening to the place of worship above-mentioned, in a sedan chair, one of the gang going before, to procure a seat among the genteeler part of the congregation, and another attending in the character of a footman.

Jenny being seated between two elderly ladies, each of whom had a gold watch by her side, she conducted herself with great seeming devotion; but when the service was nearly concluded, she seized the opportunity, when the ladies were standing up, of stealing their watches, which she delivered to an accomplice in an adjoining pew. The devotions being ended, the congregation were preparing to depart, when the ladies discovered their loss, and a violent clamour ensued: one of the injured parties exclaimed, 'that her watch must have been taken either by the devil or the pregnant woman,' on which, the other said, 'she could vindicate the pregnant lady, whose hands she was sure had not been removed from her lap during the whole time of her being in the pew.'

Flushed with success of the above adventure, our heroine determined to pursue her good fortune; and as another sermon was to be preached the same evening, she adjourned to an adjacent public-house, where, without either pain or difficulty, she soon reduced the protuberance of her waist, and having entirely changed her dress, she returned to the meeting, where she had not remained long before she picked a gentleman's pocket of a gold watch, with which she escaped unsuspected.

Her accomplices also were industrious and successful: for, on a division of the booty obtained this evening, they received thirty guineas. Jenny had now obtained an ascendency over the whole gang, who, conscious of her superior skill in the arts of thieving, came to a resolution of yielding an exact obedience to her directions.

Jenny again assumed the appearance of a pregnant woman, and attended by an accomplice as a footman, went towards St James's Park, on a day when the king was going to the House of Lords, and there being a great number of persons between the park and Spring-Gardens, she purposely slipped down, and was instantly surrounded by many of both sexes who were emulous to afford her assistance; but, affecting to be in violent pain, she intimated to them that she was desirous of remaining on the ground till she should be somewhat recovered. As she expected, the crowd increased, and her pretended footman, and a female accomplice were so industrious as to obtain two diamond girdle-buckles, a gold watch, a gold snuff-box, and two purses, containing together upward of forty guineas.

From *The New Newgate Calendar*,
edited by Andrew Knapp and William Baldwin

The Servant

THERE WAS A MISER who, when he sent his man to the cellar for wine, made him fill his mouth with water, which he was to spit out on his return, to show he had drunk no wine. But the servant kept a pitcher of water in the cellar, wherewith, after taking his fill of the better drink, he managed to deceive his master.

From Martin Luther's *Table Talk*

A Lodging for the Night

IT WAS LATE IN November 1456. The snow fell over Paris with rigorous, relentless persistence; sometimes the wind made a sally and scattered it in flying vortices; sometimes there was a lull, and flake after flake descended out of the black night air, silent, circuitous, interminable. To poor people, looking up under moist eyebrows, it seemed a wonder where it all came from. Master Francis Villon had propounded an alternative that afternoon, at a tavern window: was it only Pagan Jupiter plucking geese upon Olympus? or were the holy angels moulting? He was only a poor

Master of Arts, he went on; and as the question somewhat touched upon divinity, he durst not venture to conclude. A silly old priest from Montargis, who was among the company, treated the young rascal to a bottle of wine in honour of the jest and grimaces with which it was accompanied, and swore on his own white beard that he had been just such another irreverent dog when he was Villon's age.

The air was raw and pointed, but not far below freezing; and the flakes were large, damp, and adhesive. The whole city was sheeted up. An army might have marched from end to end and not a footfall given the alarm. If there were any belated birds in heaven, they saw the island like a large white patch, and the bridges like slim white spars, on the black ground of the river. High up overhead the snow settled among the tracery of the cathedral towers. Many a niche was drifted full; many a statue wore a long white bonnet on its grotesque or sainted head. The gargoyles had been transformed into great false noses, drooping towards the point. The crockets were like upright pillows swollen on one side. In the intervals of the wind, there was a dull sound of dripping about the precincts of the church.

The cemetery of St John had taken its own share of the snow. All the graves were decently covered; tall white house tops stood around in grave array; worthy burghers were long ago in bed, be-nightcapped like their domiciles; there was no light in all the neighbourhood but a little peep from a lamp that hung swinging in the church choir, and tossed the shadows to and fro in time to its oscillations. The clock was hard on ten when the patrol went by with halberds and a lantern, beating their hands; and they saw nothing suspicious about the cemetery of St John.

Yet there was a small house, backed up against the cemetery wall, which was still awake, and awake to evil purpose, in that snoring district. There was not much to betray it from without – only a stream of warm vapour from the chimney top, a patch where the snow melted on the roof, and a few half-obliterated footprints at the door. But within, behind the shuttered windows, Master Francis Villon the poet, and some of the thievish crew with whom he consorted, were keeping the night alive and passing round the bottle.

A great pile of living embers diffused a strong and ruddy glow from the arched chimney. Before this straddled Dom Nicolas, the Picardy monk, with his skirts picked up and his fat legs bared to the comfortable warmth. His dilated shadow cut the room in half; and the firelight only escaped on either side of his broad person, and in a little pool between his outspread feet. His face had the beery, bruised appearance of a continual drinker's; it was covered with a network of congested veins, purple in ordinary circumstances, but now pale violet, for even with his back to the fire the cold pinched him on the other side. His cowl had half fallen back, and made a strange excrescence on either side of his bull neck. So he straddled, grumbling, and cut the room in half with the shadow of his portly frame.

On the right, Villon and Guy Tabary were huddled together over a scrap of parchment, Villon making a ballade he was to call the 'Ballade of Roast Fish', and Tabary spluttering admiration at his shoulder. The poet was a rag of a man, dark, little, and lean, with hollow cheeks and thin black locks. He carried his four-and-twenty years with feverish animation. Greed had made folds about his eyes, evil smiles had puckered his mouth. The wolf and pig struggled together in his face. It was an eloquent, sharp, ugly, earthly countenance. His hands were small and prehensile, with fingers knotted like a cord; and they were continually flickering in front of him in violent and expressive pantomime. As for Tabary, a broad, complacent, admiring imbecility breathed from his squash nose and slobbering lips: he had become a thief, just as he might have become the most decent of burgesses, by the imperious chance that rules the lives of human geese and human donkeys.

At the monk's other hand, Montigny and Thevenin Pensete played a game of chance. About the first there clung some flavour of good birth and training, as about a fallen angel; something long, lithe, and courtly in the person; something aquiline and darkling in the face. Thevenin, poor soul, was in great feather: he had done a good stroke of knavery that afternoon in the Faubourg St Jacques, and all night he had been gaining from Montigny. A flat smile illuminated his face; his bald head shone rosily in a garland of red curls; his little portuberant stomach shook with silent chucklings as he swept in his gains.

'Doubles or quits?' said Thevenin.

Montigny nodded grimly.

'Some may prefer to dine in state,' wrote Villon, 'On bread and cheese on silver plate. Or, or – help me out, Guido!'

Tabary giggled.

'Or parsley on a golden dish,' scribbled the poet.

The wind was freshening without; it drove the snow before it, and sometimes raised its voice in a victorious whoop, and made sepulchral grumblings in the chimney. The cold was growing sharper as the night went on. Villon, protruding his lips, imitated the gust with something between a whistle and a groan. It was an eerie, uncomfortable talent of the poet's, much detested by the Picardy monk.

'Can't you hear it rattle in the gibbet?' said Villon. 'They are all dancing the devil's jig on nothing, up there. You may dance, my gallants, you'll be none the warmer. Whew! what a gust! Down went somebody just now! A medlar the fewer on the three-legged medlar tree! – I say, Dom Nicolas, it'll be cold to-night on the St Denis Road?' he asked.

Dom Nicolas winked both his big eyes, and seemed to choke upon his Adam's apple. Montfaucon, the great grisly Paris gibbet, stood hard by the St Denis Road, and the pleasantry touched him on the raw. As for Tabary, he laughed immoderately over the medlars; he had never heard anything more light-hearted; and he held his sides and crowed. Villon fetched him a fillip on the nose, which turned his mirth into an attack of coughing.

'Oh, stop that row,' said Villon, 'and think of rhymes to "fish".'

'Doubles or quits,' said Montigny, doggedly.

'With all my heart,' quoth Thevenin.

'Is there any more in that bottle?' asked the monk.

'Open another,' said Villon. 'How do you ever hope to fill that big hogshead, your body, with little things like bottles? And how do you expect to get to heaven? How many angels, do you fancy, can be spared to carry up a single monk from Picardy? Or do you think yourself another Elias – and they'll send the coach for you?'

'*Hominibus impossibile,*' replied the monk, as he filled his glass.

Tabary was in ecstasies.

Villon filliped his nose again.

'Laugh at my jokes, if you like,' he said.

'It was very good,' objected Tabary.

Villon made a face at him. 'Think of rhymes to "fish",' he said. 'What have you to do with Latin? You'll wish you knew none of it at the great assizes, when the devil calls for Guido Tabary, clericus – the devil with the humpback and red-hot finger-nails. Talking of the devil,' he added in a whisper, 'look at Montigny!'

All three peered covertly at the gamester. He did not seem to be enjoying his luck. His mouth was a little to a side; one nostril nearly shut, and the other much inflated. The black dog was on his back, as people say, in terrifying nursery metaphor; and he breathed hard under the gruesome burden.

'He looks as if he could knife him,' whispered Tabary with round eyes.

The monk shuddered, and turned his face and spread his open hands to the red embers. It was the cold that thus affected Dom Nicolas, and not any excess of moral sensibility.

'Come now,' said Villon, 'about this ballade. How does it run so far?' And beating time with his hand, he read it aloud to Tabary.

They were interrupted at the fourth rhyme by a brief and fatal movement among the gamesters. The round was completed, and Thevenin was just opening his mouth to claim another victory, when Montigny leaped up, swift as an adder, and stabbed him to the heart. The blow took effect before he had time to utter a cry, before he had time to move. A tremor or two convulsed his frame; his hands opened and shut, his heels rattled on the floor; then his head rolled backward over one shoulder with the eyes wide open; and Thevenin Pensete's spirit had returned to Him who made it.

Every one sprang to his feet; but the business was over in two twos. The four living fellows looked at each other in rather a ghastly fashion, the dead man contemplating a corner of the roof with a singular and ugly leer.

'My God!' said Tabary; and he began to pray in Latin.

Villon broke out into hysterical laughter. He came a step forward and ducked a ridiculous bow at Thevenin, and laughed still louder. Then he sat down suddenly, all of a heap, upon a stool, and continued laughing bitterly as though he would shake himself to pieces.

Montigny recovered his composure first.

'Let's see what he has about him,' he remarked, and he picked the dead man's pockets with a practised hand, and divided the money into four equal portions on the table. 'There's for you,' he said.

The monk received his share with a deep sigh, and a single stealthy glance at the dead Thevenin, who was beginning to sink into himself and topple sideways off the chair.

'We're all in for it,' cried Villon, swallowing his mirth. 'It's a hanging job for every man jack of us that's here – not to speak of those who aren't.' He made a shocking gesture in the air with his raised right hand, and put out his tongue and threw his head on one side, so as to counterfeit the appearance of one who has been hanged. Then he pocketed his share of the spoil, and executed a shuffle with his feet as if to restore the circulation.

Tabary was the last to help himself; he made a dash at the money, and retired to the other end of the apartment.

Montigny stuck Thevenin upright in the chair, and drew out the dagger, which was followed by a jet of blood.

'You fellows had better be moving,' he said, as he wiped the blade on his victim's doublet.

'I think we had,' returned Villon, with a gulp. 'Damn his fat head!' he broke out. 'It sticks in my throat like phlegm. What right has a man to have red hair when he is dead?' And he fell all of a heap again upon the stool, and fairly covered his face with his hands.

Montigny and Dom Nicolas laughed aloud, even Tabary feebly chiming in.

'Cry baby,' said the monk.

'I always said he was a woman,' added Montigny, with a sneer. 'Sit up, can't you?' he went on, giving another shake to the murdered body. 'Tread out that fire, Nick!'

But Nick was better employed; he was quietly taking Villon's purse, as the poet sat, limp and trembling, on the stool where he had been making a ballade not three minutes before. Montigny and Tabary dumbly demanded a share of the booty, which the monk silently promised as he passed the little bag into the bosom of his gown. In many ways an artistic nature unfits a man for practical existence.

No sooner had the theft been accomplished than Villon shook himself, jumped to his feet, and began helping to scatter and extinguish the embers. Meanwhile Montigny opened the door and cautiously peered into the street. The coast was clear; there was no meddlesome patrol in sight. Still it was judged wiser to slip out severally; and as Villon was himself in a hurry to escape from the neighbourhood of the dead Thevenin, and the rest were in a still greater hurry to get rid of him before he should discover the loss of his money, he was the first by general consent to issue forth into the street.

The wind had triumphed and swept all the clouds from heaven. Only a few vapours, as thin as moonlight, fleeted rapidly across the stars. It was bitter cold; and by a common optical effect, things seemed almost more definite than in broadest daylight. The sleeping city was absolutely still; a company of white hoods, a field full of little alps, below the twinkling stars. Villon cursed his fortune. Would it were snowing! Now, wherever he went, he left an indelible trail behind him on the glittering streets; wherever he went he was still tethered to the house by the cemetery of St John; wherever he went he must weave, with his own plodding feet, the rope that bound him to the crime and would bind him to the gallows. The leer of the dead man came back to him with a new significance. He snapped his fingers as if to pluck up his own spirits, and choosing a street at random, stepped boldly forward in the snow.

Two things preoccupied him as he went: the aspect of the gallows at Montfaucon in this bright, windy phase of the night's existence, for one; and for another, the look of the dead man with his bald head and garland of red curls. Both struck cold upon his heart, and he kept quickening his pace as if he could escape from unpleasant thoughts by mere fleetness of foot. Sometimes he looked back over his shoulder with a sudden nervous jerk; but he was the only moving thing in the white streets, except when the wind swooped round a corner and threw up the snow, which was beginning to freeze, in spouts of glittering dust.

Suddenly he saw, a long way before him, a black clump and a couple of lanterns. The clump was in motion, and the lanterns swung as though carried by men walking. It was a patrol. And though it was merely crossing his line of march, he judged it wiser to get out of eyeshot as speedily as he could. He was not in the humour to be challenged, and he was conscious of making a very conspicuous mark upon the snow. Just on his left hand there stood a great hotel, with some turrets and porch before the door; it was half ruinous, he remembered, and had long stood empty; and so he made three steps of it, and jumped into the shelter of the porch. It was pretty dark inside, after the glimmer of the snowy streets, and he was groping forward with outspread hands, when he stumbled over some substance which offered an indescribable mixture of resistances, hard and soft, firm and loose. His heart gave a leap, and he sprang two steps back and stared dreadfully at the obstacle. Then he gave a little laugh of relief. It was only a woman, and she dead. He knelt beside her to make sure upon this latter point. She was freezing cold, and rigid like a stick. A little ragged finery fluttered in the wind about her hair, and her cheeks had been heavily rouged that same afternoon. Her pockets were quite empty; but in her stocking, underneath the garter, Villon found two of the small coins that went by the name of whites. It was little enough, but it was always something; and the poet was moved with a deep sense of pathos that she should have died before she had spent her money. That seemed to him a dark and pitiable mystery; and he looked from the coins in his hand to the dead woman, and back again to the coin, shaking his head over the riddle of man's life. Henry V of England, dying at Vincennes just after he had conquered France, and this poor jade cut off by a cold draught in a great man's doorway, before she had time to spend her couple of whites – it seemed a cruel way to carry on the world. Two whites would have taken such a little while to squander; and yet it would have been one more good taste in the mouth, one more smack of the lips, before the devil got the soul, and the body was left to birds and vermin. He would like to use all his tallow before the light was blown out and the lantern broken. While these thoughts were passing through his mind, he was feeling, half mechanically, for his purse. Suddenly his heart stopped beating; a feeling of cold scales passed up the back of his legs, and a cold blow seemed to fall upon his scalp. He stood petrified for a moment; then he felt again with one feverish movement; and then his loss burst upon him, and he was covered at once with perspiration. To spendthrifts money is so living and actual – it is such a thin veil between them and their pleasures! There is only one limit to their fortune – that of time; and a spendthrift with only a few crowns is the

Emperor of Rome until they are spent. For such a person to lose his money is to suffer the most shocking reverse, and fall from heaven to hell, from all to nothing, in a breath. And all the more if he has put his head in the halter for it; if he may be hanged to-morrow for that same purse, so dearly earned, so foolishly departed! Villon stood and cursed; he threw the whites into the street; he shook his fist at heaven; he stamped, and was not horrified to find himself trampling the corpse. Then he began rapidly to retrace his steps towards the house beside the cemetery. He had forgotten all fear of the patrol, which was long gone but at any rate, and had no idea but that of his lost purse. It was in vain that he looked right and left upon the snow: nothing was to be seen. He had not dropped it in the streets. Had it fallen in the house? He would have liked dearly to go in and see; but the idea of the grisly occupant unmanned him. And he saw besides, as he drew near, that their efforts to put out the fire had been unsuccessful; on the contrary, it had broken into a blaze, and a changeful light played in the chinks of door and window, and revived his terror for the authorities and Paris gibbet.

He returned to the hotel with the porch, and groped about upon the snow for the money he had thrown away in his childish passion. But he could only find one white; the other had probably struck sideways and sunk deeply in. With a single white in his pocket, all his projects for a rousing night in some wild tavern vanished uttery away. And it was not only pleasure that fled laughing from his grasp: positive discomfort, positive pain, attacked him as he stood ruefully before the porch. His perspiration had dried upon him; and although the wind had now fallen, a binding frost was setting in stronger every hour, and he felt benumbed and sick at heart. What was to be done? Late as was the hour, improbable as was success, he would try the house of his adopted father, the chaplain of St Benoît.

He ran there all the way, and knocked timidly. There was no answer. He knocked again and again, taking heart with every stroke; and at last steps were heard approaching from within. A barred wicket fell open in the iron-studded door, and emitted a gush of yellow light.

'Hold up your face to the wicket,' said the chaplain from within.

'It's only me,' whimpered Villon.

'Oh, it's only you, is it?' returned the chaplain; and he cursed him with foul unpriestly oaths for disturbing him at such an hour, and bade him be off to hell, where he came from. 'My hands are blue to the wrist,' pleaded Villon; 'my feet are dead and full of twinges; my nose aches with the sharp air; the cold lies at my heart. I may be dead before morning. Only this once, father, and before God, I will never ask again!'

'You should have come earlier,' said the ecclesiastic, coolly. 'Young men require a lesson now and then.' He shut the wicket and retired deliberately into the interior of the house.

Villon was beside himself; he beat upon the door with his hands and feet, and shouted hoarsely after the chaplain.

'Wormy old fox!' he cried. 'If I had my hand under your twist, I would send you flying headlong into the bottomless pit.'

A door shut in the interior, faintly audible to the poet down long passages. He passed his hand over his mouth with an oath. And then the humour of the situation struck him, and he laughed and looked lightly up to heaven, where the stars seemed to be winking over his discomfiture.

What was to be done? It looked like a night in the frosty streets. The idea of the dead woman popped into his imagination, and gave him a hearty fright; what had happened to her in the early night might very well happen to him before morning. And he so young! and with such immense possibilities of disorderly amusement before him! He felt quite pathetic over the notion of his own fate, as if it had been someone else's, and made a little imaginative vignette of the scene in the morning, when they should find his body.

He passed all his chances under review, turning the white between his thumb and forefinger. Unfortunately he was on bad terms with some old friends who would once have taken pity on him in such a plight. He had lampooned them in verses; he had beaten and cheated them; and yet now, when he was in so close a pinch, he thought there was at least one who might perhaps relent. It was a chance. It was worth trying at least, and he would go and see.

On the way, two little accidents happened to him which coloured his musings in a very different manner. For, first, he fell in with the track of a patrol, and walked in it for some hundred yards, although it lay out of his direction. And this spirited him up; at least he had confused his trail; for he was still possessed with the idea of people tracking him all about Paris over the snow, and collaring him next morning before he was awake. The other matter affected him quite differently. He passed a street corner where, not so long before, a woman and her child had been devoured by wolves. This was just the kind of weather, he reflected, when wolves might take it into their heads to enter Paris again; and a lone man in these deserted streets would run the chance of something worse than a mere scare. He stopped and looked upon the place with an unpleasant interest – it was a centre where several lanes intersected each other; and he looked down them all, one after another, and held his breath to listen, lest he should detect galloping black things on the snow or hear the sound of howling between him and the river. He remembered his mother telling him the story and pointing out the spot, while he was yet a child. His mother! If he only knew where she lived, he might make sure at least of shelter. He determined he would inquire upon the morrow; nay, he would go and see her too, poor old girl! So thinking, he arrived at his destination – his last hope for the night.

The house was quite dark, like its neighbours; and yet after a few taps, he heard a movement overhead, a door opening, and a cautious voice asking who was there. The poet named himself in a loud whisper, and waited, not without some trepidation, the result. Nor had he to wait long. A window was suddenly opened, and a pailful of slops splashed down upon the doorstep. Villon had not been unprepared for something of the sort, and had put himself as much in shelter as the nature of the porch admitted; but for all that, he was deplorably drenched below the waist. His hose began to freeze almost at once. Death from cold and exposure stared him in the face; he remembered he was of phthisical tendency, and began coughing tentatively. But the gravity of the danger steadied his nerves. He stopped a few hundred yards from the door where he had been so rudely used, and reflected with his finger to his nose. He could see only one way of getting a lodging, and that was to take it. He had noticed a house not far away, which looked as if it might be easily broken into, and thither he betook himself promptly, entertaining himself on the way with the idea of a room still hot, with a table still loaded with the remains of supper, where he might pass the rest of the black hours and whence he should issue, on the morrow, with an armful of valuable plate. He even considered on what viands and what wines he should prefer; and as he was calling the roll of his favourite dainties, roast fish presented itself to his mind with an odd mixture of amusement and horror.

'I shall never finish that ballade,' he thought to himself; and then, with another shudder at the recollection, 'Oh, damn his fat head!' he repeated fervently, and spat upon the snow.

The house in question looked dark at first sight; but as Villon made a preliminary inspection in search of the handiest point of attack, a little twinkle of light caught his eye from behind a curtained window.

'The devil!' he thought. 'People awake! Some student or some saint, confound the crew! Can't they get drunk and lie in bed snoring like their neighbours! What's the good of curfew, and poor devils of bell ringers jumping at a rope's end in bell towers? What's the use of day, if people sit up all night? The gripes to them!' He grinned as he saw where his logic was leading him. 'Every man to his business, after all,' added he, 'and if they're awake, by the Lord, I may come by a supper honestly for once, and cheat the devil.'

He went boldly to the door and knocked with an assured hand. On both previous occasions, he had knocked timidly and with some dread of attracting notice; but now, when he had just discarded the thought of a burglarious entry, knocking at a door seemed a mighty simple and innocent proceeding. The sound of his blows echoed through the house with thin, phantasmal reverberations, as though it were quite empty; but these had scarcely died away before a measured tread drew near, a couple of bolts were withdrawn, and one wing was opened broadly, as though no guile or fear of guile were known to those within. A tall figure of a man, muscular and spare, but a little bent, confronted Villon. The head was massive in bulk, but finely sculptured; the nose blunt at the bottom, but refining upward to where it joined a pair of strong and honest eyebrows; the mouth and eyes surrounded with delicate markings, and the whole face based upon a thick white beard, boldly and squarely trimmed. Seen as it was by the light of a flickering hand lamp, it looked perhaps nobler than it had a right to do; but it was a fine face, honourable rather than intelligent, strong, simple, and righteous.

'You knock late, sir,' said the old man, in resonant, courteous tones.

Villon cringed, and brought up many servile words of apology; at a crisis of this sort, the beggar was uppermost in him, and the man of genius hid his head with confusion.

'You are cold,' repeated the old man, 'and hungry? Well, step in.' And he ordered him into the house with a noble enough gesture.

'Some great seigneur,' thought Villon, as his host, setting his lamp on the flagged pavement of the entry, shot the bolts once more into their places.

'You will pardon me if I go in front,' he said, when this was done; and he preceded the poet upstairs into a large apartment, warmed with a pan of charcoal and lit by a great lamp hanging from the roof. It was very bare of furniture: only some gold plate on a sideboard; some folios; and a stand of armour between the windows. Some smart tapestry hung upon the walls, representing the crucifixion of our Lord in one piece, and in another a scene of shepherds and shepherdesses by a stream. Over the chimney was a shield of arms.

'Will you seat yourself,' said the old man, 'and forgive if I leave you? I am alone in my house to-night, and if you are to eat, I must forage for you myself.'

No sooner was his host gone than Villon leaped from the chair on which he had just seated himself, and began examining the room, with the stealth and passion of a cat. He weighed the gold flagons in his hand, opened all the folios, and investigated the arms upon the shield, and the stuff with which the seats were lined. He raised the window curtains, and saw that the windows were set with rich stained glass in figures, so far as he could see, of martial import. Then he stood in the middle of the room, drew a long breath, and retaining it with puffed cheeks, looked round and round him, turning on his heels, as if to impress every feature of the apartment on his memory.

'Seven pieces of plate,' he said. 'If there had been ten, I would have risked it. A fine house, and a fine old master, so help me all the saints!'

And just then, hearing the old man's tread returning along the corridor, he stole back to his chair, and began humbly toasting his wet legs before the charcoal pan.

His entertainer had a plate of meat in one hand and a jug of wine in the other. He set down the plate upon the table, motioning Villon to draw in his chair, and going to the sideboard, brought back two goblets, which he filled.

'I drink to your better fortune,' he said, gravely touching Villon's cup with his own.

'To our better acquaintance,' said the poet, growing bold. A mere man of the people would have been awed by the courtesy of the old seigneur, but Villon was hardened in that matter; he had made mirth for great lords before now, and found them as black rascals as himself. And so he devoted himself to the viands with a ravenous gusto, while the old man, leaning backward, watched him with steady, curious eyes.

'You have blood on your shoulder, my man,' he said.

Montigny must have laid his wet right hand upon him as he left the house. He cursed Montigny in his heart.

'It was none of my shedding,' he stammered.

'I had not supposed so,' returned his host, quietly. 'A brawl?'

'Well, something of that sort,' Villon admitted with a quaver.

'Perhaps a fellow murdered?'

'Oh, no, not murdered,' said the poet, more and more confused. 'It was all fair play – murdered by accident. I had no hand in it, God strike me dead!' he added fervently.

'One rogue the fewer, I dare say,' observed the master of the house.

'You may dare to say that,' agreed Villon, infinitely relieved. 'As big a rogue as there is between here and Jerusalem. He turned up his toes like a lamb. But it was a nasty thing to look at. I dare say you've seen dead men in your time, my lord?' he added, glancing at the armour.

'Many,' said the old man. 'I have followed the wars, as you imagine.'

Villon laid down his knife and fork, which he had just taken up again.

'Were any of them bald?' he asked.

'Oh yes, and with hair as white as mine.'

'I don't think I should mind the white so much,' said Villon. 'His was red.' And he had a return of his shuddering and tendency to laughter, which he drowned with a great draught of wine. 'I'm a little put out when I think of it,' he went on. 'I knew him – damn him! And then the cold gives a man fancies – or the fancies give a man cold, I don't know which.'

'Have you any money?' asked the old man.

'I have one white,' returned the poet, laughing. 'I got it out of a dead jade's stocking in a porch. She was as dead as Caesar, poor wench, and as cold as a church, with bits of ribbon in her hair. This is a hard world in winter for wolves and wenches and poor rogues like me.'

'I,' said the old man, 'am Enguerrand de la Feuillée, seigneur de Brisetout, bailly du Patatrac. Who and what are you?'

Villon rose and made a suitable reverence. 'I am called Francis Villon,' he said, 'a poor Master of Arts of this university. I know some Latin, and a deal of vice. I can make ballades, lais, virelais, and roundels, and I am very fond of wine. I was born in a garret, and I shall not improbably die upon the gallows. I may add, my lord, that from this night forward I am your lordship's very obsequious servant to command.'

'No servant of mine,' said the knight; 'my guest for this evening and no more.'

'A very grateful guest,' said Villon, politely, and he drank in dumb show to his entertainer.

'You are shrewd,' began the old man, tapping his forehead, 'very shrewd; you have learning; you are a clerk; and yet you take a small piece of money off a dead woman in the street. Is it not a kind of theft?'

'It is a kind of theft much practised in the wars, my lord.'

'The wars are the field of honour,' returned the old man, proudly. 'There a man plays his life upon the cast; he fights in the name of his lord the king, his Lord God, and all their lordships the holy saints and angels.'

'Put it,' said Villon, 'that I were really a thief, should I not play my life also, and against heavier odds?'

'For gain, but not for honour.'

'Gain?' repeated Villon, with a shrug. 'Gain! The poor fellow wants supper, and takes it. So does the soldier in a campaign. Why, what are all these requisitions we hear so much about? If they are not gain to those who take them, they are loss enough to the others. The men-at-arms drink by a good fire, while the burgher bites his nails to buy them wine. I have seen a good many ploughmen swinging on trees about the country; ay, I have seen thirty on one elm, and a very poor figure they made; and when I asked some one how all these came to be hanged, I was told it was because they could not scrape together enough crowns to satisfy the men-at-arms.'

'These things are a necessity of war, which the lowborn must endure with constancy. It is true that some captains drive overhard; there are spirits in every rank not easily moved by pity; and, indeed, many follow arms who are no better than brigands.'

'You see,' said the poet, 'you cannot separate the soldier from the brigand; and what is a thief but an isolated brigand with circumspect manners? I steal a couple of mutton chops, without so much as disturbing people's sleep; the farmer grumbles a bit, but sups none the less wholesomely on what remains. You come up blowing gloriously on a trumpet, take away the whole sheep, and beat the farmer pitifully into the bargain. I have no trumpet; I am only Tom, Dick, or Harry; I am a rogue and a dog, and hanging's too good for me – with all my heart; but just ask the farmer which of us he prefers, just find out which of us he lies awake to curse on cold nights.'

'Look at us two,' said his lordship. 'I am old, strong, and honoured. If I were turned from my house to-morrow, hundreds would be proud to shelter me. Poor people would go out and pass the night in the streets with their children, if I merely hinted that I wished to be alone. And I find you up, wandering homeless, and picking farthings off dead women by the wayside! I fear no man and nothing; I have seen you tremble and lose countenance at a word. I wait God's summons contentedly in my own house, or, if it please the king to call me out again, upon the field of battle. You look for the gallows; a rough, swift death, without hope or honour. Is there no difference between these two?'

'As far as to the moon,' Villon acquiesced. 'But if I had been born lord of Brisetout, and you had been the poor scholar Francis, would the difference have been any the less? Should not I have been warming my knees at this charcoal pan, and would not you have been groping for farthings in the snow. Should not I have been the soldier, and you the thief?'

'A thief?' cried the old man. 'I, a thief! If you understood your words, you would repent them.'

Villon turned out his hands with a gesture of inimitable impudence. 'If your lordship had done me the honour to follow my argument!' he said.

'I do you too much honour in submitting to your presence,' said the knight. 'Learn to curb your tongue when you speak with old and honourable men, or some one hastier than I may reprove you in a sharper fashion.' And he rose and paced the lower end of the apartment, struggling with anger and antipathy. Villon surreptitiously refilled his cup, and settled himself more comfortably in the chair, crossing his knees and leaning his head upon one hand and the elbow against the back of the chair. He was now replete and warm; and he was in no wise frightened for his host, having gauged him as justly as was possible between two such different characters. The night was far spent, and in a very comfortable fashion after all; and he felt morally certain of a safe departure on the morrow.

'Tell me one thing,' said the old man, pausing in his walk. 'Are you really a thief?'

'I claim the sacred rights of hospitality,' returned the poet. 'My lord, I am.'

'You are very young,' the knight continued.

'I should never have been so old,' replied Villon, showing his fingers, 'if I had not helped myself with these ten talents. They have been my nursing mothers and my nursing fathers.'

'You may still repent and change.'

'I repent daily,' said the poet. 'There are few people more given to repentance than poor Francis. As for change, let somebody change my circumstances. A man must continue to eat, if it were only that he may continue to repent.'

'The change must begin in the heart,' returned the old man solemnly.

'My dear lord,' answered Villon, 'do you really fancy that I steal for pleasure? I hate stealing, like any other piece of work or of danger. My teeth chatter when I see a gallows. But I must eat, I must drink, I must mix in society of some sort. What the devil! Man is not a solitary animal – *Cui Deus foeminam tradit*. Make me king's pantler – make me abbot of St Denis; make me bailly of the Patatrac; and then I shall be changed indeed. But as long as you leave me the poor scholar Francis Villon, without a farthing, why, of course, I remain the same.'

'The Grace of God is all-powerful.'

'I should be a heretic to question it,' said Francis. 'It has made you lord of Brisetout and bailly of the Patatrac; it has given me nothing but the quick wits under my hat and these ten toes upon my hands. May I help myself to wine? I thank you respectfully. By God's grace, you have a very superior vintage.

The lord of Brisetout walked to and fro with his hands behind his back. Perhaps he was not yet quite settled in his mind about the parallel between thieves and soldiers; perhaps Villon had interested him by some cross thread of sympathy; perhaps his wits were simply muddled by so much unfamiliar reasoning; but whatever the cause, he somehow yearned to convert the young man to a better way of thinking, and could not make up his mind to drive him forth again into the street.

'There is something more than I can understand in this,' he said at length. 'Your mouth is full of subtleties, and the devil has led you very far astray; but the devil is only a very weak spirit before God's truth, and all his subtleties vanish at a word of true honour, like darkness at morning. Listen to me once more. I learned long ago that a gentleman should live chivalrously and lovingly to God, and the king, and his lady; and though I have seen many strange things done, I have still striven to command my ways upon that rule. It is not only written in all noble histories, but in every man's heart, if he will take care to read. You speak of food and wine, and I know very well that hunger is a difficult trial to endure; but you do not speak of other wants; you say nothing of honour, of faith to God and other men, of courtesy, of love without reproach. It may be that I am not very wise – and yet I think I am – but you seem to me like one who has lost his way and made a great error in life. You are attending to the little wants, and you have totally forgotten the great and only real ones, like a man who should be doctoring toothache on the Judgment Day. For such things as honour and love and faith are not only nobler than food and drink, but indeed I think we desire them more, and suffer more sharply for their absence. I speak to you as I think you will most easily understand me. Are you not, while careful to fill your belly, disregarding another appetite in your heart, which spoils the pleasure of your life and keeps you continually wretched?'

Villon was sensibly nettled under all this sermonising. 'You think I have no sense of honour!' he cried. 'I'm poor enough, God knows! It's hard to see rich people with their gloves, and you blowing in your hands. An empty belly is a bitter thing, although you speak so lightly of it. If you had had as many as I, perhaps you would change your tune. Anyway I'm a thief – make the most of that – but I'm not a devil from hell, God strike me dead. I would have you to know I've an honour of my own, as good as yours, though I don't prate about it all day long, as if it was a God's miracle to have any. It seems quite natural to me; I keep it in its box till it's wanted. Why now, look you here, how long have I been in this room with you? Did you not tell me you were alone in the house? Look at your gold plate! You're strong, if you like, but you're old and unarmed, and I have my knife. What did I want but a jerk of the elbow and here would have been you with the cold steel in your bowels, and there would have been me, linking in the streets, with an armful of golden cups! Did you suppose I hadn't wit enough to see that? And I scorned the action. There are your damned goblets, as safe as in a church; there are you, with your heart ticking as good as new; and here am I, ready to go out again as poor as I came in, with my one white that you threw in my teeth! And you think I have no sense of honour – God strike me dead!'

The old man stretched out his right arm. 'I will tell you what you are,' he said. 'You are a rogue, my man, an impudent and black-hearted rogue and vagabond. I have passed an hour with you. Oh! believe me, I feel myself disgraced. And you have eaten and drunk at my table. But now I am sick at your presence; the day has come, and the night bird should be off to his roost. Will you go before, or after?'

'Which you please,' returned the poet, rising. 'I believe you to be strictly honourable.' He thoughtfully emptied his cup. 'I wish I could add you were intelligent,' he went on, knocking on his head with his knuckles. 'Age! age! the brains stiff and rheumatic.'

The old man preceded him from a point of self-respect; Villon followed, whistling, with his thumbs in his girdle.

'God pity you,' said the lord of Brisetout at the door.

'Good-bye, papa,' returned Villon, with a yawn. 'Many thanks for the cold mutton.'

The door closed behind him. The dawn was breaking over the white roofs. A chill, uncomfortable morning ushered in the day. Villon stood and heartily stretched himself in the middle of the road.

'A very dull old gentleman,' he thought. 'I wonder what his goblets may be worth.'

Robert Louis Stevenson

The Sign-Language of Tramps

THE COMMON or roadside tramp is not a popular or interesting person. His appearance is usually unprepossessing, his honesty is frequently not above suspicion, and his distaste for work has passed into a proverb. Police and public alike eye him with suspicious dislike as he slouches along the highroad; and when he is forced by stress of weather or other circumstances to seek a night's lodging in some casual ward, the master first forces him to take a bath and then sets him some peculiarly obnoxious task, specially designed for the discouragement of his species.

The tramps, thus cut off by a barrier of dislike from communion with their more respectable fellow creatures, have been forced, in sheer self-defence, to aid and assist one another. There is no particular bond of sympathy between tramp and tramp; but the necessity for self-preservation compels the members of this strange fraternity of wayfarers and work-haters to co-operate to a certain extent. One of the most interesting forms which this co-operation takes is the silent, but none the less powerful, medium of a sign-language, whereby any member of the brotherhood, following in the steps of a pioneer, may learn what fate has in store for him in the way of good or bad luck at the various places he visits. The writer was recently privileged to have this curious sign-language explained to him by a venerable and grizzled member of the tramp fraternity – an interesting old ruffian who confessed that he had been tramping the highroads and by-ways of rural England for the last forty years, during which period he had done about a fortnight's honest work. My informant first told me that the amateur tramp – the out-of-work labourer looking for a job, and similar *dilettanti*; on whom the regular tramp looks down with scorn – is totally unaware of the existence of the sign-language. Knowledge of this is jealously preserved among the professional tramps – the loafers one meets camped in secluded places in the country, or hanging round farmsteads in search of food. To these men it is invaluable, enabling them to tell at a glance what sort of reception they will meet with at any house they propose to visit. The signs have the merit of being easily made; a piece of chalk or whiting and a handy wall or fence are all that is required. When made they are quite unintelligible to the layman and look very like the meaningless scrawls of schoolchildren who have purloined a fragment of the teacher's chalk. That the marks are not meaningless, however, will be abundantly proved by the following illustrations, which were prepared under the supervision of my tramp friend. The members of the fraternity not being, as a rule, artistically gifted, the marks are distinguished by their absolute simplicity; there is no sign which cannot be drawn in an instant by the most unskilled hand. Take for instance, the first sign we reproduce here. This shows a simple circle, drawn on a wall, and yet it conveys to the eye of the initiated tramp the unwelcome information: 'No good to call here.' Some other tramp has happened along the way, has called at this farmhouse with a modest request for food or money and has been repulsed. Therefore he has left behind him a warning to any fellow-tramp that might be on the same road: 'No good to call here.' And Weary Willie gives the inhospitable dwelling a wide berth.

We have seen that a plain circle is an omen of evil to the tramp, indicating a stony-hearted refusal of his gentle pleadings and the possible 'firing out' of himself from the farmyard by some indignant owner. If, however, a large cross be inserted in the circle, as in our second photograph, then the sign tells a very different story – a story which sends its travel-stained reader hurrying up the path to the back door. For now it reads: 'The people here will give you food.' And your genuine tramp never declines food that is to be had for the asking – unless it be a pie made by the newly-married *diplomée* of cookery school. The tramp is not always allowed to approach and leave a house or farm in peace. As I have before remarked, his appearance is usually distinctly against him, and some of the species have an awkward habit of annexing little unconsidered trifles which come in their way. Moreover farmers suspect them of an unhappy penchant for sleeping in stacks and accidentally setting them on fire. Hence it is that poor Weary William is as often as not forcibly ejected from the premises or else driven off by some ferocious watch-dog. When this fate happens to a tramp he is in duty bound to do his best to prevent his comrades from walking into the same trap. Therefore, if circumstances permit and no pursuit is attempted, he affixes to the farm the sign shown herewith. [The picture shows a square with four small vertical lines in the bottom right-hand corner.] Primarily this means 'Dog in the garden', but it is also used as a general strong note of caution. When placed upon a private house it means just what it says – that there is a troublesome dog stationed in the garden – but when the wandering tramp sees it on the side of a barn or farmstead he usually associates it with a choleric farmer with a horse whip or a tribe of unsympathetic labourers who are likely to throw him into the duck pond.

At certain times of the year, however, particularly at such busy seasons as seedtime and harvest, farmers can often do with the temporary services of unskilled men, and when tramps offer themselves they are frequently taken on. A tramp who has fallen upon a place of this sort sketches on some convenient fence the following sign [the picture shows a cross and the outline of a spade], which means, practically, 'Food and money here if you care to work.' As many tramps have a rooted objection to manual labour, it is not all of them who hail this sign with joy. Money, by the way, is usually indicated in the sign-language by tiny circles, but as tramps do not often receive money the sign is not much used.

What is known among this precious fraternity as a 'soft shop' is indicated by the next sign, the large V and the three triangles [the latter three are inverted]. This counsels the wayfarer to 'Pitch a yarn – three women in house.' Women are always represented by small triangles – a crude imitation of the outline of a lady's skirt. 'Pitching a tale', of course, as most people can testify from personal exerience, is an art in which the average tramp is an adept. The variety of romantic stories of distress which he can pour into the ears of sympathetic old maids and trustful servants is amazing.

In striking contrast to the 'soft shop' sign comes the portcullis arrangement next shown. This is an emblem which the tramp regards with absolute terror, passing the place on which it is placed with muttered curses against the occupier, for the criss-cross lines indicate that the occupier is so uncharitable as to give tramps in charge as rogues and vagabonds! If any country reader of this magazine wishes to protect his dwelling against tramps – at any rate against the older hands – he has only to inscribe this sign on some prominent gatepost or fence. Weary William has no desire to make the acquaintance of the village constable with the subsequent painful interview with the local bench of magistrates.

If anything could dash his hopes more than the sign we have just reproduced it is that shown in our last photograph. [The picture shows a circle with two horizontal arrows through it]. For this sign tells the foot-sore tramp that his journey has been more or less in vain: that he will meet with nothing but unkindness in the village; and that the best thing he can do is to drag his tired limbs onwards to some other and more hospitable hamlet. For the pioneer tramp tells us here: 'Get out of this village as soon as you can; there is nothing any good to be got here.' What could be more depressing after a long day's journey? There are several other signs in the tramp language, most of them more intricate than the foregoing and some of them not well known, but we have contented ourselves with reproducing the signs most commonly used by the fraternity of the road.

From *The Sign-Language of Tramps* by Victor Pitkethley

A Trampwoman's Tragedy

I

From Wynyard's Gap the livelong day,
    The livelong day,
We beat afoot the northward way
    We had travelled times before.
The sun-blaze burning on our backs,
Our shoulders sticking to our packs,
By fosseway, fields, and turnpike tracks
    We skirted sad Sedge-moor.

II

Full twenty miles we jaunted on,
    We jaunted on, –
My fancy-man, and jeering John,
    And Mother Lee, and I.
And, as the sun drew down to west,
We climbed the toilsome Poldon crest,
And saw, of landskip sights the best,
    The inn that beamed thereby.

III

For months we had padded side by side,
   Ay, side by side
Through the Great Forest, Blackmoor wide,
   And where the Parret ran.
We'd faced the gusts on Mendip ridge,
Had crossed the Yeo unhelped by bridge,
Being stung by every Marshwood midge,
   I and my fancy-man.

IV

Lone inns we loved, my man and I,
   My man and I;
'King's Stag', 'Windwhistle' high and dry,
   'The Horse' on Hintock Green,
The cosy house at Wynyard's Gap,
'The Hut' renowned on Bredy Knap,
And many another wayside tap
   Where folk might sit unseen.

V

Now as we trudged – O deadly day,
   O deadly day! –
I teased my fancy-man in play
   And wanton idleness.
I walked alongside jeering John,
I laid his hand my waist upon;
I would not bend my glances on
   My lover's dark distress.

VI

Thus Poldon top at last we won,
   At last we won,
And gained the inn at sink of sun
   Far-famed as "Marshal's Elm".
Beneath us figured tor and lea,
From Mendip to the western sea –
I doubt if finer sight there be
   Within this royal realm.

VII

Inside the settle all a-row –
　　All four a-row
We sat, I next to John, to show
　　That he had wooed and won.
And then he took me on his knee,
And swore it was his turn to be
My favoured mate, and Mother Lee
　　Passed to my former one.

VIII

Then in a voice I had never heard,
　　I had never heard,
My only Love to me: 'One word,
　　My lady, if you please!
Whose is the child you are like to bear? –
His? After all my months o' care?'
God knows 'twas not! But, O despair!
　　I nodded – still to tease.

IX

Then up he sprung, and with his knife –
　　And with his knife
He let out jeering Johnny's life,
　　Yes; there, at set of sun.
The slant ray through the window nigh
Gilded John's blood and glazing eye,
Ere scarcely Mother Lee and I
　　Knew that the deed was done.

X

The taverns tell the gloomy tale,
　　The gloomy tale,
How that at Ivel-chester jail
　　My Love, my sweetheart swung;
Though stained till now by no misdeed
Save one horse ta'en in time o' need;
(Blue Jimmy stole right many a steed
Ere his last fling he flung).

XI

Thereaft I walked the world alone,
   Alone, alone!
On his death-day I gave my groan
   And dropt his dead-born child.
'Twas nigh the jail, beneath a tree,
None tending me; for Mother Lee
Had died at Glaston, leaving me
   Unfriended on the wild.

XII

And in the night as I lay weak,
   As I lay weak,
The leaves a-falling on my cheek,
   The red moon low declined –
The ghost of him I'd die to kiss
Rose up and said: 'Ah, tell me this!
Was the child mine, or was it his?
   Speak, that I rest may find!'

XIII

O doubt not but I told him then,
   I told him then,
That I had kept me from all men
   Since we joined lips and swore.
Whereat he smiled, and thinned away
As the wind stirred to call up day . . .
-'Tis past! And here alone I stray
   Haunting the Western Moor.

Thomas Hardy

The Lincolnshire Poacher

When I was bound 'prentice in fair Lincolnshire,
I served my master for nearly seven year,
Till I got up to poaching, as quickly you shall hear,
It was my delight in a shiny night, in the season of the year.

As I and my bold comrades were setting of a snare,
The gamekeeper was watching us, for him we did not care,
For I could wrestle, or fight, my boys, or jump over anywhere,
It was my delight in a shiny night, in the season of the year.

As I and my bold comrades were setting four or five,
And going to take them up again, we found a hare alive,
I have her in the bag, my boys, and through the woods we steer,
It was my delight in a shiny night, in the season of the year.

I hung her over my shoulder, and rambled into the town,
I called at a neighbour's house, and sold her for a crown,
I sold her for a crown my boys, but I'll not tell you where,
It was my delight, in a shiny night, in the season of the year.

Here's to every poacher that lives in Lincolnshire,
And here's to every gamekeeper, that wants to buy a hare,
But not every keeper that wants to keep his deer,
It was my delight of a shiny night, in the season of the year.

Anon.

ALL
AT
SEA

Dolores Maris

'The earth is large,' said one of twain,
 'The earth is large and wide;
And it is filled with misery
 And death, on every side.'
Said the other: 'Deep as it is wide
 Is the sea, within all climes;
And it is fuller of misery
 And death a thousand times.
The land has peaceful flocks and herds,
 And sweet birds singing round;
But a myriad monstrous, hideous things
 Within the sea are found.
Things all misshapen, slimy, cold,
 Writhing, and strong, and thin;
And water-spouts, and whirlpools wild,
 That draw the fair ships in.
I have heard of divers to the depths
 Of the ocean forced to go,
To bring up pearls and twisted shells
 From the viewless caves below;
I have heard of things in those dismal gulfs,
 Like friends, that hemmed them round:
I would not lead a diver's life
 For every pearl that's found.
I have heard how the sea-snake, huge and dark,
 In the arctic flood doth roll;
He hath coiled his tail, like a cable strong,
 All round and round the Pole.
They say, when he stirs in the sea below,
 The ice-rocks split asunder,
The mountains huge of the ribbed ice,
 With a deafening crack like thunder.

There's many an isle man wots not of,
    Where the air is heavy with groans;
And the floor of the sea, the wisest say,
    Is covered with dead men's bones.
I'll tell thee what: there's many a ship
    In the wild North ocean frore,
That has lain in the ice a thousand years,
    And will lie a thousand more.
And the men – each one is frozen there,
    In the place where he did stand;
The oar he pulled, the rope he threw,
    Is frozen in his hand.
The sun shines there, but it warms them not,
    Their bodies are wintry cold;
They are wrapped in ice that grows and grows,
    All solid, and white, and old.
And there's many a haunted desert rock,
    Where seldom ship doth go,
Where unburied men with fleshless limbs
    Are moving to and fro;
They people the cliffs, they people the caves,
    A ghastly company:
I never sailed there in a ship myself,
    But I know that such there be.
And oh! that hot and horrid tract
    Of the ocean of the Line!
There are millions of the negro men
    Under that burning brine.
The ocean-sea doth moan and moan
    Like an uneasy sprite,
And the waves are wan with a fiendish fire
    That burneth all the night.
'Tis a frightful thing to sail along,
    Though a pleasant wind may blow,
When we think what a host of misery
    Lies down in the sea below.
Didst ever hear of a little boat,
    And in her there were three;
They had nought to eat, and nought to drink,
    Adrift on the desert sea.

For seven days they bore their pain;
   Then two men on the other
Did fix their longing, hungry eyes,
   And that one was their brother.
And him they killed, and ate and drank,
   Oh me! 'twas a horrid thing!
For the dead should lie in a churchyard green,
   Where the fragrant grasses spring.
And thinkest thou, but for mortal sin,
   Such frightful things would be? –
In the land of the New Jerusalem
   There will be no more sea.'

                        Mary Howitt

Honesty in Tatters

This here's what I does – I, d'ye see, forms a notion
   That our troubles, our sorrows and strife,
Are the winds and the billows that foment the ocean,
   As we work through the passage of life.
And for fear on life's sea lest the vessel should founder,
   To lament and to weep, and to wail,
Is a pop gun that tries to outroar a nine-pounder,
   All the same as a whiff in a gale.
Why now I, though hard fortune has pretty near starved me,
   And my togs are all ragged and queer,
Ne'er yet gave the bag to the friend who had served me,
   Or caused ruined beauty a tear.

Now there t'other day, when my messmate deceived me,
   Stole my rhino, my chest, and our Poll,
Do you think in revenge, while their treachery grieved me,
   I a court-martial called? – Not at all.
This here on the matter was my way of arg'ing –
   'Tis true they hadn't left me a cross;
A vile wife and false friend though are gone by the bargain,
   So the gain d'ye see's more than the loss:
For though fortune's a jilt, and has pretty near starved me,

And my togs are all ragged and queer,
I ne'er yet gave the bag to the friend who had served me,
Or caused ruined beauty a tear.

The heart's all – when that's built as it should, sound and clever,
We go 'fore the wind like a fly,
But if rotten and crank, you may luff up forever,
You'll always sail in the wind's eye:
With palaver and nonsense I'm not to be paid off,
I'm adrift, let it blow then great guns,
A gale, a fresh breeze, or the old gemman's head off,
I takes life rough and smooth as it runs:
Content, though hard fortune has pretty near starved me,
And my togs are all ragged and queer;
I ne'er yet gave the bag to a friend who had served me,
Or caused ruined beauty a tear.

Charles Dibdin

On the Famous Voyage

No more let Greece her bolder fables tell
Of Hercules, or Theseus going to hell,
Orpheus, Ulysses; or the Latin muse,
With tales of Troy's just knight, our faiths abuse.
We have a SHELTON, and a HEYDEN got,
Had power to act, what they to feign had not.
All that they boast of Styx, of Acheron,
Cocytus, Phlegethon, ours have proved in one;
The filth, stench, noise: save only what was there
Subtly distinguish'd, was confused here.
Their wherry had no sail too; ours had ne'er one:
And in it, two more horrid knaves than Charon.
Arses were heard to croak instead of frogs;
And for one Cerberus, the whole coast was dogs.
Furies there wanted not; each scold was ten.
And for the cries of ghosts, women and men,
Laden with plague-sores, and their sins, were heard,
Lash'd by their consciences, to die affeard.

Then let the former age with this content her,
She brought the poets forth, but ours th' adventer.

The Voyage Itself

I sing the brave adventure of two wights,
And pity 'tis, I cannot call them knights:
One was; and he for brawn and brain right able
To have been styled of King Arthur's table.
The other was a squire, of fair degree;
But, in the action, greater man than he,
Who gave, to take at his return from hell,
His three for one. Now, lordlings, listen well.

It was the day, what time the powerful moon
Makes the poor Bankside creature wet its shoon,
In its own hall; when these (in worthy scorn
Of those, that put out monies, on return
From Venice, Paris, or some inland passage
Of six times to and fro, without embassage
Or him that backward went to Berwick, or which
Did dance the famous morris unto Norwich)
At Bread-street's Mermaid having dined, and merry,
Proposed to go to Holborn in a wherry:
A harder task, than either his to Bristo',
Or his to Antwerp. Therefore, once more, list ho'.

A dock there is, that called is Avernus
Of some Bridewell, and may, in time, concern us
All, that are readers: but, methinks, 'tis odd
That all this while I have forgot some god,
Or goddess to invoke, to stuff my verse
And with both bombast style and phrase, rehearse
The many perils of this port, and how
Sans help of Sibyl, or a golden bough,
Or magic sacrifice, they past along! –
Alcides, be thou succouring to my song.
Thou hast seen hell, some say, and know'st all nooks there,
Canst tell me best, how every Fury looks there,
And art a god, if fame thee not abuses,

Always at hand, to aid the merry muses.
Great club-fist, though thy back and bones be sore
Still, with thy former labours; yet, once more,
Act a brave work, call it thy last adventry:
But hold my torch, while I describe the entry
To this dire passage. Say, thou stop thy nose;
'Tis but light pains: indeed, this dock's no rose.
In the first jaws appear'd that ugly monster,
Ycleped mud, which, when their oars did once stir,
Belch'd forth an air as hot, as at the muster
Of all your night-tubs, when the carts do cluster,
Who shall discharge first his merd-urinous load:
Thorough her womb they make their famous road,
Between two walls; where, on one side, to scare men,
Were seen your ugly centaurs, ye call carmen,
Gorgonian scolds, and harpies: on the other
Hung stench, diseases, and old filth, their mother,
With famine, wants, and sorrows many a dozen,
The least of which was to the plague a cousin.
But they unfrighted pass, though many a privy
Spake to them louder, than the ox in Livy;
And many a sink pour'd out her rage anenst 'em,
But still their valour and their virtue fenc'd 'em,
And on they went, like Castor brave and Pollux,
Ploughing the main. When, see (the worst of all lucks)
They met the second prodigy, would fear a
Man, that had never heard of a Chimaera.
One said, 'twas bold Briareus, or the beadle,
Who hath the hundred hands when he doth meddle,
The other thought it Hydra, or the rock
Made of the trull that cut her father's lock:
But coming near, they found it but a li'ter,
So huge, it seem'd they could by no means quite her.
Back, cried their brace of Charons: they cried, No,
No going back; on still, you rogues, and row.
How hight the place? A voice was heard, Cocytus.
Row close then, slaves. Alas! they will beshite us.
No matter, stinkards, row. What croaking sound
Is this we hear? of frogs? No, guts wind-bound,
Over your heads: well, row. At this a loud

Crack did report itself, as if a cloud
Had burst with storm, and down fell, *ab excelsis*,
Poor Mercury, crying out on Paracelsus,
And all his followers, that had so abused him;
And in so shitten sort, so long had used him
For (where he was the god of eloquence,
And subtilty of metals) they dispense
His spirits now in pills, and eke in potions,
Suppositories, cataplasms, and lotions. –
But many moons there shall not wane, quoth he,
In the mean time, let them imprison me,
But I will speak, and know I shall be heard,
Touching this cause, where they will be affeard
To answer me: and sure, it was the intent
Of the grave fart, late let in parliament,
Had it been seconded, and not in fume
Vanish'd away: as you must all presume
Their Mercury did now. by this, the stem
Of the hulk touch'd, and, as by Polypheme
The sly Ulysses stole in a sheep-skin,
The well-greased wherry now had got between,
And bade her farewell sough unto the lurden:
Never did bottom more betray her burden;
The meat-boat of Bear's-college, Paris-garden,
Stunk not so ill; nor, when she kiss'd, Kate Arden.
Yet one day in the year, for sweet 'tis voist,
And that is when it is the Lord Mayor's foist.

By this time had they reach'd the Stygian pool,
By which the masters swear, when on the stool
Of worship, they their nodding chins do hit
Against their breasts. Here, several ghosts did flit
About the shore, of farts but late departed,
White, black, blue, green, and in more forms outstarted,
Than all those *atomi* ridiculous
Whereof old Democrite, and Hill Nicholas,
One said, the other swore, the world consists.
These be the cause of those thick frequent mists
Arising in that place, through which, who goes,
Must try the unused valour of a nose:

And that ours did. For, yet, no nare was tainted,
Nor thumb, nor finger to the stop acquainted,
But open and unarm'd, encounter'd all:
Whether it languishing stuck upon the wall,
Or were precipitated down the jakes,
And after, swam abroad in ample flakes,
Or that it lay heap'd like an usurer's mass,
All was to them the same, they were to pass,
And so they did, from Styx to Acheron,
The ever-boiling flood; whose banks upon
Your Fleet-lane Furies, and hot cooks do dwell,
That with still-scalding steams, make the place hell.
The sinks ran grease, and hair of meazled hogs,
The heads, houghs, entrails, and the hides of dogs:
For to say truth, what scullion is so nasty,
To put the skins and offal in a pasty?
Cats there lay divers had been flea'd and roasted,
And after mouldy grown, again were toasted,
Then selling not, a dish was ta'en to mince 'em,
But still, it seem'd, the rankness did convince 'em.
For, here they were thrown in with th' melted pewter,
Yet drown'd they not: they had five lives in future.
But 'mongst these Tiberts, who do you think there was?
Old Banks the juggler, our Pythagoras,
Grave tutor to the learned horse; both which,
Being, beyond sea, burned for one witch,
Their spirits transmigrated to a cat:
And now, above the pool, a face right fat,
With great gray eyes, it lifted up, and mew'd;
Thrice did it spit; thrice dived: at last it view'd
Our brave heroes with a milder glare,
And in a piteous tune, began. How dare
Your dainty nostrils, in so hot a season,
When every clerk eats artichokes and peason,
Laxative lettuce, and such windy meat,
Tempt such a passage? When each privy's seat
Is fill'd with buttock, and the walls do sweat
Urine and plaisters, when the noise doth beat
Upon your ears, of discords so unsweet,
And outcries of the damned in the Fleet?

Cannot the Plague-bill keep you back, nor bells
Of loud Sepulchre's, with their hourly knells,
But you will visit grisly Pluto's hall?
Behold where Cerberus, rear'd on the wall
Of Holborn-height (three serjeants' heads) looks o'er,
And stays but till you come unto the door!
Tempt not his fury, Pluto is away:
And madam Caesar, great Proserpina,
Is now from home; you lose your labours quite,
Were you Jove's sons, or had Alcides' might.
They cry'd out, Puss. He told them he was Banks,
They had so often shew'd them merry pranks.
They laugh'd, at his laugh-worthy fate; and past
The triple-head without a sop. At last,
Calling for Rhadamanthus, that dwelt by,
A soap-boiler: and Aeacus him nigh,
Who kept an ale-house; with my little Minos,
An ancient purblind fletcher, with a high nose;
They took them all to witness of their action:
And so went bravely back without protraction.

In memory of which most liquid deed,
The city since hath raised a pyramid;
And I could wish for their eternized sakes,
My Muse had plough'd with his, that sung A-JAX.

Ben Jonson

The Spouter Inn

CROSSING THIS DUSKY ENTRY, and on through yon low-arched way –
cut through what in old times must have been a great central chimney
with fire-places all round – you enter the public room. A still duskier place
in this, with such low ponderous beams above, and such old wrinkled planks
beneath, that you would almost fancy you trod some old craft's cockpits,
especially of such a howling night, when this corner-anchored old ark
rocked so furiously. On one side stood a long, low, shelf-like table covered
with cracked glass cases, filled with dusty rarities gathered from this wide
world's remotest nooks. Projecting from the further angle of the room

stands a dark-looking den – the bar – a rude attempt at a right whale's head. Be that how it may, there stands the vast arched bone of the whale's jaw, so wide, a coach might almost drive beneath it. Within are shabby shelves, ranged round with old decanters, bottles, flasks; and in those jaws of swift destruction, like another cursed Jonah (by which name indeed they called him), bustles a little withered old man, who, for their money, dearly sells the sailors deliriums and death.

Abominable are the tumblers into which he pours his poison. Though true cylinders without – within, the villanous green goggling glasses deceitfully tapered downwards to a cheating bottom. Parallel meridians rudely pecked into the glass, surround these footpads' goblets. Fill to *this* mark, and your charge is but a penny; to *this* a penny more; and so on to the full glass – the Cape Horn measure, which you may gulp down for a shilling.

Upon entering the place I found a number of young seamen gathered about a table, examining by a dim light divers specimens of *skrimshander*. I sought the landlord, and telling him I desired to be accommodated with a room, received for answer that his house was full – not a bed unoccupied. 'But avast,' he added, tapping his forehead, 'you hain't no objections to sharing a harpooneer's blanket, have ye? I s'pose you are goin' a whalin', so you'd better get used to that sort of thing.'

I told him that I never liked to sleep two in a bed; that if I should ever do so, it would depend upon who the harpooneer might be, and that if he (the landlord) really had no other place for me, and the harpooneer was not decidedly objectionable, why rather than wander further about a strange town on so bitter a night, I would put up with the half of any decent man's blanket.

'I thought so. All right; take a seat. Supper? – you want supper? Supper'll be ready directly.'

I sat down on an old wooden settle, carved all over like a bench on the Battery. At one end a ruminating tar was still further adorning it with his jack-knife, stooping over and diligently working away at the space between his legs. He was trying his hand at a ship under full sail, but he didn't make much headway, I thought.

At last some four or five of us were summoned to our meal in an adjoining room. It was cold as Iceland – no fire at all – the landlord said he couldn't afford it. Nothing but two dismal tallow candles, each in a winding sheet. We were fain to button up our monkey jackets, and hold to our lips cups of scalding tea with our half frozen fingers. But the fare was of the most substantial kind – not only meat and potatoes, but dumplings; good heavens! dumplings for supper! One young fellow in a green box coat addressed himself to these dumplings in a most direful manner.

'My boy,' said the landlord, 'you'll have the nightmare to a dead sartainty.'

'Landlord,' I whispered, 'that ain't the harpooneer, is it?'

'Oh, no,' said he, looking a sort of diabolically funny, 'the harpooner is a dark complexioned chap. He never eats dumplings, he don't – he eats nothing but steaks, and likes 'em rare.'

'The devil he does,' says I. 'Where is that harpooneer? Is he here?'

'He'll be here afore long,' was the answer.

I could not help it, but I began to feel suspicious of this 'dark complexioned' harpooneer. At any rate, I made up my mind that if it so turned out that we should sleep together, he must undress and get into bed before I did.

Supper over, the company went back to the bar-room, when, knowing not what else to do with myself, I resolved to spend the rest of the evening as a looker on.

Presently a rioting noise was heard without. Starting up, the landlord cried, 'That's the Grampus's crew. I seed her reported in the offing this morning; a three years' voyage, and a full ship. Hurrah, boys; now we'll have the latest news from the Feegees.'

A tramping of sea boots was heard in the entry; the door was flung open, and in rolled a wild set of mariners enough. Enveloped in their shaggy watch coats, and with their heads muffled in woollen comforters, all bedarned and ragged, and their beards stiff with icicles, they seemed an eruption of bears from Labrador. They had just landed from their boat, and this was the first house they entered. No wonder, then, that they made a straight wake for the whale's mouth – the bar – when the wrinkled little old Jonah, there officiating, soon poured them out brimmers all round. One complained of a bad cold in his head, upon which Jonah mixed him a pitch-like potion of gin and molasses, which he swore was a sovereign cure for all colds and catarrhs whatsoever, never mind of how long standing, or whether caught off the coast of Labrador, or on the weather side of an ice-island.

The liquor soon mounted into their heads, as it generally does even with the arrantest topers newly landed from sea, and they began capering about most obstreperously.

It was now about nine o'clock, and the room seeming almost supernaturally quiet after these orgies, I began to congratulate myself upon a little plan that had occurred to me just previous to the entrance of the seamen.

No man prefers to sleep two in a bed. In fact, you would a good deal rather not sleep with your own brother. I don't know how it is, but people like to be private when they are sleeping. And when it comes to sleeping with an unknown stranger, in a strange inn, in a strange town, and that stranger a harpooneer, then your objections indefinitely multiply. Nor was there any earthly reason why I as a sailor should sleep two in a bed, more than anybody else; for sailors no more sleep two in a bed at sea, than bachelor kings do ashore. To be sure they all sleep together in one apartment, but you have your own hammock, and cover yourself with your own blanket, and sleep in your own skin.

The more I pondered over this harpooneer, the more I abominated the thought of sleeping with him. It was fair to presume that being a harpooneer, his linen or woollen, as the case might be, would not be of the tidiest, certainly none of the finest. I began to twitch all over. Besides, it was getting late, and my decent harpooneer ought to be home and going bedwards. Suppose now, he should tumble in upon me at midnight – how could I tell from what vile hole he had been coming?

'Landlord! I've changed my mind about that harpooneer – I shan't sleep with him. I'll try the bench here.'

'Just as you please; I'm sorry I can't spare ye a tablecloth for a mattress, and it's a plaguy rough board here' – feeling of the knots and notches. 'But wait a bit, Skrimshander; I've got a carpenter's plane there in the bar – wait, I say, and I'll make ye snug enough.' So saying he procured the plane; and with his old silk handkerchief first dusting the bench, vigorously set to planing away at my bed, the while grinning like an ape. The shavings flew right and left; till at last the plane-iron came bump against an indestructible knot. The landlord was near spraining his wrist, and I told him for heaven's sake to quit – the bed was soft enough to suit me, and I did not know how all the planning in the world could make eider down of a pine plank. So gathering up the shavings with another grin, and throwing them into the great stove in the middle of the room, he went about his business, and left me in a brown study.

I now took the measure of the bench, and found that it was a foot too short; but that could be mended with a chair. But it was a foot too narrow, and the other bench in the room was about four inches higher than the planed one – so there was no yoking them. I then placed the first bench lengthwise along the only clear space against the wall, leaving a little interval between, for my back to settle down in. But I soon found that there came such a draught of cold air over me from under the sill of the window, that this plan would never do at all, especially as another current from the rickety door met the one from the window, and both together formed a series of small whirlwinds in the immediate vicinity of the spot where I had thought to spend the night.

The devil fetch that harpooneer, thought I, but stop, couldn't I steal a march on him – bolt his door inside, and dump into his bed, not to be wakened by the most violent knockings? It seemed no bad idea; but upon second thoughts I dismissed it. For who could tell but what the next morning, so soon as I popped out of the room, the harpooneer might be standing in the entry, all ready to knock me down!

Still, looking round me again, and seeing no possible chance of spending a sufferable night unless in some other person's bed, I began to think that after all I might be cherishing unwarrantable prejudices against this unknown harpooneer. Thinks I, I'll wait awhile; he must be dropping in before long. I'll have a good look at him then, and perhaps we may become jolly good bedfellows after all – there's no telling.

But though the other boarders kept coming in by ones, twos, and threes, and going to bed, yet no sign of my harpooneer.

'Landlord!' said I, 'what sort of a chap is he – does he always keep such late hours?' It was now hard upon twelve o'clock.

The landlord chuckled again with his lean chuckle, and seemed to be mightily tickled at something beyond my comprehension. 'No,' he answered, 'generally he's an early bird – airley to bed and airley to rise – yea, he's the bird what catches the worm. But to-night he went out peddling, you see, and I don't see what on airth keeps him so late, unless, may be, he can't sell his head.'

'Can't sell his head? – What sort of a bamboozlingly story is this you are telling me?' getting into a towering rage. 'Do you pretend to say, landlord, that this harpooneer is actually engaged this blessed Saturday night, or rather Sunday morning, in peddling his head around this town?'

'That's precisely it,' said the landlord, 'and I told him he couldn't sell it here, the market's overstocked.'

'With what?' shouted I.

'With heads to be sure; ain't there too many heads in the world?'

'I tell you what it is, landlord,' said I, quite calmly, 'you'd better stop spinning that yarn to me – I'm not green.'

'May be not,' taking out a stick and whittling a toothpick, 'but I rayther guess you'll be down *brown* if that 'ere harpooneer hears you a slanderin' his head.'

'I'll break it for him,' said I, now flying into a passion again at this unaccountable farrago of the landlord's.

'It's broke a'ready,' said he.

'Broke,' said I – '*broke*, do you mean?'

'Sartain, and that's the very reason he can't sell it, I guess.'

'Landlord,' said I, going up to him as cool as Mt. Hecla in a snow storm – 'landlord, stop whittling. You and I must understand one another and that too without delay. I come to your house and want a bed; you tell me you can only give me half a one; that the other half belongs to a certain harpooneer. And about this harpooneer, whom I have not yet seen, you persist in telling me the most mystifying and exasperating stories, tending to beget in me an uncomfortable feeling towards the man whom you design for my bedfellow – a sort of connexion, landlord, which is an intimate and confidential one in the highest degree. I now demand of you to speak out and tell me who and what this harpooneer is, and whether I shall be in all respects safe to spend the night with him. And in the first place, you will be so good as to unsay that story about selling his head, which if true I take to be good evidence that this harpooneer is stark mad, and I've no idea of sleeping with a madman; and you, sir, *you* I mean, landlord, *you*, sir, by trying to induce me to do so knowingly, would thereby render yourself liable to a criminal prosecution.'

'Wall,' said the landlord, fetching a long breath, 'that's a purty long sarmon for a chap that rips a little now and then. But be easy, be easy, this here harpooneer I have been tellin' you of has just arrived from the south seas, where he bought up a lot of 'balmed New Zealand heads (great curios, you know), and he's sold all on 'em, but one, and that one he's trying to sell to-night, cause to-morrow's Sunday, and it would not do to be sellin' human heads about the streets when folks is goin' to churches. He wanted to, last Sunday, but I stopped him just as he was goin' out of the door with four heads strung on a string, for all the airth like a string of inions.'

This account cleared up the otherwise unaccountable mystery, and showed that the landlord, after all, had had no idea of fooling me – but at the same time what could I think of a harpooneer who stayed out of a Saturday night clean into the holy Sabbath, engaged in such a cannibal business as selling the heads of dead idolators?

'Depend upon it, landlord, that harpooneer is a dangerous man.'

'He pays reg'lar,' was the rejoiner. 'But come, it's getting dreadful late, you had better be turning flukes – it's a nice bed: Sal and me slept in that 'ere bed the night we were spliced. There's plenty room for two to kick about in that bed; it's an almighty big bed that. Why, afore we give it up, Sal used to put our Sam and little Johnny in the foot of it. But I got a dreaming and sprawling about one night, and somehow, Sam got pitched on the floor, and came near breaking his arm. Arter that, Sal said it wouldn't do. Come along here, I'll give ye a glim in a jiffy', and so saying he lighted a candle and held it towards me, offering to lead the way. But I stood irresolute; when looking at a clock in the corner, he exclaimed 'I vum it's Sunday – you won't see that harpooneer to-night; he's come to anchor somewhere – come along then; *do* come; *won't* ye come?'

I considered the matter a moment, and then up stairs we went, and I was ushered into a small room, cold as a clam, and furnished, sure enough, with a prodigious bed, almost big enough indeed for any four harpooneers to sleep abreast.

'There,' said the landlord, placing the candle on a crazy old sea chest that did double duty as a wash-stand and centre table; 'there, make yourself comfortable now, and good night to ye.' I turned round from eyeing the bed, but he had disappeared.

Folding back the counterpane, I stooped over the bed. Though none of the most elegant, it yet stood the scrutiny tolerably well. I then glanced round the room; and besides the bedstead and centre table, could see no other furniture belonging to the place, but a rude shelf, the four walls, and a papered fireboard representing a man striking a whale. Of things not properly belonging to the room, there was a hammock lashed up, and thrown upon the floor in one corner; also a large seaman's bag, containing the harpooneer's wardrobe, no doubt in lieu of a land trunk. Likewise, there was a parcel of outlandish bone fish hooks on the shelf over the fire-place, and a tall harpoon standing at the head of the bed.

But what is this on the chest? I took it up, and held it close to the light, and felt it, and smelt it, and tried every way possible to arrive at some satisfactory conclusion concerning it. I can compare it to nothing but a large door mat, ornamented at the edges with little tinkling tags something like the stained porcupine quills round an Indian moccasin. There was a hole or slit in the middle of this mat, as you see the same in South American ponchos. But could it be possible that any sober harpooneer would get into a door mat, and parade the streets of any Christian town in that sort of guise? I put it on, to try it, and it weighed me down like a hamper, being uncommonly shaggy and thick, and I thought a little damp, as though this mysterious harpooneer had been wearing it of a rainy day. I went up in it to a bit of glass stuck against the wall, and I never saw such a sight in my life. I tore myself out of it in such a hurry that I gave myself a kink in the neck.

I sat down on the side of the bed, and commenced thinking about this head-peddling harpooneer, and his door mat. After thinking some time on the bedside, I got up and took off my monkey jacket, and then stood in the middle of the room thinking. I then took off my coat, and thought a little more in my shirt sleeves. But beginning to feel very cold now, half undressed as I was, and remembering what the landlord said about the harpooneer's not coming home at all that night, it being so very late, I made no more ado, but jumped out of my pantaloons and boots, and then blowing out the light tumbled into bed, and commended myself to the care of heaven.

Whether that mattress was stuffed with corn-cobs or broken crockery, there is no telling, but I rolled about a good deal, and could not sleep for a long time. At last I slid off into a light doze, and had pretty nearly made a good offing towards the land of Nod, when I heard a heavy footfall in the passage, and saw a glimmer of light come into the room from under the door.

Lord save me, thinks I, that must be the harpooneer, the infernal head-peddler. But I lay perfectly still, and resolved not to say a word till spoken to. Holding a light in one hand, and that identical New Zealand head in the other, the stranger entered the room, and without looking towards the bed, placed his candle a good way off from me on the floor in one corner, and then began working away at the knotted cords of the large bag I before spoke of as being in the room. I was all eagerness to see his face, but he kept it averted for some time while employed in unlacing the bag's mouth. This accomplished, however, he turned round – when, good heavens! what a sight! Such a face! It was of a dark, purplish, yellow color, here and there stuck over with large, blackish looking squares. Yes, it's just as I thought, he's a terrible bedfellow; he's been in a fight, got dreadfully cut, and here he is, just from the surgeon. But at that moment he chanced to turn his face so towards the light, that I plainly saw they could not be sticking-plasters at all, those black squares on his cheeks. They were stains of some sort or other. At first I knew not what to make of this; but soon an inkling of the truth occurred to me. I remembered a story of a white man – a whaleman too – who, falling among the cannibals, had been tattooed by them. I concluded that this hapooneer, in the course of his distant voyages, must have met with a similar adventure. And what is it, thought I, after all! It's only his outside; a man can be honest in any sort of skin. But then, what to make of his unearthly complexion, that part of it, I mean, lying round about, and completely independent of the squares of tattooing. To be sure, it might be nothing but a good coat of tropical tanning; but I never heard of a hot sun's tanning a white man into a purplish yellow one. However, I had never been in the South Seas; and perhaps the sun there produced these extraordinary effects upon the skin. Now, while all these ideas were passing through me like lightning, this harpooneer never noticed me at all. But, after some difficulty having opened his bag, he commenced fumbling in it, and presently pulled out a sort of tomahawk, and a seal-skin wallet with the hair on. Placing these on the old chest in the middle of the room, he then took the New Zealand head – a ghastly thing enough – and crammed it down into the bag. He now took off his hat – a new beaver hat – when I came nigh singing out with fresh surprise. There was no hair on his head – none to speak of at least – nothing but a small scalp-knot twisted up on his forehead. His bald purplish head now looked for all the world like a mildewed skull. Had not the stranger stood between me and the door, I would have bolted out of it quicker than ever I bolted a dinner.

Even as it was, I thought something of slipping out of the window, but it was the second floor back. I am no coward, but what to make of this head-peddling purple rascal altogether passed my comprehension. Ignorance is the parent of fear, and being completely nonplussed and confounded about the stranger, I confess I was now as much afraid of him as if it was the devil himself who had thus broken into my room at the dead of night. In fact, I was so afraid of him that I was not game enough just then to address him, and demand a satisfactory answer concerning what seemed inexplicable in him.

Meanwhile, he continued the business of undressing, and at last showed his chest and arms. As I live, these covered parts of him were checkered with the same squares as his face; his back, too, was all over the same dark squares; he seemed to have been in a Thirty Years' War, and just escaped from it with a sticking-plaster shirt. Still more, his very legs were marked, as if a parcel of dark green frogs were running up the trunks of young palms. It was now quite plain that he must be some abominable savage or other shipped aboard of a whaleman in the South Seas, and so landed in this Christian country. I quaked to think of it. A peddler of heads too – perhaps the heads of his own brothers. He might take a fancy to mine – heavens! look at that tomahawk!

But there was no time for shuddering, for now the savage went about something that completely fascinated my attention, and convinced me that he must indeed be a heathen. Going to his heavy grego, or wrapall, or dreadnaught, which he had previously hung on a chair, he fumbled in the pockets, and produced at length a curious little deformed image with a hunch on its back, and exactly the color of a three days' old Congo baby. Remembering the embalmed head, at first I almost thought that this black manikin was a real baby preserved in some similar manner. But seeing that it was not at all limber, and that it glistened a good deal like polished ebony,

I concluded that it must be nothing but a wooden idol, which indeed it proved to be. For now the savage goes up to the empty fire-place, and removing the papered fire-board, sets up this little hunch-backed image, like a tenpin, between the andirons. The chimney jambs and all the bricks inside were very sooty, so that I thought this fire-place made a very appropriate little shrine or chapel for his Congo idol.

I now screwed my eyes hard towards the half hidden image, feeling but ill at ease meantime – to see what was next to follow. First he takes about a double handful of shavings out of his grego pocket, and places them carefully before the idol; then laying a bit of ship biscuit on top and applying the flame from the lamp, he kindled the shavings into a sacrificial blaze. Presently, after many hasty snatches into the fire, and still hastier withdrawals of his fingers (whereby he seemed to be scorching them badly), he at last succeeded in drawing out the biscuit; then blowing off the heat and ashes a little, he made a polite offer of it to the little negro. But the little devil did not seem to fancy such dry sort of fare at all – he never moved his lips. All these strange antics were accompanied by still stranger guttural noises from the devotee, who seemed to be praying in a sing-song or else singing some pagan psalmody or other, during which his face twitched about in the most unnatural manner. At last extinguishing the fire, he took the idol up very unceremoniously, and bagged it again in his grego pocket as carelessly as if he were a sportsman bagging a dead woodcock.

All these queer proceedings increased my uncomfortableness, and seeing him now exhibiting strong symptoms of concluding his business operations, and jumping into bed with me, I thought it was high time, now or never, before the light was put out, to break the spell in which I had so long been bound.

But the interval I spent in deliberating what to say was a fatal one. Taking up his tomahawk from the table, he examined the head of it for an instant, and then holding it to the light, with his mouth at the handle, he puffed out great clouds of tobacco smoke. The next moment the light was extinguished, and this wild cannibal, tomahawk between his teeth, sprang into bed with me. I sang out, I could not help it now; and giving a sudden grunt of astonishment he began feeling me.

Stammering out something, I knew not what, I rolled away from him against the wall, and then conjured him, whoever or whatever he might be, to keep quiet, and let me get up and light the lamp again. But his guttural responses satisfied me at once that he but ill comprehended my meaning.

'Who-e debel you?' – he at last said – 'you no speak-e, dam-me, I kill-e.' And so saying the lighted tomahawk began flourishing about me in the dark.

'Landlord, for God's sake, Peter Coffin!' shouted I. 'Landlord! Watch! Come! Angels! save me!'

'Speak-e! tell-ee me who-ee be, or dam-me, I kill-e!' again growled the cannibal, while his horrid flourishings of the tomahawk scattered the hot tobacco ashes about me till I thought my linen would get on fire. But thank heaven, at that moment the landlord came into the room light in hand, and leaping from the bed I ran up to him.

'Don't be afraid now,' said he, grinning again. 'Queequeg here wouldn't harm of hair of your head.'

'Stop your grinning,' shouted I, 'and why didn't you tell me that that infernal harpooneer was a cannibal?'

'I thought ye know'd it; – didn't I tell ye, he was a peddlin' heads around town? – but turn flukes again and go to sleep. Queequeg, look here – you sabbee me, I sabbee you – this man sleepe you – you sabbee?'

'Me sabbee plenty' – grunted Queequeg, puffing away at his pipe and sitting up in bed.

'You gettee in,' he added, motioning to me with his tomahawk, and throwing the clothes to one side. He really did this in not only a civil but a really kind and charitable way. I stood looking at him a moment. For all his tattooings he was on the whole a clean, comely looking cannibal. What's all this fuss I have been making about, thought I to myself – the man's a human being just as I am: he has just as much reason to fear me, as I have to be afraid of him. Better sleep with a sober cannibal than a drunken Christian.

'Landlord,' said I, 'tell him to stash his tomahawk there, or pipe, or whatever you call it; tell him to stop smoking, in short, and I will turn in with him. But I don't fancy having a man smoking in bed with me. It's dangerous. Besides, I ain't insured.'

This being told to Queequeg, he at once complied, and again politely motioned me to get into bed – rolling over to one side as much as to say – I wont touch a leg of ye.

'Good night, landlord,' said I, 'you may go.'

I turned in, and never slept better in my life.

From *Moby Dick* by Herman Melville

Janet Fisher

Where Janet Fisher lived and died,
  The Eastland marshes reach away
For miles on miles of either side,
A river desolately wide
  That is itself as drear as they.

With tufts of purple marish flowers
  The rough grey grass is islanded;
The travelling thunder broods for hours
In gathered purple, when there lowers
  The frequent tempest overhead.

Immense the eternal arch of sky;
  Immense – utterly barren, too –
The plain in which no mountains lie
To mar that vastness, bounded by
  The far horizon's shadowy blue.

Only the river's gradual bend
  Shows stunted willows set in rows,
Rank pasture, kine the children tend,
Blown curls of smoke that swerve and ascend
  From leaning hovels clustered close.

For on this barren anguish swamp,
  Even here is life, even here are men
To shake with palsy, stiffen with cramp,
To die ere fifty of the damp
  And fetid vapours of the fen.

Though how a village came to grow
  In such a vile and deathly air,
None knows; it may be long ago
The outcast of some crime or woe,
  Fleeing for refuge, sheltered there;

And through the habit of their race
  Or fearing yet the wrath of men,
Their children settled in the place,
And reaped scant harvest, in the face
  Of death, upon the poisonous fen.

And since the end was always near,
  And life so hard; and since they knew,
Save sloth and lust, no joys; each year
They served their senses less in fear,
  And more like beasts and viler grew.

Few friends were there, tho' all were kin
  There was much strife, and many raids;
The hovels that they huddled in
Housed men whose brutal love was sin,
  Nameless children, and shameless maids.

Even among this soulless herd
  Lived Janet Fisher; but she went
Along their streets, and no man stirred
Her quiet heart with look or word
  To harm the village Innocent.

They meant she was an idiot born,
  This one fair sight in foulest place;
This girl as fresh as early morn;
So fair – and yet too sad to scorn;
  Too sunk for any hind to embrace.

Their one fair thing; their one thing good,
  And she bereft of sense or will,
So were a mask of womanhood –
Sad, – but there was no heart to brood,
  Upon the irremediable ill.

Yet crazy Janet found them kind –
  They took her when her mother died
To live by turn with each; to wind
Their well-ropes, bind their sheaves, and mind
  Their cattle grazing far and wide.

Yet often by the river-brim
   She strayed, scattering seeds and flowers,
To wade in clear green shallows, and swim
Against the stream; or, through the dim
   And quiet twilight, row for hours.

Day long, night long, her spirit slept,
   And nothing shook the sullen drowse;
Yet oft a shadowy pleasure crept
All through her, where the boats were kept,
   Beneath the dangling willow boughs.

She was so strong, she liked to feel
   Her rapid stroke lend wings to the boat;
The water dashing against the keel;
The wind in her face and hair; the teal
   And plovers crying; the weeds afloat.

Then only she – who was so far
   Behind the merest child of all –
Was prouder, stronger, than others are;
And she could row to the harbour bar
   And back, ten miles, ere night-dews fall.

PART II

But all the harvest long, forlorn,
   Unloosed, the boat rocked to and fro,
While Janet slept from eve till morn,
Dead-tired with gathering in the corn
   From daybreak till the light was low.

How glad she was when autumn whirled
   The slender yellowing willow leaves,
When all the plants looked shrivelled and curled,
And no more corn or fruit in the world
   Was left to gather under eaves.

For then one evening, when the plain
   Was strangely bright i' the sun, and black
With thunder and unfallen rain
The sky, she sought her boat again,
   And bent the yielding branches back –

The thinning willow boughs – and found
   A man, half-stripped, beside the boat,
Burying hurriedly underground
And heaping yellow leaves around
   A stained and faded soldier's coat.

She stood beside him, nothing loth
   To watch his work unseen a span,
For she was neither scared nor wroth;
The splendour of the scarlet cloth
   Engrossed her, not the ragged man.

'Give me it!' eager Janet said
   At last; the man who heard her shook
Alarmed, and turned his startled head.
He was as wan and grey as the dead,
   And even Janet feared his look.

'All's up,' he moaned. 'Ay, call them out!
   I'm spent, you're strong,' he moaned; – 'hit hard,
I'm doun. Don't stare so, woman; shout!
Why, don't you know what you're about?
   I'm a deserter – there's reward.

'I'm spent.' But towards the scarlet coat
   He saw unheeding Janet go;
Then turned, and turning saw the boat,
'Oh, God!' he cried, with straining throat,
   'Girl, will you help me?' 'I can row.'

Poor Janet – all those prayers were vain
   To reach the incommunicable
Dim soul in her; and yet 'twas plain
He wished her, prayed her, to remain –
   And one thing only she could do well.

She smiled. Her masters on the fen
   Bade her: Do this, bear such a load,
Go there – for they were brutish men.
But this man spake her fair; and then
   She longed to show how well she rowed.

Within her boat she took her stand;
   He followed her unquestioningly,
Got in, sat down, at her command;
She pushed her boat off from the land,
   And, with the current, sought the sea.

Fierce yellow sunlight, beetling clouds
   Heaped up in blackness overhead;
Still air in which the beasts were cowed,
And all the sounds were over-loud –
   Yet Janet felt no thrill of dread.

Inland the sea-mews fled, that know
   The earliest tempest-mutterings;
The swallows, skimming very low,
Dipped, and a livid western glow
   Glanced off their sheeny underwings.

On through the ominous dusk the bark
   That knew no fear, that had no soul,
Made for the sea. How should it hark
The wind, or see the air grow dark
   Or feel the widening waters roll?

And soulless as itself, and rash,
   Janet rowed on elate and proud;
And thankful to escape the lash,
Her fellow heard no waters dash,
   And did not see the gathering cloud.

Speechless he drowsed for many a mile,
   Sunk to inert fatigue, half dead;
At last: 'It takes a long, long while,'
He muttered. Janet turned – her smile
   Filled all his veins with sudden dread.

He started, shook the torpid drowse
   Off him like water; all around
The river heaved in waves; and soughs
And moans of wind began to arouse
   The storm; he could not see the ground.

Black walls of stormy air shut in
   The boat; above, a gloomy vault
Shattered by lightning; roar and din
Where sea and hurtling stream begin
   Their desperate, endless rebuff and assault.

'Woman!' he shouted; 'mad-woman! speak, –
   Why did you let me sleep so long?
Is it the sea, the sea, you seek?'
The tears fell into the spray on her cheek:
   'Help me,' she wailed; 'I'm spent, you're strong.'

His words! his prayer! No safety, then,
   If she were mad; no means to avert
The end. Far backwards lay the fen,
And here, instead of a world of men,
   A danger no man shall desert.

Had she gone mad, perhaps, from fright,
   This woman? 'Oh, my God!' he cried;
'To be alone at sea by night;
Lost in a storm – no hope, no light;
   A maniac for my only guide!'

She crouched upon the lowest plank
   And cried, and dashed her hands in the wave
That drenched her dress, and made so lank,
And straight her hair – that slowly sank
   Them down towards the engulfing grave.

The man stooped down and looked at her,
   Half-blind with swirling spray of the sea.
Horror, impotent wrath, despair
At heart. What did she say? A prayer?
   'Poor crazy Janet; pity me!'

Then he was lost in very truth –
  How wild his hope! how vain his trust!
This woman – this, his angel of ruth –
Had lured him to his death; in sooth,
  To kill her would be merely just.

Should he kill her? Sea and sky,
  In answering storms heaved up, hung down;
They seemed to touch, they met so nigh,
One moment more all else must die:
  Why should he kill her? Let her drown!

'Help me!' she shrieked. But who could swim
  In such a sea, – a toppling bank
Of waves. She sprang, and clung to him,
Then noise, hate, storm, death, all grew dim;
  He caught her – tried to save her – sank.

But when the storm was stilled at last,
  The fishers found him on the strand,
One arm stretched out, still battling past
The waves, it seemed, and clasping fast
  A woman's corpse with one stiff hand.

They knew him not, but her they knew
  Poor Janet, missed a day and night,
Then wind-uncovered, stained with dew,
They found the coat; the wonder grew,
  And the sad story came to light.

A. Mary F. Robinson

The Mutiny on the Bounty

The following account puts Captain Bligh in a considerably better light than the film versions we are all familiar with.

The Mutiny

'IN THE MORNING of the 28th April [1789], the north-westernmost of the Friendly Islands, called Tofoa, bearing north-east, I was steering to the westward with a ship in most perfect order, all my plants in a most flourishing condition, all my men and officers in good health; and, in short, everything to flatter and insure my most sanguine expectations. On leaving the deck I gave directions for the course to be steered during the night. The master had the first watch; the gunner, the middle watch; and Mr Christian, the morning watch. This was the turn of duty for the night.

'Just before sunrising on Tuesday the 28th, while I was yet asleep, Mr Christian, officer of the watch, Charles Churchill, ship's corporal, John Mills, gunner's mate, and Thomas Burkitt, seaman, came into my cabin, and, seizing me, tied my hands with a cord behind my back, threatening me with instant death if I spoke or made the least noise. I called, however, as loud as I could, in hopes of assistance; but they had already secured the officers who were not of their party, by placing sentinels at their doors. There were three men at my cabin door, besides the four within; Christian had only a cutlass in his hand, the others had muskets and bayonets. I was hauled out of bed, and forced on deck in my shirt, suffering great pain from the tightness with which they had tied my hands behind my back, held by Fletcher Christian, and Charles Churchill, with a bayonet at my breast, and two men, Alexander Smith and Thomas Burkitt, behind me, with loaded muskets cocked and bayonets fixed. I demanded the reason of such violence, but received no other answer than abuse for not holding my tongue. The master, the gunner, Mr Elphinstone, the master's mate, and Nelson, were kept confined below; and the fore-hatchway was guarded by sentinels. The boatswain and carpenter, and also Mr Samuel the clerk, were allowed to come upon deck, where they saw me standing abaft the mizen-mast, with my hands tied behind my back, under a guard, with Christian at their head. The boatswain was ordered to hoist the launch out, with a threat, if he did not do it instantly, to take care of himself.

'When the boat was out, Mr Hayward and Mr Hallet, two of the midshipmen, and Mr Samuel, were ordered into it. I demanded what their intention was in giving this order, and endeavoured to persuade the people near me not to persist in such acts of violence; but it was to no effect – "Hold your tongue, sir, or you are dead this instant," was constantly repeated to me.

'The master by this time had sent to request that he might come on deck, which was permitted; but he was soon ordered back again to his cabin.

'When I exerted myself in speaking loud, to try if I could rally any with a sense of duty in them, I was saluted with "D—n his eyes, the — , blow his brains out"; while Christian was threatening me with instant death if I did not hold my tongue.

'I continued my endeavours to turn the tide of affairs, when Christian changed the cutlass which he had in his hand for a bayonet that was brought to him, and, holding me with a strong grip by the cord that tied my hands, he threatened, with many oaths, to kill me immediately, if I would not be quiet; the villains round me had their pieces cocked and bayonets fixed. Particular persons were called on to go into the boat, and were hurried over the side; whence I concluded that with these people I was to be set adrift. I therefore made another effort to bring about a change, but with no other effect than to be threatened with having my brains blown out.

'The boatswain and seamen who were to go in the boat were allowed to collect twine, canvas, lines, sails, cordage, and an eight-and-twenty-gallon cask of water; and Mr Samuel got one hundred and fifty pounds of bread, with a small quantity of rum and wine, also a quadrant and compass; but he was forbidden, on pain of death, to touch either map, ephemeris, book of astronomical observations, sextant, timekeeper, or any of my surveys or drawings.

'The mutineers having forced those of the seamen whom they meant to get rid of into the boat, Christian directed a dram to be served to each of his own crew. I then unhappily saw that nothing could be done to effect the recovery of the ship: there was no one to assist me, and every endeavour on my part was answered with threats of death.

'The officers were next called upon deck, and forced over the side into the boat, while I was kept apart from every one, abaft the mizen-mast; Christian, armed with a bayonet, holding me by the bandage that secured my hands. The guard round me had their pieces cocked; but on my daring the ungrateful wretches to fire, they uncocked them.

'Isaac Martin, one of the guard over me, I saw, had an inclination to assist me, and, as he fed me with shaddock (my lips being quite parched), we explained our wishes to each other by our looks; but this being observed, Martin was removed from me. He then attempted to leave the ship, for which purpose he got into the boat; but with many threats they obliged him to return.

'The armourer, Joseph Coleman, and two of the carpenters, McIntosh and Norman, were also kept contrary to their inclination; and they begged of me, after I was astern in the boat, to remember that they declared they had no hand in the transaction. Michael Byrne, I am told, likewise wanted to leave the ship.

'It is of no moment for me to recount my endeavours to bring back the offenders to a sense of their duty; all I could do was by speaking to them in general; but it was to no purpose, for I was kept securely bound, and no one except the guard suffered to come near me.

'To Mr Samuel (clerk) I am indebted for securing my journals and commission, with some material ship papers. Without these I had nothing to certify what I had done, and my honour and character might have been suspected, without my possessing a proper document to have defended them. All this he did with great resolution, though guarded and strictly watched. He attempted to save the timekeeper, and a box with my surveys, drawings, and remarks for fifteen years past, which were numerous; when he was hurried away with "D—n your eyes, you are well off to get what you have."

'It appeared to me that Christian was some time in doubt whether he should keep the carpenter or his mates: at length he determined on the latter, and the carpenter was ordered into the boat. He was permitted, but not without some opposition to take his tool chest.

'Much altercation took place among the mutinous crew during the whole business: some swore, "I'll be d—d if he does not find his way home, if he gets anything with him"; and when the carpenter's chest was carrying away, "D—n my eyes, he will have a vessel built in a month"; while others laughed at the helpless situation of the boat, being very deep, and so little room for those who were in her. As for Christian, he seemed as if meditating destruction on himself and every one else.

'I asked for arms; but they laughed at me, and said I was well acquainted with the people among whom I was going, and therefore did not want them; four cutlasses, however, were thrown into the boat after we were veered astern.

'The officers and men being in the boat, they only waited for me, of which the master-at-arms informed Christian; who then said, "Come, Captain Bligh, your officers and men are now in the boat, and you must go with them; if you attempt to make the least resistance, you will instantly be put to death"; and, without further ceremony, with a tribe of armed ruffians about me, I was forced over the side, when they untied my hands. Being in the boat, we were veered astern by a rope. A few pieces of pork were thrown to us, and some clothes, also the cutlasses I have already mentioned; and it was then that the armourer and carpenters called out to me to remember that they had no hand in the transaction. After having undergone a great deal of ridicule, and been kept for some time to make sport for these unfeeling wretches, we were at length cast adrift in the open ocean.'

The Open-Boat Navigation

Christian had intended to send away his captain and associates in the cutter, and ordered that it should be hoisted out for that purpose, which was done: a small wretched boat, that could hold but eight or ten men at the most, with a very small additional weight; and what was still worse, she was so worm-eaten and decayed, especially in the bottom planks, that the probability was, she would have gone down before she had proceeded a mile from the ship. In this 'rotten carcass of a boat', not unlike that into which Prospero and his lovely daughter were 'hoist',

<blockquote>

'not rigged,
Nor tackle, sail, nor mast; the very rats
Instinctively had quit it,'
</blockquote>

did Christian intend to cast adrift his late commander and his eighteen innocent companions, or as many of them as she would stow, to find, as they inevitably must have found, a watery grave. But the remonstrances of the master, boatswain, and carpenter prevailed on him to let those unfortunate men have the launch, into which nineteen persons were thrust, whose weight, together with that of the few articles they were permitted to take, brought down the boat so near to the water as to endanger her sinking with but a moderate swell of the sea, and, to all human appearance, in no state to survive the length of voyage they were destined to perform over the wide ocean, but which they did most miraculously survive.

The first consideration of Lieutenant Bligh and his eighteen unfortunate companions, on being cast adrift in their open boat, was to examine the state of their resources. The quantity of provisions which they found to have been thrown into the boat, by some few kind-hearted messmates, amounted to one hundred and fifty pounds of bread, sixteen pieces of pork, each weighing two pounds, six quarts of rum, six bottles of wine, with twenty-eight gallons of water, and four empty barricoes. Being so near to the island of Tofoa, it was resolved to seek there a supply of breadfruit and water, to preserve if possible, the above-mentioned stock entire; but after rowing along the coast, they discovered only some cocoanut trees on the top of high precipices, from which, with much danger, owing to the surf, and great difficulty in climbing the cliffs, they succeeded in obtaining about twenty nuts. The second day they made excursions into the island, but without success. They met, however, with a few natives, who came down with them to the cove where the boat was lying; and others presently followed. They made inquiries after the ship, and Bligh unfortunately advised they should say that the ship had overset and sunk, and that they only were saved. The story might be innocent, but it was certainly indiscreet to put the people in possession of their defenceless situation; however, they brought in small quantities of breadfruit, plantain, and cocoanuts, but little or no water could be procured. These supplies, scanty as they were, served to keep up the spirits of the men: 'They no longer,' says Bligh, 'regarded me with those anxious looks, which had constantly been directed towards me, since we lost sight of the ship: every countenance appeared to have a degree of cheerfulness, and they all seemed determined to do their best.'

The numbers of the natives having so much increased as to line the whole beach, they began knocking stones together, which was known to be the preparatory signal for an attack. With some difficulty on account of the surf, the seamen succeeded in getting the things that were on shore into the boat, together with all the men, except John Norton, quartermaster, who was casting off the stern-fast. The natives immediately rushed upon this poor man, and actually stoned him to death. A volley of stones was also discharged at the boat, and every one in it was more or less hurt. This induced the people to push out to sea with all the speed they were able to give to the launch; but, to their surprise and alarm, several canoes, filled with stones, followed close after them and renewed the attack; against which, the only return the unfortunate men in the boat could make, was with the stones of the assailants that lodged in her; a species of warfare in which they were very inferior to the Indians. The only expedient left was to tempt the enemy to desist from the pursuit, by throwing overboard some clothes, which fortunately induced the canoes to stop and pick them up; and night coming on, they returned to the shore, leaving the party in the boat to reflect on their unhappy situation.

The men now entreated their commander to take them towards home; and on being told that no hope of relief could be entertained till they reached Timor, a distance of full twelve hundred leagues, they all readily agreed to be content with an allowance, which, on calculation of their resources, the commander informed them would not exceed one ounce of bread, and a quarter of a pint of water, per day. Recommending them, therefore, in the most solemn manner, not to depart from their promise in this respect, 'we bore away,' says Bligh, 'across a sea where the navigation is but little known, in a small boat twenty-three feet long from stem to stern, deeply laden with eighteen men. I was happy, however, to see that every one seemed better satisfied with our situation than myself. It was about eight o'clock at night on the 2nd May, when we bore away under a reefed lug-foresail; and having divided the people into watches, and got the boat into a little order, we returned thanks to God for our miraculous preservation; and, in full confidence of His gracious support, I found my mind more at east than it had been for some time past.'

At daybreak on the 3rd, the forlorn and almost hopeless navigators saw with alarm the sun to rise fiery and red, a sure indication of a severe gale of wind; and, accordingly, at eight o'clock it blew a violent storm, and the sea ran so very high that the sail was becalmed when between the seas, and too much to have set when on the top of the sea; yet it is stated that they could not venture to take it in, as they were in very imminent danger and distress, the sea curling over the stern of the boat, and obliging them to bale with all their might. 'A situation,' observes the commander, 'more distressing has, perhaps, seldom been experienced.'

The bread, being in bags, was in the greatest danger of being spoiled by the wet, the consequence of which, if not prevented, must have been fatal, as the whole party would inevitably be starved to death, if they should fortunately escape the fury of the waves. It was determined, therefore, that all superfluous clothes, with some rope and spare sails, should be thrown overboard, by which the boat was considerably lightened. The carpenter's tool chest was cleared, and the tools stowed in the bottom of the boats and the bread secured in the chest. All the people being thoroughly wet and cold, a teaspoonful of rum was served out to each person, with a quarter of a breadfruit, which was stated to have been scarcely eatable, for dinner. Bligh having determined to preserve sacredly, and at the peril of his life, the engagement they entered into, and to make their small stock of provisions last eight weeks, let the daily proportion be ever so small.

The sea continuing to run even higher than in the morning, the fatigue of baling became very great; the boat was necessarily kept before the sea. The men were constantly wet, the night very cold, and at daylight their limbs were so benumbed that they could scarcely find the use of them. At this time a teaspoonful of rum served out to each person was found of great benefit to all. Five small cocoanuts were distributed for dinner, and every one was satisfied; and in the evening, a few broken pieces of breadfruit were served for supper, after which prayers were performed.

On the night of the 4th and morning of the 5th, the gale had abated; the first step to be taken was to examine the state of the bread, a great part of which was found to be damaged and rotten but even this was carefully preserved for use. The boat was now running among some islands, but, after their reception at Tofoa, they did not venture to land. On the 6th, they still continued to see islands at a distance; and this day, for the first time, they hooked a fish, to their great joy; 'but,' says the commander, 'we were miserably disappointed by its being lost in trying to get it into the boat.' In the evening, each person had an ounce of the damaged bread, and a quarter of a pint of water, for supper.

Lieutenant Bligh observes, 'It will readily be supposed our lodgings were very miserable, and confined for want of room'; but he endeavoured to remedy the latter defect by putting themselves at watch and watch; so that one half always sat up, while the other lay down on the boat's bottom or upon a chest, but with nothing to cover them except the heavens. Their limbs, he says, were dreadfully cramped, for they could not stretch them out; and the nights were so cold, and they were so constantly wet, that, after a few hours' sleep, they were scarcely able to move. At dawn of day on the 7th, being very wet and cold, he says, 'I served a spoonful of rum and a morsel of bread for breakfast.'

In the course of this day they passed close to some rocky isles, from which two large sailing canoes came swiftly after them, but in the afternoon gave over the chase. They were of the same construction as those of the Friendly Islands, and the land seen for the last two days was supposed to be the Fiji Islands. But being constantly wet, Bligh says, 'It is with the utmost difficulty I can open a book to write; and I feel truly sensible I can do no more than point out where these lands are to be found, and give some idea of their extent.' Heavy rain came on in the afternoon, when every person in the boat did his utmost to catch some water, and thus succeeded in increasing their stock to thirty-four gallons, besides quenching their thirst for the first time they had been able to do so since they had been at sea: but it seems an attendant consequence of the heavy rain caused them to pass the night very miserably; for being extremely wet, and having no dry things to shift or cover themselves, they experienced cold and shiverings scarcely to be conceived.

On the 8th, the allowance issued was an ounce and a half of pork, a teaspoonful of rum, half a pint of cocoanut milk, and an ounce of bread. The rum, though so small in quantity, is stated to have been of the greatest service. In the afternoon they were employed in cleaning out the boat, which occupied them until sunset before they got everything dry and in order. 'Hitherto,' Bligh says, 'I had issued the allowance by guess; but I now made a pair of scales with two cocoanut shells; and having accidentally some pistol balls in the boat, twenty-five of which weighed one pound or sixteen ounces, I adopted one of these balls as the proportion of weight that each person should receive of bread at the times I served it. I also amused all hands with describing the situations of New Guinea and New Holland, and gave them every information in my power, that in case any accident should happen to me, those who survived might have some idea of what they were about, and be able to find their way to Timor, which at present they knew nothing of more than the name, and some not even that. At night I served a quarter of a pint of water and half an ounce of bread for supper.'

On the morning of the 9th, a quarter of a pint of cocoanut milk and some of the decayed bread were served for breakfast; and for dinner, the kernels of four cocoanuts, with the remainder of the rotten bread, which, he says, was eatable only by such distressed people as themselves. A storm of thunder and lightning gave them about twenty gallons of water. 'Being miserably wet and cold, I served to the people a teaspoonful of rum each, to enable them to bear with their distressing situation. The weather continued extremely bad, and the wind increased; we spent a very miserable night, without sleep, except such as could be got in the midst of rain.'

The following day, the 10th, brought no relief except that of its light. The sea broke over the boat so much that two men were kept constantly baling, and it was necessary to keep the boat before the waves for fear of its filling. The allowance now served regularly to each person was one twenty-fifth part of a pound of bread and a quarter of a pint of water, at eight in the morning, at noon, and at sunset. Today was added about half an ounce of pork for dinner, which, though any moderate person would have considered only as a mouthful, was divided into three or four.

The morning of the 11th did not improve. 'At daybreak I served to every person a teaspoonful of rum, our limbs being so much cramped that we could scarcely move them. Our situation was now extremely dangerous, the sea frequently running over our stern, which kept us baling with all our strength. At noon the sun appeared, which gave us as much pleasure as is felt when it shows itself on a winter's day in England.

'In the evening of the 12th it still rained hard; and we again experienced a dreadful night. At length the day came, and showed a miserable set of beings, full of wants, without anything to relieve them. Some complained of great pain in their bowels, and every one of having almost lost the use of his limbs. The little sleep we got was in no way refreshing, as we were constantly covered with the sea and rain. The weather continuing, and no sun affording the least prospect of getting our clothes dried, I recommended to every one to strip and wring them through the sea water, by which means they received a warmth that, while wet with rain water, they could not have.' The shipping of seas and constant baling continued; and though the men were shivering with wet and cold, the commander was under the necessity of informing them that he could no longer afford them the comfort they had derived from the teaspoonful of rum.

On the 13th and 14th the stormy weather and heavy sea continued unabated; and on these days they saw distant land, and passed several islands. The sight of these islands, it may well be supposed, served only to increase the misery of their situation. They were as men very little better than starving with plenty in their view; yet, to attempt procuring any relief was considered to be attended with so much danger that the prolongation of life, even in the midst of misery, was thought preferable, while there remained hopes of being able to surmount their hardships.

The whole day and night of the 15th were still rainy; the latter was dark, not a star to be seen by which the steerage could be directed, and the sea was continually breaking over the boat. On the next day, the 16th, was issued for dinner an ounce of salt pork, in addition to their miserable allowance of one twenty-fifth part of a pound of bread. The night was again truly horrible, with storms of thunder, lightning, and rain; not a star visible, so that the steerage was quite uncertain.

On the morning of the 17th, at dawn of day, 'I found,' says the commander, 'every person complaining, and some of them solicited extra allowance, which I positively refused. Our situation was miserable; always wet, and suffering extreme cold in the night, without the least shelter from the weather. The little rum we had was of the greatest service: when our nights were particularly distressing, I generally served a teaspoonful or two to each person, and it was always joyful tidings when they heard of my intentions. The night was again a dark and dismal one, the sea constantly breaking over us, and nothing but the wind and waves to direct our steerage. It was my intention, if possible, to make the coast of New Holland to the southward of Endeavour Straits, being sensible that it was necessary to preserve such a situation as would make a southerly wind a fair one; that we might range along the reefs till an opening should be found into smooth water, and we the sooner be able to pick up some refreshments.'

On the 18th the rain abated, when, at their commander's recommendation, they all stripped and wrung their clothes through the sea water, from which, as usual, they derived much warmth and refreshment; but every one complained of violent pains in their bones. At night the heavy rain recommenced, with severe lightning, which obliged them to keep baling without intermission. The same weather continued through the 19th and 20th; the rain constant – at times a deluge – the men always baling; the commander, too, found it necessary to issue for dinner only half an ounce of pork.

At dawn of day, Lieutenant Bligh states that some of his people seemed half dead; that their appearances were horrible; 'and I could look,' says he, 'no way, but I caught the eye of some one in distress. Extreme hunger was now too evident; but no one suffered from thirst, nor had we much inclination to drink, that desire perhaps being satisfied through the skin. The little sleep we got was in the midst of water, and we constantly awoke with severe cramps and pains in our bones. At noon the sun broke out and revived every one.

'During the whole of the afternoon of the 21st we were so covered with rain and salt water that we could scarcely see. We suffered extreme cold, and every one dreaded the approach of night. Sleep, though we longed for it, afforded no comfort; for my own part, I almost lived without it. On the 22nd, our situation was extremely calamitous. We were obliged to take the course of the sea, running right before it, and watching with the utmost care, as the least error in the helm would in a moment have been our destruction. It continued through the day to blow hard, and the foam of the sea kept running, over our stern and quarters.

'The misery we suffered this night exceeded the preceding. The sea flew over us with great force, and kept us baling with horror and anxiety. At dawn of day I found every one in a most distressed condition, and I began to fear that another such night would put an end to the lives of several, who seemed no longer able to support their sufferings. I served an allowance of two teaspoonfuls of rum; after drinking which, and having wrung our clothes and taken our breakfast of bread and water, we became a little refreshed.

'On the evening of the 24th, the wind moderated, and the weather looked much better, which rejoiced all hands, so that they ate their scanty allowance with more satisfaction than for some time past. The night also was fair; but being always wet with the sea, we suffered much from the cold. I had the pleasure to see a fine morning produce some cheerful countenances; and for the first time during the last fifteen days, we experienced comfort from the warmth of the sun. We stripped and hung up our clothes to dry, which were by this time become so threadbare that they could not keep out either wet or cold. In the afternoon we had many birds about us, which are never seen far from land, such as boobies and noddies.'

As the sea now began to run fair, and the boat shipped but little water, Lieutenant Bligh took the opportunity to examine into the state of their bread; and it was found that, according to the present mode of living, there was a sufficient quantity remaining for twenty-nine days' allowance, by which time there was every reason to expect they would be able to reach Timor. But as this was still uncertain, and it was possible that, after all, they might be obliged to go to Java, it was determined to proportion the allowance, so as to make the stock hold out six weeks. 'I was apprehensive,' he says, 'that this would be ill received, and that it would require my utmost resolution to enforce it; for, small as the quantity was which I intended to take away for our future good, yet it might appear to my people like robbing them of life; and some who were less patient than their companions, I expected, would very ill brook it. However, on my representing the necessity of guarding against delays that might be occasioned by contrary winds, or other causes, and promising to enlarge upon the allowance as we got on, they cheerfully agreed to my proposal.' It was accordingly settled that every person should receive one twenty-fifth part of a pound of bread for breakfast, and the same quantity for dinner as usual, but that the proportion for supper should be discontinued; this arrangement left them forty-three days' consumption.

On the 25th, about noon, some noddies came so near to the boat that one of them was caught by hand. This bird was about the size of a small pigeon. 'I divided it,' says Bligh, 'with its entrails, into eighteen portions, and by a well-known method at sea, of "Who shall have this?" it was distributed with the allowance of bread and water for dinner, and eaten up, bones and all, with salt water for sauce. In the evening, several boobies flying very near to us, we had the good fortune to catch one of them. The bird is as large as a duck. They are the most presumptive proof of being near land of any sea fowl we are acquainted with. I directed the bird to be killed for supper, and the blood to be given to three of the people who were the most distressed for want of food. The body, with the entrails, beak, and feet, I divided into eighteen shares, and with the allowance of bread, which I made a merit of granting, we made a good supper compared with our usual fare.

'On the next day, the 26th, we caught another booby, so that Providence appeared to be relieving our wants in an extraordinary manner. The people were overjoyed at this addition to their dinner, which was distributed in the same manner as on the preceding evening; giving the blood to those who were the most in want of food. To make the bread a little savoury, most of the men frequently dipped it in salt water; but I generally broke mine into small pieces, and ate it in my allowance of water, out of a cocoanut shell, with a spoon, economically avoiding to take too large a piece at a time; so that I was as long at dinner as if it had been a much more plentiful meal.'

The weather was now serene, which, nevertheless, was not without its inconveniences; for, it appears, they began to feel distress of a different kind from that which they had hitherto been accustomed to suffer. The heat of the sun was now so powerful that several of the people were seized with a languor and faintness, which made life indifferent. But the little circumstance of catching two boobies in the evening, trifling as it may appear, had the effect of their spirits. The stomachs of these birds contained several flying fish, and small cuttlefish, all of which were carefully saved to be divided for dinner the next day; which were accordingly divided, with their entrails, and the contents of their maws, into eighteen portions; and as the prize was a very valuable one, it was distributed as before, by calling out, 'Who shall have this?' – 'so that today,' says the Lieutenant, 'with the usual allowance of bread at breakfast and dinner, I was happy to see that every person thought he had feasted.' From the appearance of the clouds in the evening, Mr Bligh had no doubt they were then near the land, and the people amused themselves with conversing on the probability of what they would meet with on it.

Accordingly at one in the morning of the 28th, the person at the helm heard the sound of breakers. It was the 'barrier reef' which runs along the eastern coast of New Holland, through which it now became their anxious object to discover a passage: Mr Bligh says this was now become absolutely necessary, without a moment's loss of time. The idea of getting into smooth water and finding refreshments kept up the people's spirits. The sea broke furiously over the reef in every part; within, the water was so smooth and calm that every man already anticipated the heartfelt satisfaction he was about to receive, as soon as he should have passed the barrier. At length a break in the reef was discovered, a quarter of a mile in width; and through this the boat rapidly passed with a strong stream running to the westward, and came immediately into smooth water, and all the past hardships seemed at once to be forgotten.

They now returned thanks to God for his generous protection, and with much content took their miserable allowance of the twenty-fifth part of a pound of bread, and a quarter of a pint of water for dinner.

The coast now began to show itself very distinctly, and in the evening they landed on the sandy point of an island, when it was soon discovered there were oysters on the rocks, it being low water. The party sent out to reconnoitre returned highly rejoiced at having found plenty of oysters and fresh water. By the help of a small magnifying glass, a fire was made; and among the things that had been thrown into the boat was a tinderbox and a piece of brimstone, so that in future they had the ready means of making a fire. One of the men, too, had been so provident as to bring away with him from the ship a copper pot; and thus, with a mixture of oysters, bread, and pork, a stew was made, of which each person received a full pint. It is remarked that the oysters grew so fast to the rocks that it was with great difficulty they could be broken off: but they at length discovered it to be the most expeditious way to open them where they were fixed.

The general complaints among the people were a dizziness in the head, great weakness of the joints, and violent tenesmus; but none of them are stated to have been alarming; and notwithstanding their sufferings from cold and hunger, all of them retained marks of strength. Mr Bligh had cautioned them not to touch any kind of berry or fruit that they might find; yet it appears they were no sooner out of sight than they began to make free with three different kinds that grew all over the island, eating without any reserve. The symptoms of having eaten too much began at last to frighten some of them; they fancied they were all poisoned, and regarded each other with the strongest marks of apprehension, uncertain what might be the issue of their imprudence: fortunately the fruit proved to be wholesome and good.

'This day (29th May) being,' says Lieutenant Bligh, 'the anniversary of the restoration of King Charles II, and the name not being inapplicable to our present situation (for we were restored to fresh life and strength), I named this "Restoration Island"; for I thought it probable that Captain Cook might not have taken notice of it.'

With oysters and palm tops stewed together the people now made excellent meals, without consuming any of their bread. In the morning of the 30th, Mr Bligh saw with the great delight a visible alteration in the men for the better, and he sent them away to gather oysters, in order to carry a stock of them to sea; for he determined to put off again that evening. They also procured fresh water, and filled all their vessels to the amount of nearly sixty gallons. On examining the bread, it was found there still remained about thirty-eight days' allowance.

Being now ready for sea, every person was ordered to attend prayers; but just as they were embarking, about twenty naked savages made their appearance, running and hallooing, and beckoning the strangers to come to them; but, as each was armed with a spear or lance, it was thought prudent to hold no communication with them. They now proceeded to the northward, having the continent on their left, and several islands and reefs on their right.

On the 31st they landed on one of these islands, to which was given the name of 'Sunday'. 'I sent out two parties,' says Bligh, 'one to the northward and the other to the southward, to seek for supplies, and others I ordered to stay by the boat. On this occasion fatigue and weakness so far got the better of their sense of duty, that some of the people expressed their discontent at having worked harder than their companions, and declared that they would rather be without their dinner than go in search of it. One person, in particular, went so far as to tell me, with a mutinous look, that he was as good a man as myself. It was not possible for one to judge where this might have an end, if not stopped in time; to prevent, therefore, such disputes in future, I determined either to preserve my command or die in the attempt; and seizing a cutlass, I ordered him to lay hold of another and defend himself; on which he called out that I was going to kill him, and immediately made concessions. I did not allow this to interfere further with the harmony of the boat's crew, and everything soon became quiet.'

On this island they obtained oysters, clams, and dogfish; also a small bean, which Nelson, the botanist, pronounced to be a species of dolichos. On the 1st of June, they stopped in the midst of some sandy islands, such as are known by the name of *keys*, where they procured a few clams and beans. Here Nelson was taken very ill with a violent heat in his bowels, a loss of sight, great thirst, and inability to walk. A little wine, which had carefully been saved, with some pieces of bread soaked in it, was given to him in small quantities, and he soon began to recover. The boatswain and carpenter were also ill, and complained of headache and sickness of the stomach. Others became shockingly distressed with tenesmus; in fact, there were few without complaints.

A party was sent out by night to catch birds; they returned with only twelve noddies; but it is stated that, had it not been for the folly and obstinacy of one of the party, who separated from the others and disturbed the birds, a great many more might have been taken. The offender was Robert Lamb, who acknowledged when he got to Java, that he had that night eaten nine raw birds, after he separated from his two companions. The birds, with a few clams, were the whole of the supplies afforded at these small islands.

On the 3rd of June, after passing several keys and islands, and doubling Cape York, the north-easternmost point of New Holland, at eight in the evening, the little boat and her brave crew once more launched into the open ocean. 'Miserable,' says Lieutenant Bligh, 'as our situation was in every respect, I was secretly surprised to see that it did not appear to affect any one so strongly as myself; on the contrary, it seemed as if they had embarked on a voyage to Timor in a vessel sufficiently calculated for safety and convenience. So much confidence gave me great pleasure, and I may venture to assert that to this cause our preservation is chiefly to be attributed. I encouraged every one with hopes that eight or ten days would bring us to a land of safety; and after praying to God for a continuance of His most gracious protection, I served out an allowance of water for supper, and directed our course to the west south-west.

'We had been just six days on the coast of New Holland, in the course of which we found oysters, a few clams, some birds, and water. But a benefit, probably not less than this, was that of being relieved from the fatigue of sitting constantly in the boat, and enjoying good rest at night. These advantages certainly preserved our lives; and, small as the supply was, I am very sensible how much it alleviated our distresses. Before this time nature must have sunk under the extremes of hunger and fatigue. Even in our present situation, we were most deplorable objects; but the hopes of a speedy relief kept up our spirits. For my own part, incredible as it may appear, I felt neither extreme hunger nor thirst. My allowance contented me, knowing that I could have no more.' In his manuscript journal he adds, 'This, perhaps, does not permit me to be a proper judge on a story of miserable people like us being at last driven to the necessity of destroying one another for food; but if I may be allowed, I deny the fact in its greatest extent. I say, I do not believe that, among us, such a thing could happen, but death through famine would be received in the same way as any mortal disease.'

On the 5th a booby was caught by the hand, the blood of which was divided among three of the men who were weakest, and the bird kept for next day's dinner; and on the evening of the 6th the allowance for supper was recommenced, according to a promise made when it had been discontinued. On the 7th, after a miserably wet and cold night, nothing more could be afforded than the usual allowance for breakfast; but at dinner each person had the luxury of an ounce of dried clams, which consumed all that remained. The sea was running high and breaking over the boat the whole of this day. Mr Ledward, the surgeon, and Lawrence Lebogue, an old hardy seaman, appeared to be giving way very fast. No other assistance could be given to them than a teaspoonful or two of wine, that had been carefully saved for such a melancholy occasion, which was not at all unexpected.

On the 8th the weather was more moderate, and a small dolphin was caught, which gave about two ounces to each man: in the night it again blew wet and cold. The surgeon and Lebogue still continued very ill, and the only relief that could be afforded them was a small quantity of wine, and encouraging them with the hope that a very few days more, at the rate they were then sailing, would bring them to Timor.

'In the morning of the 10th, after a very comfortless night, there was a visible alteration for the worse,' says Mr Bligh, 'in many of the people, which gave me great apprehensions. An extreme weakness, swelled legs, hollow and ghastly countenances, a more than common inclination to sleep, with an apparent debility of understanding, seemed to me the melancholy presages of an approaching dissolution. The surgeon and Lebogue, in particular, were most miserable objects; I occasionally gave them a few teaspoonfuls of wine, out of the little that remained, which greatly assisted them. The hope of being able to accomplish the voyage was our principal support. The boatswain very innocently told me that he really thought I looked worse than any in the boat. The simplicity with which he uttered such an opinion amused me, and I returned him a better compliment.'

On the 11th Lieutenant Bligh announced to his wretched companions that he had no doubt they had now passed the meridian of the eastern part of Timor, a piece of intelligence that diffused universal joy and satisfaction. Accordingly, at three in the morning of the following day, Timor was discovered at the distance only of two leagues from the shore.

'It is not possible for me,' says this experienced navigator, 'to describe the pleasure which the blessing of the sight of this land diffused among us. It appeared scarcely credible to ourselves that, in an open boat, and so poorly provided, we should have been able to reach the coast of Timor in forty-one days after leaving Tofoa, having in that time run, by our log, a distance of three thousand six hundred and eighteen nautical miles; and that, notwithstanding our extreme distress, no one should have perished in the voyage.'

On Sunday, the 14th, they came safely to anchor in Coupang Bay, where they were received with every mark of kindness, hospitality, and humanity. The houses of the principal people were thrown open for their reception. The poor sufferers when landed were scarcely able to walk; their condition is described as most deplorable. 'The abilities of a painter could rarely, perhaps, have been displayed to more advantage than in the delineation of the two groups of figures which at this time presented themselves to each other. An indifferent spectator (if such could be found) would have been at a loss which most to admire, the eyes of famine sparkling at immediate relief, or the horror of their preservers at the sight of so many spectres, whose ghastly countenances, if the cause had been unknown, would rather have excited terror than pity. Our bodies were nothing but skin and bones, our limbs were full of sores, and we were clothed in rags: in this condition, with the tears of joy and gratitude flowing down our cheeks, the people of Timor beheld us with a mixture of horror, surprise, and pity.

'When,' continues the commander, 'I reflect how providentially our lives were saved at Tofoa, by the Indians delaying their attack; and that, with scarcely anything to support life, we crossed a sea of more than twelve hundred leagues, without shelter from the inclemency of the weather; when I reflect that, in an open boat, with so much stormy weather, we escaped foundering, that not any of us were taken off by disease, that we had the great good fortune to pass the unfriendly natives of other countries without accident, and at last to meet with the most friendly and best of people to relieve our distresses – I say, when I reflect on all these wonderful escapes, the remembrance of such great mercies enables me to bear with resignation and cheerfulness the failure of an expedition the success of which I had so much at heart, and which was frustrated at a time when I was congratulating myself on the fairest prospect of being able to complete in a manner that would fully have answered the intention of His Majesty, and the humane promoters of so benevolent a plan.'

Having recruited their strength by a residence of two months among the friendly inhabitants of Coupang, they proceeded to the westward on the 20th August, in a small schooner, which was purchased and armed for the purpose, and arrived on the 1st October in Batavia Road, where Mr Bligh embarked in a Dutch packet, and was landed on the Isle of Wight on the 14th March, 1790. The rest of the people had passages provided for them in ships of the Dutch East India Company, then about to sail for Europe. All of them, however, did not survive to reach England. Nelson, the botanist, died at Coupang; Mr Elphinstone, master's mate, Peter Linkletter and Thomas Hall, seamen, died at Batavia; Robert Lamb, seaman (the booby eater) died on the passage; and Mr Ledward, the surgeon, was left behind, and not afterwards heard of. These six, with John Norton, who was stoned to death, left twelve of the nineteen, forced by the mutineers into the launch, to survive the difficulties and dangers of this unparalleled voyage, and to revisit their native country.

From *The Mutiny and Piratical Seizure of HMS 'Bounty'* by Sir John Barrow

Grieving's a Folly

Spanking Jack was so comely, so pleasant, so jolly,
    Though winds blew great guns, still he'd whistle and sin,
For Jack loved his friend, and was true to his Molly,
    And, if honour gives greatness, was great as a king.
One night as we drove with two reefs in the mainsail,
    And the scud came on low'ring upon a lee shore,
Jack went up aloft for to hand the topg'ant sail –
    A spray washed him off, and we ne'er saw him more:
        But grieving's a folly,
        Come let us be jolly;
If we've troubles on sea, boys, we've pleasures on shore.

Whiffling Tom, still of mischief or fun in the middle,
    Through life in all weathers at random would jog;
He'd dance, and he'd sing, and he'd play on the fiddle,
    And swig with an air his allowance of grog:
'Longside of a Don, in the 'Terrible' frigate,
    As yardarm and yardarm we lay off the shore,
In and out Whiffling Tom did so caper and jig it,
    That his head was shot off, and we ne'er saw him more;
        But grieving's a folly,
        Come let us be jolly;
If we've troubles on sea, boys, we've pleasures on shore.

Bonny Ben was to each jolly messmate a brother,
    He was manly and honest, good-natured and free;
If ever one tar was more true than another
    To his friend and his duty, that sailor was he:
One day with the davit to weigh the kedge anchor,
    Ben went in the boat on a bold craggy shore –
He overboard tipped, when a shark and a spanker
    Soon nipped him in two, and we ne'er saw him more;
        But grieving's a folly,
        Come let us be jolly;
If we've troubles on sea, boys, we've pleasures on shore.

But what of it all, lads? shall we be downhearted
    Because that mayhap we now take our last sup?
Life's cable must one day or other be parted,
    And Death in safe moorings will bring us all up.
But 'tis always the way on't – one scarce finds a brother
    Fond as pitch, honest, hearty, and true to the core,
But by battle, or storm, or some damned thing or other,
    He's popped off the hooks, and we ne'er see him more!
        But grieving's a folly,
        Come let us be jolly;
If we've troubles on sea, boys, we've pleasures on shore.

Charles Dibdin

Skipper Ireson's Ride

Of all the rides since the birth of time
Told in story or sung in rhyme –
On Apuleius's Golden Ass,
Or one-eyed Calendar's horse of brass,
Witch astride of a human hack,
Islam's prophet on Al-Borák –
The strangest ride that ever was sped
Was Ireson's, out from Marblehead!
    Oh! Floyd Ireson, for his hard heart,
      Tarred and feathered and carried in a cart
        By the women of Marblehead!

Body of turkey, head of owl,
Wings adroop like a rained-on fowl,
Feathered and ruffled in every part,
Skipper Ireson stood in the cart.
Scores of women, old and young,
Strong of muscle, and glib of tongue,
Pushed and pulled up the rocky lane,
Shouting and singing the shrill refrain:
    'Here's Flud Oirson, fur his horrd horrt,
      Torr'd an' furtherr'd an' corr'd in a corrt
        By the women o' Morble'ead!'

Wrinkled scolds with hands on hips,
Girls in bloom of cheek and lips,
Wild-eyed, free-limbed, such as chase
Bacchus round some antique vase,
Brief of skirt with ankles bare,
Loose of kerchief and loose of hair,
With conch-shells blowing and fish-horns' twang,
Over and over the Maenads sang:
  'Here's Flud Oirson, fur his horrd horrt,
  Torr'd an' furtherr'd and corr'd in a corrt
    By the women o' Morble'ead!'

Small pity for him – He sailed away
From a leaking ship, in Chaleur Bay –
Sailed away from a sinking wreck
With his own town's-people on her deck!
'Lay by! lay by!' they called to him.
Back he answered, 'Sink or swim!
Brag of your catch of fish again!'
And off he sailed through the fog and rain!
  Old Floyd Ireson, for his hard heart,
  Tarred and feathered and carried in a cart
    By the women of Marblehead!

Fathoms deep in dark Chaleur
That wreck shall lie for evermore.
Mother and sister, wife and maid,
Looked from the rocks of Marblehead
Over the moaning and rainy sea –
Looked for the coming that night not be!
What did the winds and the sea-birds say
Of the cruel captain who sailed away? –
  Old Floyd Ireson, for his hard heart,
  Tarred and feathered and carried in a cart
    By the women of Marblehead!

Through the street, on either side,
Up flew windows, doors swung wide;
Sharped-tongued spinsters, old wives grey,
Treble lent the fish-horn's bray.

Sea-worn grandsires, cripple-bound,
Hulks of old sailors run aground,
Shook head, and fist, and hat, and cane,
And cracked with curses the hoarse refrain;
　　'Here's Flud Oirson, fur his horrd horrt,
　　Torr'd an' furtherr'd an' corr'd in a corrt
　　　　By the women o' Morble'ead!'

Sweetly along the Salem road
Bloom of orchard and lilac showed.
Little the wicked skipper knew
Of the fields so green and the sky so blue.
Riding there in his sorry trim,
　　Like an Indian idol glum and grim,
Scarcely he seemed tho sound to hear
Of voices shouting, far and near:
　　'Here's Flud Oirson, fur his horrd horrt,
　　Torr'd an' furtherr'd an' corr'd in a corrt
　　　　By the women o' Morble'ead!'

'Hear me, neighbours!' at last he cried –
'What to me is this noisy ride?
What is the shame that clothes the skin
To the nameless horror that lives within?
Waking or sleeping, I see a wreck,
And hear a cry from a reeling deck!
Hate me and curse me – I only dread
The hand of God, and the face of the dead!'
　　Said old Floyd Ireson, for his hard heart,
　　Tarred and feathered and carried in a cart
　　　　By the women of Marblehead!

Then the wife of the skipper lost at sea
Said, 'God has touched him! why should we?'
Said an old wife mourning her only son,
'Cut the rogue's tether and let him run!'
So with soft relentings and rude excuse,
Half scorn, half pity, they cut him loose,
And gave him a cloak to hide him in,
And left him alone with his shame and sin.

Poor Floyd Ireson, for his hard heart,
Tarred and feathered and carried in a cart
By the women of Marblehead.

John Greenleaf Whittier

'Sans Teeth, sans Eyes, sans Taste'

The Prison Hospital

BY DEGREES I took in my surroundings. As far as I could see, those who were really ill were suffering from scurvy and affections of the eye – diseases frequent in that region. There were several such in the ward. Of the others who were really ill, some had fever, skin diseases or consumption. This was not like other wards – here patients of all kinds were collected together, even those suffering from venereal diseases. I speak of 'those who were *really* ill', because there were some here who had come without any disease, 'to have a rest'. The doctors readily admitted such sham invalids from sympathy, especially when there were many beds empty. Detention in the guard-houses and prisons seemed so disagreeable, compared with the hospital, that many convicts were glad to come to the hospital in spite of the bad air and the locked ward. There were indeed some people, especially from the disciplinary battalion, who were fond of lying in bed and of hospital life in general. I looked at my new companions with interest, but I remember my curiosity was especially aroused by one from our prison, a man who was dying, also consumptive, and also at the last gasp. He was in the bed next but one beyond Ustyantsev, and so almost opposite me. His name was Mihailov; a fortnight before I had seen him in the prison. He had been ill a long while and ought to have been in the doctor's hands long before; but with obstinate and quite unnecessary patience he had controlled himself, and gone on, and only at Christmas he had come into the hospital to die three weeks later of galloping consumption; it was like a fire consuming him. I was struck this time by the awful change in his face, which was one of the first I noticed when I entered the prison; it somehow caught my eye then. Near him was a soldier of the disciplinary battalion, an old man of filthy and revolting habits . . . However, I cannot go over all the patients. I have mentioned this old man now simply because he made some impression on me at the time, and in the course of one minute gave me a full idea of some peculiarities of the convict ward. This old fellow, I remember, had a very heavy cold at the time. He was constantly sneezing, and went on sneezing for the whole of the following week, even in his sleep, in fits of five or six sneezes at a time, regularly repeating each time, 'Oh Lord, what an affliction.' At that minute he was sitting on the bed greedily stuffing his nose with snuff from a paper parcel, so that his sneezes might be more violent and complete. He sneezed into a checked cotton handkerchief of his own, that had been washed a hundred times and was faded to the last extreme; and as he sneezed he wrinkled up his nose in a peculiar way into tiny innumerable creases, and showed the relics of ancient blackened teeth between his red dribbling jaws. Then at once he opened his handkerchief, scrutinised the phlegm in it, and immediately smeared it on his brown hospital dressing-gown, so that the handkerchief remained comparatively clean. He did this the whole week. This persistent miserly care of his own handkerchief at the sacrifice of the hospital dressing-gown aroused no sort of protest from the other patients, though one of them would have to wear that dressing-gown after him. But our peasants are not squeamish and are strangely lacking in fastidiousness. I winced at that moment and I could not help at once beginning to examine with disgust and curiosity the dressing-gown I had just put on. Then I realised that it had been attracting my attention for a long time by its strong smell; by now it had become warm on me and smelt more and more strongly of medicines, plasters, and, as I thought, of some decomposing, which was not to be wondered at, since it had been for immemorial years on the backs of patients. Possibly the linen lining may have been washed sometimes; but I am not sure of that. At the present, anyway, it was saturated with all sorts of unpleasant discharges, lotions, matter from broken blisters, and so on. Moreover, convicts who had just received corporal punishment were constantly coming into the convict wards with wounded backs. Compresses were applied and then the dressing-gown being put on straight over the wet shirt could not possibly escape getting messed, and everything that dropped on it remained.

And the whole time I was in prison, that is, several years, I used to put on the dressing-gown with fear and mistrust whenever I had to be in hospital (and I was there pretty often). I particularly disliked the huge and remarkably fat lice I sometimes came across in those dressing-gowns. The convicts enjoyed killing them, so that when one was squashed under the convict's thick, clumsy nail, one could see from the hunter's face the satisfaction it gave him. We particularly disliked bugs, too, and sometimes the whole ward joined in their destruction on a long dreary winter evening.

From *The House of the Dead* by Fyodor Dostoevsky,
translated by Constance Garnett

Christmas Day in the Workhouse

It is Christmas Day in the Workhouse,
And the cold bare walls are bright
With garlands of green and holly,
And the place is a pleasant sight:
For with clean-washed hands and faces,
In a long and hungry line
The paupers sit at their tables,
For this is the hour they dine.

And the guardians and their ladies,
Although the wind is east,
Have come in their furs and wrappers,
To watch their charges feast:
To smile and be condescending,
Put pudding on pauper plates,
To be hosts at the workhouse banquet
They've paid for – with the rates.

Oh, the paupers are meek and lowly
With their 'Thank'ee kindly, mum'
So long as they fill their stomachs,
What matter it whence it comes?
But one of the old men mutters,
And pushes his plate aside:
'Great God!' he cried; 'but it chokes me!
For this is the day *she* died.'

The guardians gazed in horror,
The master's face went white;
'Did a pauper refuse their pudding?'
'Could their ears believe aright?'
Then the ladies clutched their husbands,
Thinking the man would die,
Struck by a bolt, or something,
By the outraged One on high.

But the pauper sat for a moment
Then rose 'mid a silence grim,

For the others had ceased to chatter
And trembled in every limb.
He looked at the guardians' ladies,
Then, eyeing their lords, he said,
'I eat not the food of villains
Whose hands are foul and red:

'Whose victims cry for vengeance
From their dank, unhallowed graves.'
'He's drunk!' said the workhouse master,
'Or else he's mad, and raves.'
'Not drunk or mad,' cried the pauper,
'But only a hunted beast,
Who, torn by the hounds and mangled,
Declines the vulture's feast.

'I care not a curse for the guardians,
And I won't be dragged away.
Just let me have the fit out,
It's only on Christmas Day
That the black past comes to goad me,
And prey on my burning brain;
I'll tell you the rest in a whisper, –
I swear I won't shout again.

'Keep your hands off me, curse you!
Hear me right out to the end.
You come here to see how paupers
The season of Christmas spend.
You come here to watch us feeding,
As they watch the captured beast.
Hear why a penniless pauper
Spits on your paltry feast.

'Do you think I will take your bounty,
And let you smile and think
You're doing a noble action
With the parish's meat and drink?
Where is my wife, you traitors –
The poor old wife you slew?

Yes, by the God above us,
My Nance was killed by you!

'Last winter my wife lay dying,
Starved in a filthy den;
I had never been to the parish, –
I came to the parish then.
I swallowed my pride in coming,
For, ere the ruin came,
I held up my head as a trader,
And I bore a spotless name.

'I came to the parish, craving
Bread for a starving wife,
Bread for the woman who'd loved me
Through fifty years of life;
And what do you think they told me,
Mocking my awful grief?
That "the House" was open to us,
But they wouldn't give "out relief".

'I slunk to the filthy alley –
'Twas a cold, raw Christmas eve –
And the bakers' shops were open,
Tempting a man to thieve;
But I clenched my fists together,
Holding my head awry,
So I came to her empty-handed,
And mournfully told her why.

'Then I told her "the House" was open;
She had heard of the way of *that*,
For her bloodless cheeks went crimson,
And up in her rags she sat,
Crying, "Bide the Christmas here, John,
We've never had one apart;
I think I can bear the hunger, –
The other would break my heart."

'All through that eve I watched her,
Holding her hand in mine,
Praying the Lord, and weeping
Till my lips were salt as brine.
I asked her once if she hungered,
And as she answered "No,"
The moon shone in at the window
Set in a wreath of snow.

'Then the room was bathed in glory,
And I saw in my darling's eyes
The far-away look of wonder
That comes when the spirit flies;
And her lips were parched and parted,
And her reason came and went,
For she raved of our home in Devon,
Where our happiest years were spent.

'And the accents, long forgotten,
Came back to the tongue once more,
For she talked like the country lassie
I woo'd by the Devon shore.
Then she rose to her feet and trembled,
And fell on the rags and moaned,
And, "Give me a crust – I'm famished –
For the love of God!" she groaned.

'I rushed from the room like a madman,
And flew to the workhouse gate,
Crying, "Food for a dying woman!"
And the answer came, "Too late."
They drove me away with curses;
Then I fought with a dog in the street,
And tore from the mongrel's clutches
A crust he was trying to eat.

'Back, through the filthy by-lanes!
Back, through the trampled slush!
Up to the crazy garret,
Wrapped in an awful hush.

My heart sank down at the threshold,
And I paused with a sudden thrill,
For there in the silv'ry moonlight
My Nance lay, cold and still.

'Up to the blackened ceiling
The sunken eyes were cast –
I knew on those lips all bloodless
My name had been the last;
She'd called for her absent husband –
O God! had I but known! –
Had called in vain, and in anguish
Had died in that den – *alone*.

'Yes, there, in a land of plenty
Lay a loving woman dead,
Cruelly starved and murdered
For a loaf of the parish bread.
At yonder gate, last Christmas,
I craved for a human life.
You, who would feast us paupers,
What of my murdered wife!

'There, get ye gone to your dinners;
Don't mind me in the least;
Think of the happy paupers
Eating your Christmas feast;
And when you recount their blessings
In your smug parochial way,
Say what you did for *me*, too,
Only last Christmas Day.'

George R. Sims

Auld Robin Gray

When the sheep are in the fauld, and the kye at hame,
And a' the warld to rest are gane,
The waes o' my heart fa' in showers frae my e'e,
While my gudeman lies sound by me.

Young Jamie lo'ed me weel, and sought me for his bride;
But saving a croun he had naething else beside:
To make the croun a pund, young Jamie gaed to sea;
And the croun and the pund were baith for me.

He hadna been awa' a week but only twa,
When my father brak his arm, and the cow was stown awa';
My mother she fell sick, and my Jamie at the sea –
And auld Robin Gray came a-courtin' me.

My father couldna work, and my mother couldna spin;
I toil'd day and night, but their bread I couldna win;
Auld Rob maintain'd them baith, and wi' tears in his e'e
Said, 'Jennie, for their sakes, O, marry me!'

My heart it said nay; I look'd for Jamie back;
But the wind it blew high, and the ship it was a wrack.
His ship was a wrack – why didna Jamie dee,
Or why do I live to cry, Wae's me.

My father urgit sair: my mother didna speak;
But she look'd in my face till my heart was like to break:
They gi'ed him my hand, but my heart was at the sea:
Sae auld Robin Gray he was gudeman to me.

I hadna been a wife a week but only four,
When mournfu' as I sat on the stane at the door,
I saw my Jamie's wraith, for I couldna think it he –
Till he said, 'I'm come hame to marry thee.'

—O sair, sair did we greet, and muckle did we say;
We took but ae kiss, and I bad him gang away:

I wish that I were dead, but I'm no like to dee;
And why was I born to say, Wae's me!

I gang like a ghaist, and I carena to spin;
I daurna think on Jamie, for that wad be a sin;
But I'll do my best a gude wife aye to be,
For auld Robin Gray he is kind unto me.

Lady A. Lindsay

The Mischievous Ape

IN THE time of Lodovico Sforza, the unfortunate Duke of Milan, there was kept, among other living curiosities in the ducal palace, a large and beautiful ape, whose amusing yet harmless manners, full of practical jests and witticisms, had long obtained for him the liberty of going at large. Such indeed was his reputation for prudence and good conduct, that he was not merely permitted the range of the whole palace, but frequently visited the outskirts, in the vicinity of Maine, of Cusano, and San Giovanni, and was not infrequently seen conversing with some friend upon the walls. In fact most people were eager to show their respect for him by presenting him with fruits and other dainties, no less from regard to his ducal patron, than to his own intrinsic merits. The singular pleasure he afforded to all classes of society, by his happy talents of various kinds, was always a sufficient passport from place to place. But his favourite resort, among many others, was the house of an ancient gentlewoman, situated in the parish of San Giovanni, upon the walls; where he cultivated the society of her two sons, one of whom in particular, though at the head of a family, invariably received his monkey guest in the most amiable manner, making him as much at home as if he had been the lady's favourite lap dog. These young men, perceiving their aged mother amused with the animal's unequalled exhibitions of his art, vied with each other in paying the most gratifying attentions to his monkeyship; and would certainly, had he not happened to have been ducal property, either have purchased or stolen him, merely out of regard to their mother. The whole household, likewise, received orders to treat him with the same invariable kindness and respect, studying what appeared most agreeable to his taste, so as to give him an affection for the old lady's house. This last motive weighed so greatly with his apeship, that he almost deserted his other neighbours, in order to enjoy more of the society of these very agreeable friends; although he was careful to return to his own ducal residence at the castle in the evening. During this time the aged lady, becoming very infirm, no longer left her chamber, where she was affectionately attended by her whole family, who supplied her with every alleviation in the power of medical advice to bestow. Thither, occasionally, our facetious hero was also introduced for the purpose of awakening a smile on the wan features of the patient, by his strange and amusing manners, receiving some delicate morsels in return from the poor lady's own hand. As he possessed a natural taste, in common with most of his race, for every kind of sweets, he was in the habit of besieging the old lady's room with great perseverance and assiduity, feasting upon the best confectionery with far higher zest than the poor patient herself. Worn out at length, by long infirmities and age, she soon after departed this world, having first with becoming piety confessed herself, and received the holy sacraments of our church, with the communion and extreme unction at the final close.

While the funeral ceremonies were preparing, and the last offices rendered to the deceased, the monkey appeared to pay remarkable attention to all that was going forward. The corpse being dressed, and placed on the funeral bier, the holy sisterhood then attended with the usual ceremonies, offering up hymns and aves to the Virgin for the soul of the deceased. The body was afterwards borne to the parish church not far distant, not unobserved by the monkey, who watched the procession depart. But he soon turned his attention to the state of things around him; and after feasting on the cake and wine being a little elevated, he began to empty the boxes and drawers, and examine the contents. Having observed the deceased in her last habiliments, and the form of her head-dress when she was laid out, the facetious ape immediately began to array himself in the cast-off garments, exactly in the manner he had witnessed, and so perfect was the resemblance that when he had covered himself up in bed, the physician himself would have been puzzled to detect the cheat. Here the false patient lay, when the domestics entered the chamber and suddenly perceiving the monkey thus dexterously laid out they ran back in the utmost terror and surprise, believing that they had really seen either the corpse or the spirit of the deceased. After recovering sufficient presence of mind to speak, they declared, as they hoped to be saved, that they had seen their mistress reposing upon her sick couch as usual. On the return of the two brothers with their friends and relatives from church, they directly resolved to ascend in a body into the sick chamber; and night already approaching, they all felt, in spite of their affected indifference, an unpleasant sensation on entering the room. Drawing near the bedside, they not only fancied they saw and heard a person breathe, but observing the coverings move, as if the patient were about to spring from the couch, they retreated with the utmost precipitation and alarm. When they had recovered their spirits a little, the guests requested that a priest might be sent for, to whom, on his arrival, they proceeded to explain the case. On hearing the nature of it, the good friar, being of a truly prudent and pious turn, dispatched a person back for his clerk, with orders to bring him the large ivory crucifix, and the illuminated psalter. These, with the help of holy water, the wafer, and the priest's stole, were judged a sufficient match for the devices of the Evil One, and thus armed, repeating the seven psalms, with due ejaculations to the Virgin, they once more ascended the stairs, the clerk, in obedience to the friar bearing the huge ivory crucifix at their head. He had previously exhorted the brothers to have no fears for the final salvation of their parent, as the number and excellence of her confessions were an effectual preservative against the most diabolical efforts of the adversary. He maintained that there was not the least cause for alarm, for what the servants had beheld were merely Satanic illusions, which he had frequently been in the habit of dispelling with singular success; and that having made use of his exorcisms, he would then bless the house, and with the Lord's help, lay such a curse upon the bad spirits, as would deprive them of the least inclination to return.

When they arrived at the chamber door, all the guests, in spite of these encouraging exhortations and the sprinkling of holy water, drew back, while the bold friar ordered his clerk to advance in the name of the Lord; which he did, followed only by his superior. Approaching the sick bed, they perceived Monna Bertuccia, our facetious ape, laid out as we have said, in perfect personification of the deceased. After mumbling some prayers, and flourishing the cross in vain, for some time, they began to entertain doubts of their success, though at the same time they felt ashamed to retreat. So sprinkling the holy water with a more liberal hand, crying: '*Asperges me, domine; asperges me,*' they complimented the ape with a portion of it in his face. Expecting upon this to be next saluted with a blow of the huge cross, he suddenly began to grin and chatter in so horrible a manner that the sacred vessel fell from the priest's hands, and the clerk at the same time dropping the crucifix, they both fled together. Such was their haste that they stumbled, one over the other, down the stairs, the priest falling upon his clerk, when they reached the bottom.

On hearing the sudden crash, and the terrified exclamations of the good friar, '*Jesus, Jesus, Domine, adjuva me,*' the brothers, followed by the rest of the party, rushed towards the spot, eagerly inquiring what dreadful accident had occurred. Both of the holy personages gazed on the guests, without being able to utter a word; but their pallid looks spoke volumes sufficient to answer all demands. The poor clerk fainted away, no less from excess of fear than from the terrible fall he had just received. Having obliged both to partake of some restoratives, the priest at length summoned courage enough to say: 'It is true, my dear children, I have indeed seen your poor departed mother in the form of a fierce demon,' when just as he had finished these words, the cause of all their disturbance, desirous of securing the remnants of the feast, was heard approaching at a pretty brisk and clattering pace down the unlucky stairs. Without giving any of the party time to discover a fresh place of refuge, or even to prepare their minds for his reception, he bounced suddenly into the room, armed cap-à-pie, in the fearful petticoats of the deceased. His head was dressed to a nicety exactly in the same manner as the old lady's and his whole body very decently arrayed in her late habiliments. He placed himself in the midst of the company, all of whom stood rooted to the spot, silent and awe-stricken, awaiting the dreadful scene that might ensue. The wrinkles in his countenance certainly bore no small resemblance to those the features of the deceased, to which his very serious demeanour added not a little. Yet after a few secret ejaculations for divine protection on the part of the guests, the facetious visitor was soon recognised by one of the brothers, the only person who had possessed courage to look the monkey in the face, on his sudden entrance into the room. Momentary prayers and exclamations were then as suddenly converted into bursts of laughter; and in a few minutes, the author of all their sufferings began to resume the usual hilarity of his disposition, to exhibit his best manoeuvres in the saltic art, and with the greatest politeness, severally to accost the company. He evinced, however, the utmost aversion to disrobing himself of his new honours, snapping at anyone who ventured to approach him, while he performed his antics in the ablest and most whimsical manner. In full dress he thus set out on his return to the castle, meeting with reiterated plaudits, as he passed along the streets. In this state, he was welcomed home by the domestics of the castle, producing infinite diversion among the courtiers and all those who witnessed his exploits. Nor did the two brothers punish him for his involuntary fault; rather kindly permitting him to return to his old haunts, where he feasted and frolicked away his days, until he attained to be a happy and respectable old age.

Matteo Bandello, translated by Thomas Roscoe

Dirty Dick of Leadenhall Street

EARLY IN THE present century[1] there was living in Leadenhall Street an eccentric person named Nathaniel Bentley, who, by reason of his disregard for appearances, obtained the unenviable name of 'Dirty Dick'. He kept a large emporium for all sorts of wares: the number of the house was 46, now divided into two tenements. Bentley's shop was one of the curiosities of the town, whither strangers flocked 'less to buy than to stare', and it was usually confessed,

> Though the dirt was so frightful,
> The dirty man's manners were truly delightful.

In his early days he was called 'the Beau of Leadenhall Street', and might be seen at public places of resort, dressed as a man of fashion. He not only spoke French and Italian fluently, but, as the rhyme implies, his demeanour was that of a polished gentleman. Whence the cause of his decadence into dirt? As the story goes, our young tradesman had made proposals of marriage to the daughter of a wealthy citizen, and had been accepted; but the lady died suddenly, and Bentley's hopes were wrecked. Time passed on, and our fashionable beau became the inveterate enemy of soap and towels; and hence 'Dirty Dick'. His house was equally neglected. That wonderful room, whose inside no mortal might brag to have viewed, and the circumstances in which it became so, are described in *The Dirty Old Man, a Lay of Leadenhall*, by William Allingham, who notes that the verses accord with the accepted account of the man and his house: –

> That room – forty years since folks settled and deck'd it,
> The luncheon's prepared, and the guests are expected;
> The handsome young host he is gallant and gay,
> For his love and her friends will be with him to-day.

> With solid and dainty the table is drest,
> The wine beams its brightest, the flowers bloom their best;
> Yet the host need not smile, and no guests will appear,
> For his sweetheart is dead, as he shortly shall hear.

1 i.e. the nineteenth century.

Full forty years since, turned the key in that door;
'Tis a room deaf and dumb 'mid the city's uproar.

★   ★   ★

Cup and platter are mask'd in thick layers of dust;
The flow'rs fall'n to powder, the wines swath'd in crust;
A nosegay was laid before one special chair,
And the faded blue ribbon that bound it lies there.

In February 1804, Bentley finally quitted his warehouse in Leadenhall Street, in which the forty years he had conducted business, among cobwebs and dust. He then took a house in Jewry Street, Aldgate, where he lived for three years; but his landlord refusing to renew the lease, he removed to Leonard Street, Shoreditch, taking with him a stock of spoiled goods, to the amount of £10,000. Here he was robbed of a considerable sum by a woman with whom he was imprudent enough to associate in his old age. To divert his mind, after this misfortune, he travelled for a time until he reached Haddington, in Scotland. Almost penniless, and suffering severely from ill-health, he took up his abode at the Crown Inn, where he died about the close of the year 1809, and was buried in the churchyard of that town.

From *The Romance of London* by John Timbs

THE END

The Golden Ass

How Socrates and Aristomenus slept together in one Chamber, and how they were handled by Witches.

IN SPEAKING THESE WORDS, and devising with my selfe of our departing the next morrow, lest Meroe the Witch should play by us as she had done by divers other persons, it fortuned that Socrates did fall asleepe, and slept very soundly, by reason of his travell, and plenty of meat and wine wherewithall hee had filled himselfe. Wherefore I closed and barred fast the doores of the chamber, and put my bed behinde the doore, and so layed mee downe to rest. But I could in no wise sleepe, for the great feare which was in my heart, untill it was about midnight, and then I began to slumber. But alas, behold suddenly the chamber doores brake open, and lockes, bolts, and posts fell downe, that you would verily have thought that some Theeves had beene presently come to have spoyled and robbed us. And my bed whereon I lay being a truckle bed, fashioned in forme of a Cradle, and one of the feet broken and rotten, by violence was turned upside downe, and I likewise was overwhelmed and covered lying in the same. Then perceived I in my selfe, that certaine affects of the minde by nature doth chance contrary. For as tears oftentimes trickle down the cheekes of him that seeth or heareth some joyfull newes, so I being in this fearefull perplexity, could not forbeare laughing, to see how of Aristomenus I was made like unto a snail his shell. And while I lay on the ground covered in this sort, I peeped under the bed to see what would happen. And behold there entred in two old women, the one bearing a burning torch, and the other a sponge and a naked sword; and so in this habit they stood about Socrates being fast asleep. Then shee which bare the sword sayd unto the other, Behold sister Panthia, this is my deare and sweet heart, which both day and night hath abused my wanton youthfulnesse. This is he, who little regarding my love, doth not onely defame me with reproachfull words, but also intendeth to run away. And I shall be forsaken by like craft as Ulysses did use, and shall continually bewaile my solitarinesse as Calipso. Which said, shee pointed towards mee that lay under the bed, and shewed me to Panthia. This is hee, quoth she, which is his Counsellor, and perswadeth him to forsake me, and now being at the point of death he lieth prostrate on the ground covered with his bed, and hath seene all our doings, and hopeth to escape scot-free from my hands, but I will cause that hee shall repent himselfe too late, nay rather forthwith, of his former untemperate language, and his present curiosity. Which words when I heard I fell into a cold sweat, and my heart trembled with feare, insomuch that the bed over me did likewise rattle and shake. Then spake Panthia unto Meroe and said, Sister let us by and by teare him in pieces, or tye him by the members, and so cut them off. Then Meroe (being so named because she was a Taverner, and loved wel good wines) answered, nay rather let him live, and bury the corps of this poore wretch in some hole of the earth; and therewithall shee turned the head of Socrates on the other side, and thrust her sword up to he hilts into the left part of his necke, and received the bloud that gushed out, into a pot, that no drop thereof fell beside: which things I saw with myne owne eyes, and as I thinke to the intent she might alter nothing that pertained to sacrifice, which she accustomed to make, she thrust her hand downe into the intrals of his body, and searching about, at length brought forth the heart of my miserable companion Socrates, who having his throat cut in such sort, yeelded out a dolefull cry and gave up the ghost. Then Panthia stopped the wide wound of his throat with the Sponge, and said, O Sponge sprung and made of the sea, beware that thou passe nat by running River. This being sayd, the one of them moved and turned up my bed, and then they strid over mee, and clapped their buttocks upon my face, and all bepissed mee till I was wringing wet. When this was ended they went their wayes, and the doores closed fast, the posts stood in their old places, and the lockes and bolts were shut againe. But I that lay upon the ground like one without soule, naked and cold, and wringing wet with pisse, like to one that were more than halfe dead, yet reviving my selfe, and appointed as I thought for the Gallowes, began to say, Alasse what shall become of me to morrow, when my companion shall be found murthered here in the chamber? To whom shall I seeme to tell any similitude of truth, when as I shal tell the trueth in deed? They will say, If thou wert unable to resist the violence of the women, yet shouldest thou have cried for helpe; Wouldst thou suffer the man to be slaine before thy face and say nothing? Or why did they not slay thee likewise? Why did they spare thee that stood by and saw them commit that horrible fact? Wherefore although thou hast escaped their hands, yet thou shalt not escape ours. While I pondered these things with my selfe the night passed on, and so I resolved to take my horse before day, and goe forward on my journey.

Howbeit the wayes were unknowne unto me, and thereupon I tooke up my packet, unlocked and unbarred the doors, but those good and faithfull doores which in the night did open of their owne accord, could then scantly be opened with their keys. And when I was out I cried, O sirrah Hostler where art thou? open the stable doore, for I will ride away by and by. The Hostler lying behinde the stable doore upon a pallet, and halfe asleepe, What (quoth hee) doe you not know that the wayes be very dangerous? What meane you to rise at this time of night? If you perhaps guilty of some heynous crime, be weary of your life, yet thinke you not that wee are such Sots that we will die for you. Then said I, It is well nigh day, and moreover, what can Theeves take from him that hath nothing? Doest thou not know (Foole as thou art) if thou be naked, if ten Gyants should assaile thee, they could not spoyle or rob thee? Whereunto the drowsie Hostler halfe asleepe, and turning on the other side, answered, What know I whether you have murthered your Companion whom you brought in yesternight, or no, and now seeke the meanes to escape away? O Lord, at that time I remember the earth seemed to open, and me thought I saw at hell gate the Dog Cerberus ready to devour mee; and then I verily beleeved, that Meroe did not spare my throat, mooved with pitty, but rather cruelly pardoned mee to bring mee to the Gallowes. Wherefore I returned to my chamber, and there devised with my selfe in what sort I should finish my life. But when I saw that fortune would minister unto mee no other instrument, than that which my bed profered mee, I sayd, O bed, O bed, most dear unto me at this present, which hast abode and suffered with me so many miseries, Judge and arbiter of such things as were done here this night, whome onely I may call to witnesse for my innocency, render (I say) unto me some wholsome weapon to end my life, that am most willing to dye. And therewithal I pulled out a piece of the rope wherewith the bed was corded, and tyed one end thereof about a rafter by the window, and with the other end I made a sliding knot, and stood upon my bed, and so put my neck into it, and when I leaped from the bed, thinking verily to strangle my selfe and so dye, behold the rope beeing old and rotten burst in the middle, and I fell downe tumbling upon Socrates that lay under: And even at that same very time the Hostler came in crying with a loud voyce, and sayd, Where are you that made such hast at midnight, and now lies wallowing abed? Whereupon (I know not whether it was by my fall, or by the great cry of the Hostler) Socrates as waking out of a sleepe, did rise up first and sayd, It is not without cause that strangers do speake evill of all such Hostlers, for this Caitife in his comming in, and with his crying out, I thinke under a colour to steale away somthing, hath waked me out of a sound sleepe. Then I rose up joyfull with a merry countenance, saying, behold good Hostler, my friend, my companion and my brother, whom thou didst falsly affirme to be slaine by mee this night. And therewithall I embraced my friend Socrates and kissed him: but hee smelling the stinke of the pisse wherewith those Hagges had embrued me, thrust me away and sayd, Clense thy selfe from this filthy odour, and then he began gently to enquire, how that noysome sent hapned unto mee. But I finely feigning and colouring the matter for the time, did breake off his talk, and tooke him by the hand and sayd, Why tarry we? Why lose wee the pleasure of this faire morning? Let us goe, and so I tooke up my packet, and payed the charges of the house and departed: and we had not gone a mile out of the Towne but it was broad day, and then I diligently looked upon Socrates throat, to see if I could espy the place where Meroe thrust in her sword: but when I could not perceive any such thing, I thought with my selfe, What a mad man am I, that being overcome with wine yester night, have dreamed such terrible things? Behold, I see Socrates is sound, safe, and in health. Where is his wound? where is the Sponge? Where is his great and new cut? And then I spake to him and sayd, Verily it is not without occasion, that Physitians of experience do affirme, That such as fill their gorges abundantly with meat and drinke, shall dreame of dire and horrible sights: for I my selfe, not tempering my appetite yester night from the pots of wine, did seeme to see this night strange and cruel visions, that even yet I think my self sprinkled and wet with human blood: whereunto Socrates laughing made answer and said, Nay, thou art not wet with the blood of men, but thou art imbrued with stinking pisse; and verily I my selfe dreamed this night that my throat was cut, and that I felt the paine of the wound, and that my heart was pulled out of my belly, and the remembrance thereof makes me now to feare, for my knees do so tremble that I can scarce goe any further, and therefore I would faine eat somewhat to strengthen and revive my spirits. Then said I, Behold here thy breakefast, and therwithall I opened my script that hanged upon my shoulder, and gave him bread and cheese, and we sate downe under a great Plane tree, and I eat part with him; and while I beheld him eating greedily, I perceived that he waxed meigre and pale, and that his lively colour faded away, insomuch that beeing in great fear, and remembring those terrible furies of whom I lately dreamed, the first morsell of bread that I put in my mouth (which was but very small) did so sticke in my jawes, that I could neither swallow it downe, nor yet yeeld it up, and moreover the small time of our being together increased my feare, and what is hee that seeing his companion die in the highway before his face, would not greatly lament and bee sorry? But when that Socrates had eaten sufficiently he waxed very thirsty, for indeed he had well nigh devoured all a whole Cheese: and behold evill fortune! there was behinde the Plane tree a pleasant running water as cleere as Crystal, and I sayd unto him, Come hither Socrates to this water and drinke thy fill. And then he rose and came to the River, and kneeled downe upon the side of the banke to drinke, but he had scarce touched the water with his lips when as behold the wound of his throat opened wide, and the Sponge suddenly fell into the water, and after issued out a little remnant of bloud, and his body being then without life, had fallen into the river, had not I caught him by the leg and so pulled him up. And after that I had lamented a good space the death of my wretched companion, I buried him in the sands there by the river.

Which done, in great feare I rode through many Outwayes and desart places, and as culpable of the death of Socrates, I forsooke my countrey, my wife, and my children and came to Etolia where I married another Wife.

Lucius Apuleius, translated by William Adlington

Isolina

The opening pages of *Isolina* give a brief summation of the facts of a celebrated Veronese case as the prelude to a latter-day investigation by the novelist Dacia Maraini.

VERONA. 16 January 1900. Two washerwomen were bent over, soaping sheets in the river bed of the Adige just under the Garibaldi Bridge.

From photographs of the time we can reconstruct how the river must have looked then: muddy, turbulent, just held back by its new banks (the Adige overflowed in 1882, destroying half the city); animated by the continual passage of boats carrying sand, barges with wide, brown sails, ferries that would go back and forth from one side to the other. Where the water ran more deeply and swiftly, floating water mills emerged, turning their dirty dripping paddles with a noisy creaking.

Along the banks, whether the day were fine or not, on the strips of stony beach there were lines of well-wrapped-up women, bent over their washing, chattering cheerfully amongst themselves.

Today the Garibaldi Bridge roots its granite arches in the pale water. A wall supports the pavement of the embankment on top of which cars run. Along the brick wall you can still see traces of the steps where the washerwomen would go down to the river.

It was at this point, where the water accumulates bits of plastic, old milk cans, and rags, that the washerwoman Maria Menapace, on the morning of

16 January 1900, saw a bag caught up in the undergrowth.

She showed it to her friend Luigia Marconcini saying, as she would later be quoted in the evidence, 'It must be cheap meat, someone's trying to avoid the tax on it.'

Not far off there was a boy fishing. He was bundled up in a black jerkin, a threadbare cap on his head, and a pair of patched ankle boots made of canvas. His name was Paride Baggio. He was fifteen. Menapace asked him to help her drag the bag to the bank.

The river police later described it as a 'voluminous bundle tied up with string'. 'That has to be something being smuggled in,' they heard someone say from the bank. The two women left their washing to open it. The boy took out a knife with a wooden handle. He cut the string. Four curious hands unwrapped the cloth. And there they found 'six pieces of human flesh weighing 13,400 kg' as *L'Adige* reported next day.

The pieces were identified as 'the right side of the thorax with the whole breast wrapped up in a piece of scarlet cloth. The left side of the thorax with the breast wrapped up in the same kind of material. The lower part of the stomach wrapped up in green material of the same shade. A piece of the pelvic bone, from which the flesh had been stripped, wrapped up in the same green material. Part of the left leg wrapped up in a tablecloth. The thighbone, from which the flesh had been stripped, wrapped up in a pair of women's pants trimmed with lace'.

One detail was noted: a corner of the tablecloth was cut off as if to destroy a mark by which it might be recognised.

At twelve o'clock the Royal Prosecutor made his written report. The next day sappers from the 4th Genio regiment began to drag the river. In a few hours other pieces of the woman's body were retrieved: two bundles containing the intestines and another with the oesophagus, a placenta with the umbilical cord still attached to it.

When the pieces were put together, the experts established that it was the body of a young woman (aged between 16 and 22) who had an obvious curvature of the spine and was about three months pregnant. On the stage of the pregnancy there were to be conflicting opinions and endless discussions.

The whole city was alarmed. All of Verona was gripped by this crime. The hunt for the murderer began. Many people went to drag the river to try to find the head, which had not yet been retrieved.

On 17 January a miller found another piece: a hipbone wrapped up in a piece of skirt. In the folds of the skirt, hidden in a pocket, was a shopping list. The handwriting was shaky, rough and childish; it covered a piece of squared paper from an exercise book: 'Trousers for papa: 15 lire. Socks: 0.30 lira. Muslin and flannel: 8.35 lire. Red wool: 1.50 lire. Total: 25.15 lire.'

The chief constable, Cavalier Cacciatori, who was conducting the preliminary enquiries, asked about various girls who had disappeared. In the registers it appeared that on 5 January a certain Felice Canuti had reported the disappearance of his daughter, Isolina. They sent for him and showed him the list. The man recognised his daughter's handwriting.

Felice Canuti, whom the *Corriere della Sera* described as 'a stooped old man who moves slowly, with long white hair and beard, a long hooked nose, large sunken eyes, high cheekbones, thin, wearing threadbare clothes', was sixty-one and spoke very lovingly about his daughter Isolina: 'She was my idol,' he said, 'I lived for her glance'; 'I can't take it in that she's dead . . . she went away the morning of the 5th and hasn't been back since . . .'

'And where was she going?'

'I don't know . . . my daughter Clelia saw her walking in the direction of the Officers' Club and the gasometer.'

From *Isolina* by Dacia Maraini, translated by Siân Williams

A Witness

Wild and eerie was the night,
And the snow fell thick and white,
And across the moaning sea
Sped the spirits wearily;
And the north wind from the moor
Railed and rattled at the door;
And against the window-pane
Smote the bitter hail and rain.

Wild and eerie was the night,
But the fire within burned bright,
And my mother span apace,
With the red light on her face;
And my father, as he sat,
Slowly stroked the purring cat,
While she lay upon my knee; –
For no fear or care had we.

Wild and eerie was the night,
Yet no cause had we for fright,
And the moaning of the sea
Seemed a cradle-song to me;
And the loose wind-rattled pane,
Smitten sharply by the rain,
But a playmate singing low,
Not the harbinger of woe.

Wild and eerie was the night,
Yet in Mary's blessed sight
Darkest night is clear as day;
And the sweet saints ever pray
To the dear Lord on His throne,
When the nights are dark and lone,
So our priest says constantly,
And his words seemed true to me.

Wild and eerie was the night,
Yet the faint and chequered light
Of the log-fire, cast athwart
Wheel and worker, subtly wrought
From the old forms that I knew,
Visions strange, and weird, and new,
Till I slept the young child's sleep,
Dreamless, visionless, and deep.

Sudden woke I, with a start,
And a cold fear at my heart.
Through the clamour at the pane
Came a sound that was not rain,
Wind, or hail, or storm, or sea,
But a deadlier enemy!
With a crash, the fast-barred door
At my feet fell, on the floor!

Three men, through the open space
Rushed into our dwelling-place;
Seized my father by the hair,
While my mother, in despair,

Strove to shield him with her breast.
God! how shall I tell the rest?
Swift they dragged him from our sight,
Out into the fearful night!

Never, while I live, shall I
Lose the utter misery
Of my mother's maddened eyes!
Always to my ears will rise
Her despairing shriek, as they
Tore him from her arms away –
Bleeding, wounded, scarce alive,
How should he with three men strive?

Out into that awful night
Rushed they, from her tortured sight.
For an instant, with shrill groan,
Sank she fainting, cold as stone;
But full soon her face flushed red:
'Hear that sound, my child!' she said;
''Tis your father's dying cry,
As they murder him hard-by!

'When he's dead (heed carefully
What I say; ah, woe is me!
Father's blood and mother's tears
Yield you strength beyond your years!)
Then will come my turn to die.
(Darling listen heedfully)
In yon cupboard must you hide;
By the small crack in its side.

'Set your face, where you can see
All the bitter tragedy.
I will struggle as I may.
See, the fire is bright as day'; –
Here she flung logs fresh and dry,
And the fire blazed clear and high –
'In this light your eyes can scan
Face and form of every man.'

Then she set me in my place,
With a smile on her wan face;
And she kissed me, held me near
Her poor heart, till I could hear
Its swift beats; and then she said,
'Help will come when I am dead;
And, my child, your voice must be
Raised to tell the truth for me.

'At each face look well, my own;
Never think you are alone;
See, I lay upon your knee
Pussy for sweet company.
Very soon the sun will rise,'
(Oh, the anguish of her eyes!)
'Then my darling, you will tell
What you saw. Watch well! watch well!'

As she kissed me, last of all,
Said she, 'Let no whisper fall
From your lips, but silently
Heed whate'er you hear or see.'
Hasty footsteps filled the place;
Muttered curses fell apace;
Back the murderers had sped.
God! and was my father dead?

Lurid flashed the new-fed fire,
Springing upward, brighter, higher –
On her white face as she strove,
Strong in vengeance and in love,
'Gainst those red knives, dripping wet
With my father's life-blood yet.
Oh, my God! I know not well
How time sped! At last she fell!

Stricken through and through again,
With no feeling left but pain,
She had striven, that each man
Well her child might note and scan:

Think you I forget these three
Not till life forgetteth me!
Silent watched I till they fled,
Then I crept out to the dead,

And ye found me. Here I stand,
God's own book within my hand:
In His awful sight I swear
That the murderers stand there!

Evelyn Pyne

Spontaneous Combustion

MR GUPPY sitting on the window-sill, nodding his head and balancing all these possibilities in his mind, continues thoughtfully to tap it, and clasp it, and measure it with his hand, until he hastily draws his hand away.

'What, in the devil's name,' he says, 'is this! Look at my fingers!'

A thick, yellow liquor defiles them, which is offensive to the touch and sight and more offensive to the smell. A stagnant, sickening oil, with some natural repulsion in it that makes them both shudder.

'What have you been doing here? What have you been pouring out of the window?'

'I pouring out of window? Nothing, I swear. Never, since I have been here!' cries the lodger.

And yet look here – and look here! When he brings the candle, here, from the corner of the window-sill, it slowly drips, and creeps away down the bricks; here, lies in a little thick nauseous pool.

'This is a horrible house,' says Mr Guppy, shutting down the window. 'Give me some water, or I shall cut my hand off.'

He so washes, and rubs, and scrubs, and smells and washes, that he has not long restored himself with a glass of brandy, and stood silently before the fire, when Saint Paul's bell strikes twelve, and all those other bells strike twelve from their towers of various heights in the dark air, and in their many tones. When all is quiet again, the lodger says:

'It's the appointed time at last. Shall I go?'

Mr Guppy nods, and gives him a 'lucky touch' on the back; but not with the washed hand, though it is his right hand.

He goes down-stairs; and Mr Guppy tries to compose himself, before the fire, for waiting a long time. But in no more than a minute or two the stairs creak, and Tony comes swiftly back.

'Have you got them?'

'Got them! No. The old man's not there.'

He has been so horribly frightened in the short interval that his terror seizes the other, who makes a rush at him and asks loudly, 'What's the matter?'

'I couldn't make him hear, and I softly opened the door and looked in. And the burning smell is there – and the soot is there, and the oil is there – and he is not there!' – Tony ends this with a groan.

Mr Guppy takes the light. They go down, more dead than alive, and holding one another, push open the door of the back shop. The cat has retreated close to it, and stands snarling – not at them; at something on the ground, before the fire. There is a very little fire left in the grate, but there is a smouldering suffocating vapour in the room, and a dark greasy coating on the walls and ceiling. The chairs and table, and the bottle so rarely absent from the table, all stand as usual. On one chair-back, hang the old man's hairy cap and coat.

'Look!' whispers the lodger, pointing his friend's attention to these objects with a trembling finger. 'I told you so. When I saw him last, he took his cap off, took out the little bundle of old letters, hung his cap on the back of the chair – his coat was there already, for he had pulled that off before he went to put the shutters up – and I left him turning the letters over in his hand, standing just where that crumbled black thing is upon the floor.'

Is he hanging somewhere? They look up. No.

'See!' whispers Tony. 'At the foot of the same chair there lies a dirty bit of thin red cord that they tie up pens with. That went round the letters. He undid it slowly, leering and laughing at me, before he began to turn them over, and threw it there. I saw it fall.'

'What's the matter with the cat?' says Mr Guppy. 'Look at her!'

'Mad, I think. And no wonder in this evil place.'

They advance slowly, looking at all these things. The cat remains where they found her, still snarling at the something on the ground, before the fire and between the two stairs. What is it? Hold up the light.

Here is a small burnt patch of flooring; here is the tinder from a little bundle of burnt paper, but not so light as usual, seeming to be steeped in something; and here is – is it the cinder of a small charred and broken log of wood sprinkled with white ashes, or is it coal? O Horror, he IS here! and this from which we run away, striking out the light and overturning one another into the street, is all that represents him.

Help, help, help! come into this house for Heaven's sake!

Plenty will come in, but none can help. The Lord Chancellor of that Court, true to his title in his last act, has died the death of all Lord Chancellors in all Courts, and of all authorities in all places under all names soever, where false pretences are made, and where injustice is done. Call the death by any name Your Highness will, attribute it to whom you will, or say it might have been prevented how you will, it is the same death eternally – inborn, inbred, engendered in the corrupted humours of the vicious body itself, and that only – Spontaneous Combustion, and none other of all the deaths that can be died.

From *Bleak House* by Charles Dickens

Vilikins and His Dinah

The following was popular as a street song or on stage. The parts in italics were spoken.

> Oh! 'tis of a rich merchant,
> In London did dwell,
> He had but one daughter,
> An uncommon nice young gal!
> Her name it was Dinah,
> Scarce sixteen years old,
> She had a large fortune
> In silver and gold.
>   Singing Too-ral-loo, Too-ral-loo, Too-ral-loo, Ay.

> As Dinah was valking
> In the garden vun day,
> *(It was the front garden, not the back garden.)*
> Her papa came up to her,
> And thus he did say,
> Go, dress yourself, Dinah,
> In gor-ge-ous array
> And I'll get you a husband,
> Both val-ly-ant and gay.
>   Singing Too-ral-loo, etc.

This is what the infant progeny said to the author of her being.
Oh, papa! oh, papa!
I've not made up my mind,
To marry just yet
I do not feel inclined,
And all my large fortune,
I'll freely give o'er,
If you'll let me stay single
A year or two more.
　　Singing Too-ral-loo, etc.

This is what the indignant parient replied. I represent the father.
Then go, boldest daughter,
The parient replied,
If you don't consent to be
This here young man's bride,
I'll leave your large fortune
To the nearest of kin,
And you shan't have the benefit
Of one single pin.
　　Singing Too-ral-loo, etc.

Now comes the epiflabbergastrinum of the lovier.
As Vilikins vas valking
The garden around
(The aforesaid front garden)
He spied his dear Dinah
Lying dead on the ground,
A cup of cold pison
It laid by her side,
And a billy dux stating
By pison she died.
Taken inwardly, Singing Too-ral-loo, etc.

This is what the lovier did.
Then he kissed her cold corpus
A thousand times o'er,
He called her his Dinah
Though she was no more!
He swallowed the pison

Like a true lovier brave,
And Vilikins and his Dinah
Lie a-buried in one grave.
Both on 'em Singing Too-ral-loo, etc.

Moral:

Now all you young vimmen,
Take a warning by her,
And never by any means
Disobey the guv'ner:
And all you young fellers,
Mind who you clap eyes on,
Think on Vilikins and Dinah
And the cup of cold pison
Else you'll be singing Too-ral-loo, etc.

Anon.

The Bride of Lammermoor

GLANCING WIDE over hill and dale, the fair bridal procession at last reached the parish church, which they nearly filled; for besides domestics, above a hundred gentlemen and ladies were present upon the occasion. The marriage ceremony was performed according to the rites of the Presbyterian persuasion, to which Bucklaw of late had judged it proper to conform.

On the outside of the church a liberal dole was distributed to the poor of the neighbouring parishes, under the direction of Johnny Mortsheugh, who had lately been promoted from his desolate quarters at the hermitage, to fill the more eligible situation of sexton at the parish church of Ravenswood. Dame Gourlay with two of her contemporaries, the same who assisted at Alice's late wake, seated apart upon a flat monument, or throughstane, sate enviously comparing the shares which had been allotted to them in dividing the dole.

'Johnny Mortsheugh,' said Annie Winnie, 'might hae minded auld lang syne and thought of his auld kimmers, for as braw as he is with his new black coat. I hae gotten but five herring instead o' sax, and this disna look like a gude saxpennies, and I dare say this bit morsel o' beef is unce lighter than ony that's been dealt round; and it's a bit o' the tenony hough, mair by token, that yours Maggie, is out o' the back sey.'

'Mine, quo' she?' mumbled the paralytic hag, 'mine is half banes, I trow. If grit folk gie poor bodies ony thing for coming to their weddings and burials, it suld be something that wad do them gude, I think.'

'Their gifts,' said Ailsie Gourlay, 'are dealt for nae love of us – nor out of respect for whether we feed or starve. They wad gie us whinstanes for loaves, if it would serve their ain vanity, and yet they expect us to be as gratefu', as they ca' it, as if they served us for true love and liking.'

'And that's truly said,' answered her companion.

'But Ailsie Gourlay, ye're the auldest o' us three, did ye ever see a mair grand bridal?'

'I winna say that I have,' answered the hag; 'but I think soon to see as braw a burial.'

'And that wad please me as weel,' said Annie Winnie; 'for there's as large a dole, and folk are no obliged to girn and laugh, and mak murgeons, and wish joy to these hellicat quality, that lord it ower us like brute beasts. I like to pack the dead-dole in my lap, and rin ower the old rhyme, –

My loaf in my lap, my penny in my purse,
Thou art ne'er the better, and I'm ne'er the worse.'

'That's right, Annie,' said the paralytic woman; 'God send us a green Yule and a fat kirkyard!'

'But I wad like to ken, Luckie Gourlay, for ye're the auldest and wisest amang us, whilk o' these revellers' turns it will be to be streekit first?'

'D'ye see yon dandilly maiden,' said Dame Gourlay, 'a' glistenin' wi' gold and jewels, that they are lifting up on the white horse behind that harebrained callant in scarlet, wi' the lang sword at his side?'

'But that's the bride?' said her companion, her cold heart touched with some sort of compassion; 'that's the very bride hersell! Eh, whow! sae young, sae braw, and saw bonny – and is her time sae short?'

'I tell ye,' said the sibyl, 'her winding-sheet is up as high as her throat already, believe it wha list. Her sand has but few grains to rin out, and nae wonder – they've been weel shaken. The leaves are withering fast on the trees, but she'll never see the Martinmas wind gar them dance in swirls like the fairy rings.'

'Ye waited on her for a quarter,' said the paralytic woman, 'and got twa red pieces, or I am far beguiled.'

'Ay, ay,' answered Ailsie, with a bitter grin; 'and Sir William Ashton promised me a bonny red gown to the boot o' that – a stake, and a chain, and a tar-barrel, lass? – what think ye o' that for a propine? for being up early and doun late for fourscore nights and mair wi' his dwining daugher. But he may keep it for his ain leddy, cummers.'

'I hae heard a sough,' said Annie Winnie, 'as if Leddy Ashton was nae canny body.'

'D'ye see her yonder,' said Dame Gourlay, 'as she prances on her gey gelding out at the kirkyard? – there's mair o' utter deevilry in that woman as brave and fair-fashioned as she rides yonder, than in a' the Scotch witches that ever flew by moonlight ower North-Berwick Law.'

'What's that ye say about witches, ye damned hags!' said Johnny Mortsheugh; 'are ye casting yer cantrips in the very kirkyard, to mischieve the bride and bridegroom? Get awa hame, for if I tak my souple t'ye, I'll gar ye find the road faster than ye wad like.'

'Hech, sirs!' answered Ailsie Gourlay – 'how bra' are we wi' our new black coat and our weel-pouthered head, as if we had never kend hunger nor thirst oursells! and we'll be screwing up our bit fiddle, doubtless, in the ha' the night, amang a' the other elbo'-jiggers for miles round. Let's see if the pins haud, Johnny – that's a', lad.'

'I take ye a' to witness, gude people,' said Mortsheugh, 'that she threatens me wi' mischief, and forespeaks me. If ony thing but gude happens to me or my fiddle this night, I'll make it the blackest night's job she ever stirred in. I'll hae her before Presbytery and Synod – I'm half a minister mysell, now that I'm a bedral in an inhabited parish.'

Sir Walter Scott

Hon. Mr Suckle Thumbkin's Story

The Execution: A Sporting Anecdote

My Lord Tomnoddy got up one day;
    It was half after two,
    He had nothing to do,
So his lordship rang for his cabriolet.

    Tiger Tim
    Was clean of limb,
His boots were polished, his jacket was trim;

With a very smart tie in his smart cravat,
And a smart cockade on the top of his hat;
Tallest of boys or shortest of men,
He stood in his stockings just four foot ten;
And he asked as he held the door on the swing,
'Pray did your Lordship please to ring?'

My Lord Tomnoddy he raised his head,
And thus to Tiger Tim he said,
    'Malibran's dead,
    Duvernay's fled,
Taglioni has not yet arrived in her stead;
Tiger Tim come tell me true,
What may a nobleman find to do?'
    Tim looked up, and Tim looked down,
He paused, and he put on a thoughtful frown,
And he held up his hat, and he peeped in the crown,
He bit his lip, and he scratched his head,
He let go the handle, and thus he said,
As the door, released, behind him banged:
'An't please you, my Lord, there's a man to be hanged.'

My Lord Tomnoddy jumped up at the news,
    'Run to M'Fuze,
    And Lieutenant Tregooze,
And run to Sir Barnaby Jenks, of the Blues.
    Ropedancers a score
    I've seen before –
Madame Sacchi, Antonio, and Master Black-more:
    But to see a man swing
    At the end of a string,
With his neck in a noose, will be quite a new thing!"

My Lord Tomnoddy stepped into his cab –
Dark rifle green, with a lining of drab:
    Through street, and through square,
    His high-trotting mare,
Like one of Ducrow's, goes pawing the air,
Adown Piccadilly and Waterloo Place
Went the high-trotting mare at a very quick pace;

She produced some alarm,
But did no great harm,
Save frightening a nurse with a child on her arm,
Spattering with clay
Two urchins at play,
Knocking down – very much to the sweeper's dismay –
An old woman who wouldn't get out of the way,
And upsetting a stall
Near Exeter Hall,
Which made all the pious Church-mission folks squall;

But eastward afar,
Through Temple Bar,
My Lord Tomnoddy directs his car;
Never heeding their squalls,
Or their calls, or their bawls,
He passes by Waithman's Emporium for shawls,
And, merely just catching a glimpse of St Paul's,
Turns down the Old Bailey,
Where, in front of the jail, he
Pulls up at the door of the ginshop, and gayly
Cries, 'What must I fork out to-night, my trump,
For the whole first floor of the Magpie and Stump?'

★ ★ ★

The clock strikes twelve – it is dark midnight –
Yet the Magpie and Stump is one blaze of light.
The parties are met;
The tables are set;
There is 'punch', 'cold *without*', 'hot *within*', 'heavy wet',
Ale glasses and jugs,
And rummers and mugs,
And sand on the floor, without carpets or rugs,
Cold fowl and cigars,
Pickled onions in jars,
Welsh rabbits and kidneys – rare work for the jaws, –
And very large lobsters, with very large claws;
And there is M'Fuze,
And Lieutenant Tregooze,

And there is Sir Barnaby Jenks, of the Blues,
        All come to see a man 'die in his shoes!'

        The clock strikes One!
        Supper is done,
And Sir Barnaby Jenks is full of his fun,
Singing 'Jolly companions every one!'
        My Lord Tomnoddy
        Is drinking gin toddy,
And laughing at everything, and everybody.

The clock strikes Two! and the clock strikes Three!
–'Who so merry, so merry as we?'
        Save Captain M'Fuze,
        Who is taking a snooze,
While Sir Barnaby Jenks is busy at work,
Blacking his nose with a piece of burnt cork.
        The clock strikes four!
        Round the debtor's door
Are gathered a couple of thousand or more;
        As many await
        At the press-yard gate,
Till slowly its folding doors open, and straight
The mob divides, and between their ranks
A wagon comes loaded with posts and with planks.
        The clock strikes Five!
        The Sheriffs arrive,
And the crowd is so great that the street seems alive;
        But Sir Barnaby Jenks
        Blinks, and winks,
A candle burns down in the socket, and sinks,
        Lieutenant Tregooze
        Is dreaming of Jews,
And acceptances all the bill brokers refuse;
        My Lord Tomnoddy
        Has drunk all his toddy,
And just as dawn is beginning to peep,
The whole of the party are fast asleep.

Sweetly, oh! sweetly, the morning breaks,

      With roseate streaks,
Like the first faint blush on a maiden's cheeks;
It seemed that the mild and clear blue sky
Smiled upon all things far and nigh,
On all – save the wretch condemned to die!
Alack that ever so fair a sun
As that which its course has now begun,
Should rise on such a scene of misery –
Should gild with rays so light and free
That dismal, dark-frowning gallows tree!

And hark! – a sound comes, big with fate;
The clock from St Sepulchre's tower strikes – Eight! –
List to that low funereal bell:
It is tolling, alas! a living man's knell –
And see, – from forth that opening door
They come! – He steps that threshold o'er
Who never shall tread upon threshold more.
–God! 'tis a fearsome thing to see
That pale, wan man's mute agony,
The glare of that wild, despairing eye,
Now bent on the crowd, now turned to the sky,
As though 'twere scanning, in doubt and in fear,
The path of the Spirit's unknown career;
Those pinioned arms, those hands that ne'er
Shall be lifted again, not even in prayer;
That heaving chest! – Enough, – 'tis done!
The bolt has fallen! – the spirit is gone –
For weal or for woe is known but to One! –
–Oh! 'twas a fearsome sight! – Ah me!
A deed to shudder at, not to see.

Again that clock! 'tis time, 'tis time!
The hour is past; – with its earliest chime
The chord is severed, its lifeless clay
By 'dungeon villains' is borne away:
Nine! – 'twas the last concluding stroke!
And then – my Lord Tomnoddy awoke!
And Tregooze and Sir Barnaby Jenks arose,
And Captain M'Fuze, with the black on his nose:

And they stared at each other, as much as to say
     'Hollo! hollo!
     Here's a rum Go!
Why, Captain! – my Lord! – Here's the devil to pay!
The fellow's been cut down and taken away! –
     What's to be done?
     We've missed all the fun! –
Why, they'll laugh at and quiz us all over the town.
We are all of us done so uncommonly brown!'

What *was* to be done? – 'twas perfectly plain
That they could not well hang the man over again.
What was to be done! – The man was dead!
Naught *could* be done – naught could be said;
So – my Lord Tomnoddy went home to bed!

From the *Ingoldsby Legends* by Richard Harris Barham

The Slave

WHEN I WAS TRAVELLING through North Carolina, a black man, who was outlawed, being shot by one of his pursuers, and left wounded in the woods, they came to the ordinary where I had stopped to bait my horse, in order to procure a cart to bring the poor wretched object in. Another, I was credibly informed, was shot, his head cut off, and carried in a bag by the perpetrators of the murder, who received the reward, which was said to have been two hundred dollars, and that the head was stuck on a coal-house at an iron-works in Virginia. His crime was going, without leave, to visit his wife, who was in slavery at some distance.

From *The New Newgate Calendar*, edited by Andrew Knapp
and William Baldwin

Sweet Meat Has Sour Sauce; or, The Slave-Trader in the Dumps

A trader I am to the African shore,
But since that my trading is like to be o'er,
I'll sing you a song that you ne'er heard before,
    Which nobody can deny, deny,
    Which nobody can deny.

When I first heard the news it gave me a shock,
Much like what they call an electrical knock,
And now I am going to sell off my stock,
    Which nobody, &c.

'Tis a curious assortment of dainty regales,
To tickle the negroes with when the ship sails,
Fine chains for the neck, and a cat with nine tails,
    Which nobody, &c.

Here's supple-jack plenty, and store of ratan,
That will wind itself round the sides of a man,
As close as a hoop round a bucket or can,
    Which nobody, &c.

Here's padlocks and bolts, and screws for the thumbs,
That squeeze them so lovingly till the blood comes;
They sweeten the temper like comfits or plums,
    Which nobody, &c.

When a negro his head from his victuals withdraws,
And clenches his teeth and thrusts out his paws,
Here's a notable engine to open his jaws,
    Which nobody, &c.

Thus going to market, we kindly prepare
A pretty black cargo of African ware,
For what they must meet with when they get there,
    Which nobody, &c.

'Twould do your heart good to see 'em below
Lie flat on their backs all the way as we go,
Like sprats on a gridiron, scores in a row,
    Which nobody, &c.

But ah! if in vain I have studied an art
So gainful to me, all boasting apart,
I think it will break my compassionate heart,
    Which nobody, &c.

For oh! how it enters my soul like an awl;
This pity, which some people self-pity call,
Is sure the most heart-piercing pity of all,
    Which nobody, &c.

So this is my song, as I told you before;
Come, buy off my stock, for I must no more
Carry Caesars and Pompeys to sugar-cane shore,
    Which nobody, &c.

William Cowper

Epigram

To purify their wine, some people bleed
A lamb into the barrel, and succeed;
No nostrum, planters say, is half so good
To make fine sugar, as a negro's blood.
Now lambs and negroes both are harmless things,
And hence perhaps this wondrous virtue springs.
'Tis in the blood of innocence alone –
Good cause why planters never try their own.

William Cowper

Going to See a Man Hanged

X, who had voted with Mr Ewart for the abolition of the punishment of death, was anxious to see the effect on the public mind of an execution, and asked me to accompany him to see Courvoisier killed. We had not the advantage of a sheriff's order, like the 'six hundred noblemen and gentlemen' who were admitted within the walls of the prison; but determined to mingle with the crowd at the foot of the scaffold, and take up our positions at a very early hour.

As I was to rise at three in the morning, I went to bed at ten, thinking that five hours' sleep would be amply sufficient to brace me against the fatigues of the coming day. But, as might have been expected, the event of the morrow was perpetually before my eyes through the night, and kept them wide open. I heard all the clocks in the neighbourhood chime the hours in succession; a dog from some court hard by kept up a pitiful howling; at one o'clock, a cock set up a feeble, melancholy crowing; shortly after two the daylight came peeping grey through the window-shutters; and by the time that X arrived, in fulfilment of his promise, I had been asleep about half-an-hour. He, more wise, had not gone to rest at all, but had remained up all night at the Club, along with Dash and two or three more. Dash is one of the most eminent wits in London, and had kept the company merry all night with appropriate jokes about the coming event. It is curious that a murder is a great inspirer of jokes. We all like to laugh and have our fling about it; there is a certain grim pleasure in the circumstance – a perpetual jingling antithesis between life and death, that is sure of its effect.

In mansion or garret, on down or straw, surrounded by weeping friends and solemn oily doctors, or tossing unheeded upon scanty hospital beds, there were many people in this great city to whom that Sunday night was to be the last of any that they should pass on earth here. In the course of half-a-dozen dark, wakeful hours, one had leisure to think of these (and a little, too, of that certain supreme night, that shall come at one time or other, when he who writes shall be stretched upon the last bed, prostrate in the last struggle, taking the last look of dear faces that have cheered us here, and lingering – one moment more – ere we part for the tremendous journey); but, chiefly, I could not help thinking, as each clock sounded, what is *he* doing now? has *he* heard it in his little room in Newgate yonder? Eleven o'clock. He has been writing until now. The gaoler says he is a pleasant man enough to be with; but he can hold out no longer, and is very weary. 'Wake me at four,' says he, 'for I have still much to put down.' From eleven to twelve the gaoler hears how he is grinding his teeth in his sleep. At twelve he is up in his bed, and asks, 'Is it the time?' He has plenty more time yet for sleep; and he sleeps, and the bell goes on tolling. Seven hours more – five hours more. Many a carriage is clattering through the streets, bringing ladies away from evening parties; many bachelors are reeling home after a jolly night; Covent Garden is alive; and the light coming through the cell-window turns the gaoler's candle pale. Four hours more! 'Courvoisier,' says the gaoler, shaking him, 'it's four o'clock now, and I've woke you as you told me; but there's no call for you to get up yet.' The poor wretch leaves his bed, however, and makes his last toilet; and then falls to writing, to tell the world how he did the crime for which he has suffered. This time he will tell the truth, and the whole truth. They bring him his breakfast 'from the coffee-shop opposite – tea, coffee, and thin bread and butter'. He will take nothing, however, but goes on writing. He has to write to his mother – the pious mother far away in his own country – who reared him and loved him; and even now has sent him her forgiveness and her blessing. He finishes his memorials and letters, and makes his will, disposing of his little miserable property of books and tracts that pious people have furnished him with. '*Ce 6 Juillet, 1849. François Benjamin Courvoisier vous donne ceci, mon ami, pour souvenir.*' He has a token for his dear friend the gaoler; another for his dear friend the under-sheriff. As the day of the convict's death draws nigh, it is painful to see how he fastens upon everybody who approaches him, how pitifully he clings to them and loves them.

While these things are going on within the prison (with which we are made accurately acquainted by the copious chronicles of such events which are published subsequently), X's carriage has driven up to the door of my lodgings, and we have partaken of an elegant *déjeuner* that has been prepared for the occasion. A cup of coffee at half-past three in the morning is uncommonly pleasant; and X enlivens us with the repetition of the jokes that Dash has just been making. Admirable, certainly – they must have had a merry night of it, that's clear; and we stoutly debate whether, when one has to get up so early in the morning, it is best to have an hour or two of sleep, or wait and go to bed afterwards at the end of the day's work. That fowl is extraordinarily tough – the wing, even, is as hard as a board; a slight disappointment, for there is nothing else for breakfast. 'Will any gentleman have some sherry and soda-water before he sets out? It clears the brains famously.' Thus primed, the party sets out. The coachman has dropped asleep on the box, and wakes up wildly as the hall-door opens. It is just four o'clock. About this very time they are waking up poor – pshaw! who is for a cigar? X does not smoke himself; but vows and protests, in the kindest way in the world, that he does not care in the least for the new drab-silk linings in his carriage. Z, who smokes, mounts, however, the box.

'Drive to Snow Hill,' says the owner of the chariot. The policemen, who are the only people in the street, and are standing by, look knowing – they know what it means well enough.

How cool and clean the streets look, as the carriage startles the echoes that have been asleep in the corners all night. Somebody has been sweeping the pavements clean in the night-time surely; they would not soil a lady's white satin shoes, they are so dry and neat. There is not a cloud or a breath in the air, except Z's cigar, which whiffs off, and soars straight upwards in volumes of white, pure smoke. The trees in the squares look bright and green – as bright as leaves in the country in June. Those who keep late hours don't know the beauty of London air and verdure; in the early morning they are delightful – the most fresh and lively companions possible. But they cannot bear the crowd and the bustle of midday. You don't know them then – they are no longer the same things. We have come to Gray's Inn; there is actually dew upon the grass in the gardens; and the windows of the stout old red houses are all in a flame.

As we enter Holborn the town grows more animated; and there are already twice as many people in the streets as you see at midday in a German *Residenz* or an English provincial town. The ginshop keepers have many of them taken their shutters down, and many persons are issuing from them pipe in hand. Down they go along the broad bright street, their blue shadows marching after them; for they are all bound the same way, and are bent like us upon seeing the hanging.

It is twenty minutes past four as we pass St Sepulchre's: by this time many hundred people are in the street, and many more are coming up Snow Hill. Before us lies Newgate Prison; but something a great more awful to look at, which seizes the eye at once, and makes the heart beat, is[1]

There it stands black and ready, jutting out from a little door in the prison. As you see it, you feel a kind of dumb electric shock, which causes one to start a little, and give a sort of gasp for breath. The shock is over in a second; and presently you examine the object before you with a certain feeling of complacent curiosity. At least, such was the effect that the gallows produced upon the writer, who is trying to set down all his feelings as they occurred, and not to exaggerate them at all.

After the gallows-shock had subsided, we went down into the crowd, which was very numerous, but not dense as yet. It was evident that the day's *business* had not begun. People sauntered up, and formed groups, and talked; the new-comers asking those who seemed *habitués* of the place about

1 Thackeray inserts a sketch of the scaffold at this point

former executions; and did the victim hang with his face towards the clock or towards Ludgate Hill? and had he the rope round his neck when he came on the scaffold, or was it put on by Jack Ketch afterwards? and had Lord W taken a window, and which was he?

Various political arguments follow amongst the groups in the crowd.

What is the meaning of this unconscionable republican tirade – *à propos* of a hanging? Such feelings, I think, must come across any man in a vast multitude like this. What good sense and intelligence have most of the people by whom you are surrounded; how much sound humour does one hear bandied about from one to another! A great number of coarse phrases are used, that would make ladies in drawing-rooms blush; but the morals of the men are good and hearty. A ragamuffin in the crowd (a powdery baker in a white sheep's-wool cap) uses some indecent expression to a woman near: there is an instant cry of shame, which silences the man, and a dozen people are ready to give the woman protection. The crowd has grown very dense by this time, it is about six o'clock, and there is great heaving, and pushing, and swaying to and fro; but round the women the men have formed a circle, and keep them as much as possible out of the rush and trample. In one of the houses near us, a gallery has been formed on the roof. Seats were here let, and a number of persons of various degrees were occupying them. Several tipsy, dissolute-looking young men, of the Dick Swiveller cast, were in this gallery. One was lolling over the sunshiny tiles, with a fierce sodden face, out of which came a pipe, and which was shaded by long matted hair, and a hat cocked very much on one side. This gentleman was one of a party which had evidently not been to bed on Sunday night, but had passed it in some of those delectable night-houses in the neighbourhood of Covent Garden. The debauch was not over yet, and the women fo the party were giggling, drinking, and romping, as is the wont of these delicate creatures; sprawling here and there, and falling upon the knees of one or other of the males. Their scarfs were off their shoulders, and you saw the sun shining down upon the bare white flesh, and the shoulder-points glittering like burning-glasses. The people about us were very indignant at some of the proceedings of this debauched crew, and at last raised up such a yell as frightened them into shame, and they were more orderly for the remainder of the day. The windows of the shops opposite began to fill apace, and our before-mentioned friend with ragged elbows pointed out a celebrated fashionable character who occupied one of them, and, to our surprise, knew as much about him as the *Court Journal* or the

Morning Post. Presently he entertained us with a long and pretty accurate account of the history of Lady — , and indulged in a judicious criticism upon her last work. I have met with many a country gentleman who had not read half as many books as this honest fellow, this shrewd *prolétaire* in a black shirt. The people about him took up and carried on the conversation very knowingly, and were very little behind him in point of information. It was just as good a company as one meets on common occasions. I was in a genteel crowd in one of the galleries at the Queen's coronation; indeed, in point of intelligence, the democrats were quite equal to the aristocrats. How many more such groups were there in this immense multitude of nearly forty thousand, as some say? How many more such throughout the country? I never yet, as I said before, have been in an English mob, without the same feeling for the persons who composed it, and without wonder at the vigorous, orderly good sense and intelligence of the people.

The character of the crowd was as yet, however, quite festive. Jokes bandying about here and there, and jolly laughs breaking out. Some men were endeavouring to climb up a leaden pipe on one of the houses. The landlord came out, and endeavoured with might and main to pull them down. Many thousand eyes turned upon this contest immediately. All sorts of voices issued from the crowd, and uttered choice expressions of slang. When one of the men was pulled down by the leg, the waves of this black mob-ocean laughed innumerably; when one fellow slipped away, scrambled up the pipe, and made good his lodgment on the shelf, we were all made happy, and encouraged him by loud shouts of admiration. What is there so particularly delightful in the spectacle of a man clambering up a gas-pipe? Why were we kept for a quarter of an hour in deep interest gazing upon this remarkable scene? Indeed it is hard to say a man does not know what a fool he is until he tries; or, at least, what mean follies will amuse him. The other day I went to Astley's, and saw a clown come in with a fool's cap and pinafore, and six small boys who represented his schoolfellows. To them enters schoolmaster; horses clown, and flogs him hugely on the back part of his pinafore. I never read anything in Swift, Boz, Rabelais, Fielding, Paul de Kock, which delighted me so much as this sight, and caused me to laugh so profoundly. And why? What is there so ridiculous in the sight of one miserably rouged man beating another on the breech? Tell us where the fun lies in this and the before-mentioned episode of the gas-pipe? Vast, indeed, are the capacities and ingenuities of the human soul that can find, in incidents so wonderfully small, means of contemplation and amusement.

Really the time passed away with extraordinary quickness. A thousand things of the sort related here came to amuse us. First the workmen knocking and hammering at the scaffold, mysterious clattering of blows was heard within it, and a ladder painted black was carried round, and into the interior of the edifice by a small side-door. We all looked at this little ladder and at each other – things began to be very interesting. Soon came a squad of policemen; stalwart, rosy-looking men, saying much for City feeding; well dressed, well limbed, and of admirable good-humour. They paced about the open space between the prison and the barriers which kept in the crowd from the scaffold. The front line, as far as I could see, was chiefly occupied by blackguards and boys – professional persons, no doubt, who saluted the policemen on their appearance with a volley of jokes and ribaldry. As far as I could judge from faces, there were more blackguards of sixteen and seventeen than of any maturer age; stunted, sallow, ill-grown lads, in rugged fustian, scowling about. There were a considerable number of girls, too, of the same age; one that Cruikshank and Boz might have taken as a study for Nancy. The girl was a young thief's mistress evidently; if attacked, ready to reply without a particle of modesty; could give as good ribaldry as she got; made no secret (and there were several inquiries) as to her profession and means of livelihood. But with all this, there was something good about the girl; a sort of devil-may-care candour and simplicity that one could not fail to see. Her answers to some of the coarse questions put to her, were very ready and good-humoured. She had a friend with her on the same age and class, of whom she seemed to be very fond, and who looked up to her for protection. Both of these women had beautiful eyes. Devil-may-care's were extraordinarily bright and blue, an admirably fair complexion, and a large red mouth full of white teeth. *Au reste*, ugly, stunted, thick-limbed, and by no means a beauty. Her friend could not be more than fifteen. They were not in rags, but had greasy cotton shawls, and old, faded, rag-shop bonnets. I was curious to look at them, having, in late fashionable novels, read many accounts of such personages. Bah! what figments these novelists tell us! Boz, who knows life well, knows that his Miss Nancy is the most unreal fantastical personage possible, no more like a thief's mistress than one of Gesner's sheperdesses resembles a real country wench. He dare not tell the truth concerning such young ladies. They have, no doubt, virtues like other human creatures; nay, their position engenders virtues that are not called into exercise among other women. But on these an honest painter of human nature has no right to dwell; not being able to paint the whole portrait, he has no right to present one or two favourable points as characterising the whole; and therefore, in fact, had better leave the picture alone altogether. The new French literature is essentially false and worthless from this very error – the writers giving us favourable pictures of monsters, and (to say nothing of decency or morality) pictures quite untrue to nature.

But yonder, glittering through the crowd in Newgate Street – see, the Sheriffs; carriages are slowly making their way. We have been here three hours! Is it possible that they can have passed so soon? Close to the barriers where we are, the mob has become so dense that it is with difficulty a man can keep his feet. Each man, however, is very careful in protecting the women, and all are full of jokes and good-humour. The windows of the shops opposite are now pretty nearly filled by the persons who hired them. Many young dandies are there with moustaches and cigars; some quiet, fat, family-parties, of simple, honest tradesmen and their wives, as we fancy, who are looking on with the greatest imaginable calmness, and sipping their tea. Yonder is the sham Lord W, who is flinging various articles among the crowd; one of his companions, a tall, burly man, with large moustaches, has provided himself with a squirt, and is aspersing the mob with brandy-and-water. Honest gentleman! high-bred aristocrat! genuine lover of humour and wit! I would walk some miles to see thee on the tread-mill, thee and thy Mohawk crew!

We tried to get up a hiss against these ruffians, but only had a trifling success; the crowd did not seem to think their offence very heinous; and our friend, the philosopher in the ragged elbows, who had remained near us all the time, was not inspired with any such savage disgust at the proceedings of certain notorious young gentlemen, as I must confess fills my own particular bosom. He only said, 'So-and-so is a lord, and they'll let him off,' and then discoursed about Lord Ferrers being hanged. The philosopher knew the history pretty well, and so did most of the little knot of persons about him, and it must be a gratifying thing for young gentlemen to find that their actions are made the subject of this kind of conversation.

Scarcely a word had been said about Courvoisier all this time. We were all, as far as I could judge, in just such a frame of mind as men are in when they are squeezing at the pit-door of a play, or pushing for a review or a Lord Mayor's show. We asked most of the men who were near us, whether they had seen many executions? most of them had, the philosopher especially; whether the sight of them did any good? 'For the matter of that, no; people did not care about them at all; nobody ever thought of it after a bit.' A countryman, who had left his drove in Smithfield, said the same thing; he had seen a man hanged at York, and spoke of the ceremony with perfect good sense, and in a quiet, sagacious way.

J.S., the famous wit, now dead, had, I recollect, a good story upon the subject of executing, and of the terror which the punishment inspires. After

Thistlewood and his companions were hanged, their heads were taken off, according to the sentence, and the executioner, as he severed each, held it up to the crowd, in the proper orthodox way, saying, 'Here is the head of a traitor!' At the sight of the first ghastly head the people were struck with terror, and a general expression of disgust and fear broke from them. The second head was looked at also with much interest, but the excitement regarding the third head diminished. When the executioner had come to the last of the heads, he lifted it up, but, by some clumsiness, allowed it to drop. At this the crowd yelled out, '*Ah, Butter-fingers!*' – the excitement had passed entirely away. The punishment had grown to be a joke – Butter-fingers was the word – a pretty commentary, indeed, upon the august nature of public executions, and the awful majesty of the law.

It was past seven now; the quarters rang and passed away; the crowd began to grow very eager and more quiet, and we turned back every now and then and looked at St Sepulchre's clock. Half-an-hour, twenty-five minutes. What is he doing now? He has his irons off by this time. A quarter: he's in the press-room now, no doubt. Now at last we had come to think about the man we were going to see hanged. How slowly the clock crept over the last quarter! Those who were able to turn round and see (for the crowd was now extraordinarily dense) chronicled the time, eight minutes, five minutes; at last – ding, dong, dong, dong! – the bell is tolling the chimes of eight.

Between the writing of this line and the last, the pen has been put down, as the reader may suppose, and the person who is addressing him has gone through a pause of no very pleasant thoughts and recollections. The whole of the sickening, ghastly, wicked scene passes before the eyes again; and, indeed, it is an awful one to see, and very hard and painful to describe.

As the clock began to strike, an immense sway and movement swept over the whole of that vast dense crowd. They were all uncovered directly, and a great murmur arose, more awful, bizarre, and indescribable than any sound I had ever before heard. Women and children began to shriek horribly. I don't know whether it was the bell I heard; but a dreadful quick, feverish kind of jangling noise mingled with the noise of the people, and lasted for about two minutes. The scaffold stood before us, tenantless and black; the black chain was hanging down ready from the beam. Nobody came. 'He has been respited,' some one said; another said, 'He has killed himself in prison.'

Just then, from under the black prison-door, a pale, quiet head peered out. it was shockingly bright and distinct; it rose up directly, and a man in black appeared on the scaffold, and was silently followed by about four more dark figures. The first was a tall grave man: we all knew who the second man was. '*That's he – that's he!*' you heard the people say, as the devoted man came up.

I have seen a cast of the head since, but, indeed, should never have known it. Courvoisier bore his punishment like a man, and walked very firmly. He was dressed in a new black suit, as it seemed: his shirt was open. His arms were tied in front of him. He offered his hands in a helpless kind of way, and clasped them once or twice together. He turned his head here and there, and looked about him for an instant with a wild, imploring look. His mouth was contracted into a sort of pitiful smile. he went and placed himself at once under the beam, with his face towards St Sepulchre's. The tall, grave man in black twisted him round swiftly in the other direction, and, drawing from his pocket a night-cap, pulled it tight over the patient's head and face. I am not ashamed to say that I could look no more, but shut my eyes as the last dreadful act was going on, which sent this wretched, guilty soul into the presence of God.

If a public execution is beneficial – and beneficial it is, no doubt or else the wise laws would not encourage forty thousand people to witness it – the next useful thing must be a full description of such a ceremony, and all its entourages, and to this end the above pages are offered to the reader. How does an individual man feel under it? In what way does he observe it, – how does he view all the phenomena connected with it, – what induces him, in the first instance, to go and see it, – and how is he moved by it afterwards? The writer has discarded the magazine 'We' altogether, and spoken face to face with the reader, recording every one of the impressions felt by him as honestly as he could.

I must confess, then (for 'I' is the shortest word, and the best in this case), that the sight has left on my mind an extraordinary feeling of terror and shame. It seems to me that I have been abetting an act of frightful wickedness and violence, performed by a set of men against one of their fellows; and I pray God that it may soon be out of the power of any man in England to witness such a hideous and degrading sight. Forty thousand persons (say the Sheriffs), of all ranks and degrees, – mechanics, gentlemen, pickpockets, members of both Houses of Parliament, street-walkers, newspaper-writers, gather together before Newgate at a very early hour; the most part of them give up their natural quiet night's rest, in order to partake of this hideous debauchery, which is more exciting than sleep, or than wine, or the last new ballet, or any other amusement they can have. Pickpocket and Peer, each is tickled by the sight alike, and has that hidden lust after blood which influences our race. Government, a Christian government, gives us a feast every now and then: it agrees – that is to say, a majority in the two Houses agrees – that for certain crimes it is necessary that a man should be hanged by the neck. Government commits the criminal's soul to the mercy of God, stating that here on earth he is to look for no mercy; keeps him for a fortnight to prepare, provides him with a clergyman to settle his religious matters (if there be time enough, but Government can't wait); and on a Monday morning, the bell tolling, the clergyman reading out the word of God, 'I am the resurrection and the life,' 'The Lord giveth and the Lord taketh away,' – on a Monday morning, at eight o'clock, this man is placed under a beam, with a rope connecting it and him; a plank disappears from under him, and those who have paid for good places may see the hands of the Government agent, Jack Ketch, coming up from his black hole, and seizing the prisoner's legs, and pulling them, until he is quite dead – strangled.

From *Sketches and Travels in London* by William Makepeace Thackeray

The Hamburg Executioner

CLOSE BY THE JAIL I espied a house of free stone, round and flat roofed, and leaded, upon the which was erected the true picture of a most unmatchable Hangman: and now I am entered into a discourse of this brave abject, or subject, you must understand that this fellow, is a merry, a mad, and a subsidy Hangman, to whom our Tyburn tatterdemalion, or our Wapping wind-pipe stretcher, is but a raggamuffin, not worth the hanging: for this tear-throat termagant is a fellow in folio, a commander of such great command, and of such greatness to command, that I never saw any that in that respect could countermand him: for his making is almost past description, no Saracen's head seems greater, and sure I think his brainpan if it were emptied, (as I think he hath not much brain in it,) would well contain half a bushel of malt, his shaggy hair and beard would stuff a cushion for Charon's boat, his embossed nose and embroidered face, would furnish a Jeweller; his eyes well dried, would make good tennis-balls, or shot for a small piece of ordnance, his yawning mouth would serve for a cony-burrow, and his two ragged rows of teeth, for a stone wall, or a pale; then hath he a neck like one of Hercules his pillars, with a windpipe, (or rather a beer pipe) as big as the boar of a demiculvering, or a wooden pump;

through which conduit half a brewing of Hamburgh beer doth run down into his unmeasurable paunch, wherein is more midriff, guts and garbage than three tripewives could be able to utter before it stunk. His post-like legs were answerable to the rest of the great frame which they supported, and to conclude, Sir Bevis, Ascapart, Gogmagog, or our English Sir John Falstaff, were but shrimps to this bezzling bombard's longitude, latitude, altitude, and crassitude, for he passes, and surpasses the whole German multitude.

And as he is great in corpulency, so is he powerful in potency, for figuratively he hath spiritual resemblance of Romish authority, and in some sort he is a kind of demi-Pope, for once a year in the dog-days he sends out his men with baits instead of Bulls, with full power from his greatness, to knock down all the curs without contradiction, whose masters or owners will not be at the charge to buy a pardon for them of his mightiness, which pardon is more durable than the Popes of wax or parchment, for his is made of a piece of the hide of an ox, a horse, or such lasting stuff, which with his stigmatical stamp or seal is hanged about every dog's neck who is freed from his fury by the purchase of his pardon. And sure I am persuaded that these dogs are more sure of their lives with the hangman's pardon, than the poor besotted blinded Papists are of their seduced souls from any pardon of the Popes.

The privileges of this grand halter-master are many, as he hath the emptying of all the vaults or draughts in the city, which no doubt he gains some favour by. Besides all oxen, kine, horses, hogs, dogs, or any such beasts, if they die themselves, or if they be not like to live, the hangman, must knock them on the heads, and have their skins: and whatsoever inhabitant in his jurisdiction doth any of these things aforesaid himself, is abhorred and accounted as a villain without redemption. So that with hangings, headings, breakings, pardoning and killing of dogs, flaying of beasts, emptying of vaults, and such privy commodities, his whole revenue sometimes amounts to 4 or 5 hundred pounds a year. And he is held in that regard and estimation, that any man will converse and drink with him, nay sometimes the Lords of the town will feast with him, and it is accounted no impeachment to their honours; for he is held in the rank of a gentleman, (or a rank gentleman) and he scorns to be called in the cast weeds of executed offenders: No, he goes to the mercers, and hath his satin, his velvet, or what stuff he pleases, measured out by the yard or the ell, with his gold and silver lace, his silk stockings, laced spangled garters and roses, hat and feather, with four or five brave villains attending him in livery cloaks, who have stipendiary means from his ignominious bounty.

Monday the 19 of August, about the hour of 12 at noon, the people of the town in great multitudes flocked to the place of execution; which is half a mile English without the gates, built more like a sconce than a gallows, for it is walled and ditched about with a drawbridge and the prisoner came on foot with a Divine with him, all the way exhorting him to repentance, and because death should not terrify him, they had given him many rouses and carouses of wine and beer: for it is the custom there to make such poor wretches drunk, whereby they may be senseless either of God's mercy or their own misery; but being prayed for by others, they themselves may die resolutely, or (to be feared) desperately.

But the prisoner being come to the place of death, he was by the officers delivered to the hangman, who entering his strangling fortification with two grand hangmen more and their men, which were come from the city of Lübeck, and another town (which I cannot name) to assist their Hamburghian brother in this great and weighty work: the drawbridge was drawn up, and the prisoner mounted on a mount of earth, built high on purpose that the people without may see the execution a quarter of a mile round about: four of the hangman's men takes each of them a small halter, and by the hands and the feet they hold the prisoners extended all abroad lying on his back: then the Arch-hangman, or the great Master of this mighty business took up a wheel, much about the bigness of one of the fore wheels of a coach: and first, having put off his doublet, his hat, and being in his shirt, as if he meant to play at tennis, he took the wheel, and set it on the edge, and turned it with one hand like a top or a whirligig, then he took it by the spokes, and lifting it up with a mighty stroke he beat one of the poor wretch's legs in pieces, (the bones I mean) at which he roared grievously; then after a little pause he breaks the other leg in the same manner, and consequently breaks his arms, and then he stroke four or five main blows on his breast, and burst all his bulk and chest in shivers, lastly he smote his neck, and missing, burst his chin and jaws to mammocks; then he took the broken mangled corpse, and spread it on the wheel, and thrust a great post or pile into the nave or hole of the wheel, and then fixed the post into the earth some six foot deep, being in height above the ground, some ten or twelve foot, and there the carcass must lie till it be consumed by all-consuming time, or ravening fowls.

This was the terrible manner of this horrid execution, and at this place are twenty posts with those wheels or pieces of wheels, with heads of men nailed on the top of the posts, with a great spike driven through the skull. The several kinds of torments which they inflict upon offenders in those parts makes me to imagine our English hanging to be but a flea-biting.

Moreover, if any men in those parts are to be beheaded, the fashion is, that the prisoner kneels down, and being blinded with a napkin, one takes hold of the hair of the crown of the head, holding the party upright, whilst the hangman with a backward blow with a sword will take the head from a man's shoulders so nimbly, and with such dexterity, that the owner of the head shall never want the miss of it.

From *Three Weekes, three daies and three houres Observations and Travel from London to Hamburgh in Germanie* by John Taylor

The Death of Falstaff

London. Mistress Quickly's House in Eastcheap.
Enter Mistress Quickly, Nym, Bardolph and Boy.

QUICK: Pr'ythee, honey-sweet husband, let me bring
   thee to Staines.
PIST: No; for my manly heart doth yearn. –
   Bardolph, be blithe: Nym, rouse thy vaunting veins;
   Boy, bristle thy courage up: for Falstaff he is dead,
   And we must yearn therefore.
BARD: Would I were with him, wheresome'er he is, either in
   heaven, or in hell.
QUICK: Nay, sure he's not in hell: he's in Arthur's bosom, if ever man
   went to Arthur's bosom. 'A made a finer end, and went away, an it had
   been any cristom child: 'a parted even just between twelve and one,
   even at the turning o' the tide: for after I saw him fumble with the
   sheets, and play with flowers, and smile upon his fingers' ends, I knew
   there was but one way: for his nose was as sharp as a pen, and 'a
   babbled of green fields. 'How now, Sir John?' quoth I: 'what, man! be of
   good cheer.' So 'a cried out – 'God, God, God!' three or four times:
   now I, to comfort him, bid him, 'a should not think of God; I hoped,
   there was no need to trouble himself with any such thoughts yet. So, 'a
   bade me lay more clothes on his feet: I put my hands into the bed, and
   felt them, and they were as cold as any stone, then I felt to his knees,
   and so upward, and upward, and all was cold as any stone.
NYM: They say, he cried out of sack.
QUICK: Ay, that 'a did.
BARD: And of women.

QUICK: Nay, that 'a did not.

BOY: Yes, that 'a did; and said they were devils incarnate.

QUICK: 'A could never abide carnation; 'twas a colour he never liked.

BOY: 'A said once, the devil would have him about women.

QUICK: 'A did in some sort, indeed, handle women but then he was rheumatic, and talked of the whore of Babylon.

BOY: Do you not remember, 'a saw a flea stick upon Bardolph's nose, and 'a said it was a black soul burning in Hell?

BARD: Well, the fuel is gone that maintained that fire: that's all the riches I got in his service.

From *Henry V*, Act II, Scene 3, by William Shakespeare

Mr Tod

A T A SUMMER ASSIZES holden at Hertford, while the judge was sitting on the bench, comes this old Tod into court, clothed in a green suit, with his leathern girdle in his hand, his bosom open, and all in a dung sweat, as if he had run for his life; and being come in, he spake aloud as follows: 'My lord,' said he, 'here is the veriest rogue that breathes upon the face of the earth. I have been a thief from a child. When I was but a little one I gave myself to rob orchards, and to do other such like wicked things, and I have continued a thief ever since. My lord, there has not been a robbery committed these many years, within so many miles of this place, but I have been either at it, or privy to it!' The judge thought the fellow was mad, but after some conference with some of the justices, they agreed to indict him; and so they did of several felonious actions; to all of which he confessed guilty, and so was hanged with his wife at the same time.

John Bunyan

He That Is Down

He that is down need fear no fall,
　　He that is low, no pride;
He that is humble ever shall
　　Have God to be his guide.

I am content with what I have,
　　Little be it or much:
And, Lord, contentment still I crave,
　　Because Thou gavest such.

Fullness to such a burden is
　　That go on pilgrimage;
Here little, and hereafter bliss,
　　Is best from age to age.

From *The Pilgrim's Progress* by John Bunyan

Charon

THE BOAT is made of nothing but the wormeaten ribs of coffins, nayl'd together with the splinters of fleshlesse shin-bones, dig'd out of graves, beeing broken in pieces. The sculls that hee rowes with, are made of sextons spades, which had bene hung up at the end of some great Plague, the bench he sits upon, a ranke of dead mens sculls, the worst of them having bene an Emperor, as great as Charlemaine: and a huge heap of their beards serving for his cushion: the mast of the boat is an arme of a yew tree, whose boughs (in stead of Rosemary) had wont to be worn at buryals: the sayle, two patcht winding sheets, wherein a broker and an usurer had bin laid for their linnen, will last longest, because it comes commonly out of lavender and is seldom worn.

　　The waterman himselfe is an old grisly-fac'd fellow: a beard filthyer then a bakers mawkin[1] that hee sweeps his oven with, which hung full of knotted elf-locks, and serves him for a swabber in fowle weather to clense his hulke: a payre of eyes staring so wide (by beeing bleard with the wind) as if the liddes were lifted up with gags to keepe them open: more salt rewmatick

1 Mawkin – merkin, i.e. a pubic wig.

water runnes out of them, than would pickle all the Herrings that shall come out of Yarmouth: a payre of hands so hard and scal'd over with durt, that passengers thinke hee weares gantlets, and more stinkingly musty are they than the fists of night-men, or the fingers of bribery, which are never cleane: his breath belches out nothing but rotten damps, which lye so thick and foggie, on the face of the waters, that his fare is halfe choakt, ere they can get to land: the sea-cole furnaces of ten brew-howses, make not such a smoke, nor the tallow pans of fifteene chaundlers (when they melt,) send out such a smell: hee's dreadfull in looks, and currish in language, yet as kind as a courtyer where he takes. Hee sits in all stormes bare headed, for if he had a cap, he would not put it of to a Pope: a gowne girt to him (made all the Wolves skins) tanned (figuring his greedynes) but worne out so long, that it has almost worn away his elbows: hee's thick of hearing to them that sue to him, but to those against whose wils hee's fent for, a fiddler heares not the creeking of a window sooner.

As touching the River, looke how Moore-ditch shews, when the water is three quarters dreyn'd out, and by reason the stomacke of it is over-laden, is ready to fal to casting, so does that, it stinks almost worse, is almost pysonous, altogether so muddy, altogether so black: in tast very bitter, yet (to those that know how to distill these deadly waters), very wholsome.

From *The Devils Answer to Pierce Pennylesse* by Thomas Dekker

INDEX OF AUTHORS

(titles are used where poems are anonymous)